Robert E. L. Krick
May 31, 2003

The Peninsula Campaign of 1862:

Yorktown to the Seven Days

Essays on the American Civil War

Volume Two

Series Editor
William J. Miller

Savas Woodbury Publishers
1475 South Bascom Avenue, Suite 204
Campbell, California 95008
phone: 1-800-848-6585   fax: 1-408-879-9327

Manufactured in the United States of America

The Peninsula Campaign of 1862:
Yorktown to the Seven Days, Volume Two

edited by William J. Miller

Savas Publishing Company
1475 S. Bascom Avenue, Suite 204,
Campbell, California 95008   (800) 848-6585

Includes bibliographic references and index

Printing Number
10 9 8 7 6 5 4 3

ISBN 1-882810-76-7

This book is printed on 50-lb. Glatfelter acid-free paper

The paper in this book meets or exceeds the guidelines for permanence and durability
of the Committee on Production Guidelines for Book Longevity of the Council on Library Resources

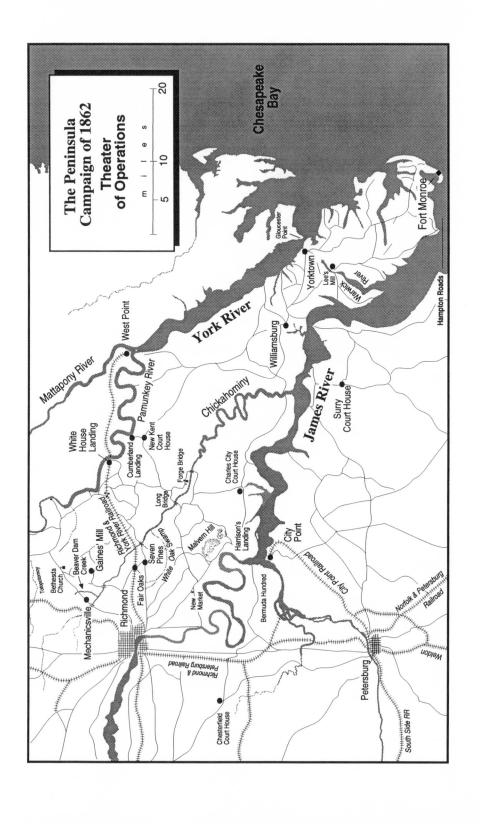

The Peninsula
Campaign of 1862
Theater
of Operations

miles
5   10   20

Chesapeake
Bay

Fort Monroe

Hampton Roads

Gloucester
Point

Yorktown

Lee's
Mill

Warwick River

Williamsburg

York River

West Point

Mattapony River

Pamunkey River

Chickahominy

James River

Surry
Court House

White House
Landing

New Kent
Court House

Cumberland
Landing

Forge Bridge

Long
Bridge

Charles City
Court House

Richmond & York River Railroad

Beaver Dam
Creek

Gaines' Mill

Seven
Pines

White Oak Swamp

Malvern Hill

Harrison's
Landing

City
Point

Totopotomoy

Bethesda
Church

Mechanicsville

Richmond

Fair Oaks

New
Market

Bermuda Hundred

City Point Railroad

Norfolk & Petersburg
Railroad

Richmond & Petersburg Railroad

Chesterfield
Court House

Petersburg

Waldon

South Side RR

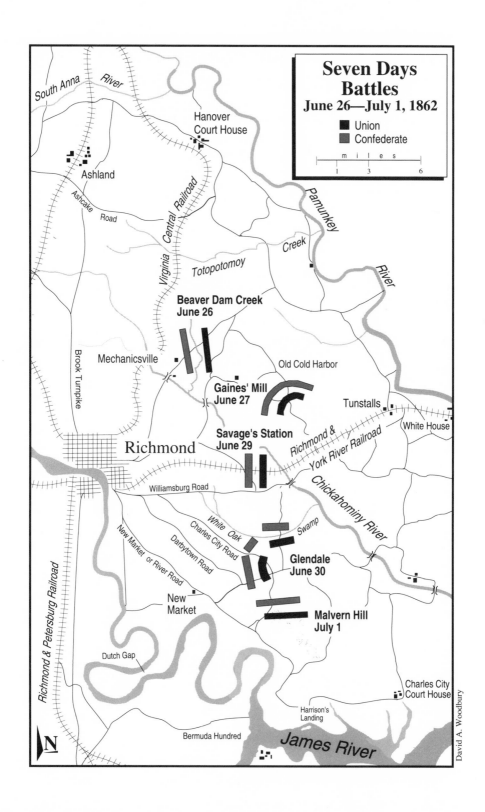

Seven Days Battles
June 26—July 1, 1862

■ Union
■ Confederate

m i l e s
1   3   6

South Anna River

Hanover Court House

Ashland

Ashcake Road

Virginia Central Railroad

Pamunkey Creek

River

Totopotomoy

Beaver Dam Creek
June 26

Brook Turnpike

Mechanicsville

Old Cold Harbor

Gaines' Mill
June 27

Tunstalls

White House

Savage's Station
June 29

Richmond

Richmond & York River Railroad

Williamsburg Road

Chickahominy River

White Oak Swamp

New Market or River Road

Charles City Road

Darbytown Road

Glendale
June 30

New Market

Malvern Hill
July 1

Richmond & Petersburg Railroad

Dutch Gap

Charles City Court House

Harrison's Landing

Bermuda Hundred

James River

N

David A. Woodbury

TABLE OF CONTENTS

List of Maps & Photos

Prelude to the Seven Days:
The Battle of Slash Church, May 27, 1862

Down the Peninsula with Richard Ewell:
Capt. Campbell Brown's Memoirs of the Seven Days Campaign

Military Advisor to Stanton and Lincoln:
Quartermaster General Montgomery C. Meigs
and the Peninsula Campaign, January—August, 1862

continued

List of Maps & Photos (continued)

Publisher's Preface

In his introduction to the first volume of this series, editor William J. Miller wrote that George B. McClellan's 1862 effort to capture Richmond "was one of the most monumental campaigns of the war. From the Federal perspective, the Peninsula Campaign was the most complex and ambitious operation of the war to that point, as well as the most expensive. . . .For the Confederacy, the Peninsula Campaign was the greatest crisis the young government would face in the first three years of the war."

It remains somewhat of a mystery that, in the literature on the war, a campaign of the magnitude of the Peninsula Campaign has historically taken a back seat to many smaller-scale operations with fewer battles. There are innumerable, and important reasons why—as students of the Civil War—we should be drawn to the study of this complex military and political drama, and *The Peninsula Campaign of 1862: Yorktown to the Seven Days* continues to explore those reasons in greater depth than has previously been attempted.

This collection of essays marks the second volume in the ongoing *Campaign Chronicles* series examining events on the Virginia peninsula in the spring and summer of 1862. Essays in this assemblage include detailed looks at some of the prominent personalities associated with George B. McClellan's movement against the Confederate capital, two of the battles in which they participated, and the logistical problems with which they grappled. From the under-studied fighting at Slash Church in Hanover County, to the climactic showdown a month later at Malvern

Hill; from Quartermaster General Montgomery Meigs to the Confederacy's "boy artillerist," Willie Pegram, the six articles brought together here add significant new information to the growing body of work on this largely overlooked campaign.

Leading off this volume is "Prelude to the Seven Days: the Battle of Slash Church (Hanover Court House)" by Richmond historian Robert E. L. Krick. Nervous about the vulnerable right flank of the Army of the Potomac, McClellan dispatched a division under Fitz John Porter to eliminate the threat posed by assorted Confederate forces in upper Hanover County, which included a brigade of North Carolinians. On May 27, 1862, Porter's men crashed into a regiment of Carolinians near the home of Dr. Thomas H. Kinney, and the carnage was underway. Krick chronicles the events of that sanguinary afternoon in a cogent and compelling narrative highlighted with precise maps and modern views of the battlefield. "Slash Church," Krick writes, "magnified many times is Sharpsburg, Gettysburg, or Gaines' Mill. While those encounters consumed thousands of men, featured vast hordes of combatants, and produced far-reaching strategic ramifications, they were not much different from Slash Church to the farmers and factory workers doing the shooting."

Terry Jones, assistant professor of history at Northeast Louisiana University and author of *Lee's Tigers: The Louisiana Infantry in the Army of Northern Virginia*, contributed the second selection in this volume, an outstanding excerpt from the memoirs of Campbell Brown, assistant adjutant general to Maj. Gen. Richard S. Ewell. As his memoirs illustrates, Brown was a highly educated, keenly observant, and well-spoken witness to the participation of "Stonewall" Jackson's column in The Seven Days Battles. Enhanced by Jones' generously informative and pertinent annotations, Campbell Brown's recollections of the campaign provide us with an unusually unique on-the-scene perspective of events from Beaver Dam Creek to Malvern Hill.

Professor Carmen Grayson of Williamsburg, Virginia, rendered exceptional service in the study of this campaign with the contribution of her essay, "Military Advisor to Lincoln and Stanton: Quartermaster General Montgomery C. Meigs." Even long-time students of the war will be surprised to learn of Meigs substantial influence with Lincoln

and Secretary of War Stanton during the critical operations on the peninsula. Among other things, Meigs directed the Union's initial responses
to Stonewall Jackson's Shenandoah Valley Campaign; was instrumental
in the disposition of Irvin McDowell's corps; signed Stanton's name to
official orders without the secretary's knowledge; and played a large role
in Lincoln's decision to evacuate the Army of the Potomac from the
peninsula after the Seven Days fighting had ended. Grayson adroitly
reports on these events and others with an insightful analysis which
ultimately conveys to the reader a still clearer picture of an exceedingly
complicated campaign.

Following Grayson's contribution is Mac Wyckoff's "Our Loss Was
Great: Joseph B. Kershaw's South Carolina Brigade in the Battle of
Savage's Station." Wyckoff, a National Park Service historian for the
past 15 years—the last seven years at Fredericksburg & Spotsylvania
NMP—delivers a fast-paced, blow-by-blow account of the service rendered by Brig. Gen. Joseph Brevard Kershaw and his brigade of South
Carolinians at the June 29 Battle of Savage's Station. After Lee's
sledgehammer attacks on the right of McClellan's army at
Mechanicsville and Gaines' Mill caused "Little Mac" to begin a hasty
but guarded flight for the protection of his James River gunboats, Lee
instructed "Prince John" Magruder—to whose command Kershaw's brigade belonged—to interdict the Federal "change of base." Wyckoff
presents the ensuing battle on a solid foundation of disparate primary
sources, focusing in detail on the valiant efforts and grievous suffering
of the four South Carolina regiments under Kershaw's able command.

Series editor William Miller, in "Scarcely any Parallel in History:
Logistics, Friction, and McClellan's Strategy for the Peninsula Campaign" examines, from a broader perspective, the premises upon which
the Federal campaign for Richmond were based, the unhappy alliance
between McClellan's headquarters and Washington, and most impor-
tantly, the specific logistical demands of feeding, supplying, and effi-
ciently moving more than 100,000 soldiers in a country ill-suited for
such large-scale operations. That the officers of the Federal quartermaster department succeeded as well as they did in the face of seemingly insurmountable obstacles—and yet go virtually overlooked and
unnamed in the vast sea of books on the war—suggests that most us,

however well read, have a weak understanding of one of the most important aspects of *any* campaign. Miller, in brilliant fashion, has taken a big
step toward remedying that oversight. "While there might have been
good logisticians who were bad generals," Miller tells us, "it is unlikely
that there were good generals who were bad logisticians."

Completing this volume is a gripping look at a young artillery officer who for the Confederacy became the personification of daring and
courage, William R. J. Pegram. In "The Merits of this Officer Will Not
Go Unrewarded: William R. J. Pegram & the Purcell Battery in the
Seven Days," Peter S. Carmichael, author of the forthcoming *Lee's
Young Artillerist: William R. J. Pegram* (Lexington, 1995), delivers a
compelling account of the all-but-suicidal service of Pegram and the
Purcell Artillery in The Seven Days Battles. As Carmichael points out,
not only did the Seven Days set the stage for "unnecessarily high standards for acceptable losses in later battles," it also "served as an intensive,
week-long seminar in tactics" in the early stages of the war. One lesson,
learned the hard way, was the brutal efficiency of artillery on the tactical
defensive. Compounding the problem for the Confederates was their
habit of dispersing batteries to separate commands throughout the army.
Consequently, the Southern artillery battery worked more or less alone
against the mass fire of the enemy. Carmichael's essay on Pegram and
the Purcell Battery is the story of brave men doing dangerous work.
Before Mechanicsville, Pegram counted 80 to 90 men in his command.
During three engagements of The Seven Days Battles, at least 57 of
those men were killed or wounded.

These essays, it is hoped, along with many others in subsequent
volumes, will help provide a fuller understanding of this colossal—and
colossally important—campaign.

Volume Two

Robert E. L. Krick

Robert E. L. Krick, a Richmond-based historian, is the author of *The 40th Virginia Infantry* (Lynchburg, 1985) and is a regular contributor to many journals, including *Civil War* magazine. He specializes in the Army of Northern Virginia's battles and personnel, and is at work on a biographical register of the army's staff officers.

Prelude to the Seven Days

The Battle of Slash Church (Hanover Court House)
May 27, 1862

A s George B. McClellan inched his army toward the Confederate capital city in May 1862, few observers doubted that the climax of the war was at hand. The "Young Napoleon" apparently had only to marshal and unleash his substantial forces before the defenders could regroup and maneuver for advantage. In the event, the Peninsula Campaign proved to be a mismanaged duel dominated by the floundering of awkward neophytes. The battles that began at Yorktown and concluded at Malvern Hill exposed several leaders on both sides as fumblers with no future in the main theater of the war; the campaign culled these men out via natural selection. The Battle of Slash Church-known among Northern participants as the Battle of Hanover Court House-was a part of this testing process. It featured as its star performer Brig. Gen. Lawrence O'Bryan Branch of North Carolina, certainly a suspect figure for such a weighty position. Branch's reaction to unaccustomed military responsibility, the behavior of the raw infantrymen on both sides, and the ferocity of this obscure action make the Battle of Slash Church an interesting component of the 1862 campaign for Richmond.

The northern section of Hanover County, Virginia, oozed history long before the contending armies began crowding its roads. Patrick

Henry and Henry Clay lived their early years just south of Hanover Court House. Henry even suffered matrimony at a nearby mansion that figured prominently in Civil War operations many decades later. In 1862, the area offered a patchwork of open farmland and thick, immature woods. One particularly dense section earned the local designation of "The Slash," a term inspired by an abundance of briars and swamps. Two features of the landscape gave upper Hanover County military significance in the operations around Richmond in May 1862. The Virginia Central Railroad sliced through northern Hanover, passing villages bearing names like Peake's Turnout and Atlee's Station. The evolving status of railroad transportation and supply increased the Virginia Central's importance. Upper Hanover fell only a few miles short of being the mid-way point between Richmond and Fredericksburg. Those two cities marked the flanks of the opposing armies, each of which had elements scattered over the 60 intervening miles. Whatever troops dominated northern Hanover and controlled the railroad line in that section enjoyed the advantage of position.

* * *

By the middle of May 1862, General McClellan apparently had determined his pattern for the next phase of the campaign. While predicting an orderly reduction of Richmond, he still fretted incessantly over the dispersal of the Union troops in the central part of the state. He viewed their presence with the Army of the Potomac as an essential ingredient to the success of his enterprise.

Irvin McDowell, stoic in the face of his public relations nightmare at First Manassas, commanded the most substantial outpost of Union troops between Richmond and Washington. His mission was to remain around Fredericksburg, near enough to Washington to react in case the unpredictable Maj. Gen. Thomas J. "Stonewall" Jackson broke loose from his tormentors in the Shenandoah Valley. McClellan craved the presence of McDowell's troops to further his plan of victory through method and statistical superiority. Abraham Lincoln was accustomed by mid-May to McClellan's harangues on the subject of reinforcements. In this case, he agreed with his top-ranking general. McClellan received the happy intelligence on May 17 that McDowell, with an entire corps, would march toward Richmond to reinforce the Army of the Potomac.[1]

This promising development ended in disaster. In a well-timed movement, Stonewall Jackson commenced his rampage in the Valley, driving Union armies before him as he indirectly threatened Washington. Jackson's victories had the desired effect: Lincoln succumbed to his fears and recalled McDowell to northern Virginia to help protect the Republican Party's capital city. Thus a series of relatively small battles more than 100 miles distant had a significant role in the successful Confederate defense of Richmond.

Since aid from McDowell now seemed doubtful, McClellan found himself in a difficult position. Much of his army-including the corps commanded by Fitz John Porter-languished on the north side of the Chickahominy River, stretching hopefully toward Fredericksburg. Thus, the textbook soldier George McClellan found himself in violation of the fundamental concepts of flank protection. Not only did Porter's flank dangle unprotected in Hanover County, but a bad dose of weather could flood the Chickahominy and isolate Porter and the other Union troops north of the river.

The Confederates' situation by May 25 hardly differed from that of their Federal counterparts. The Southerners, too, maintained an isolated force in Hanover County. These troops were commanded by Brig. Gen. Lawrence O'B. Branch and were, in theory, situated for defense. Branch, however, barely controlled enough soldiers to merit attention as a strategic force.[2] Joseph E. Johnston had telegraphed Branch on May 18 and 19 to move from his post near Gordonsville eastward to Hanover Court House. Branch grappled with railroad transportation, and finally began assembling his force at Hanover Court House early on May 22.[3]

---

[1] U. S. War Department, *The War of the Rebellion: The Official Records of the Union and Confederate Armies,* 128 vols. (Washington, D. C., 1890-1901), series I, vol. 11, pt. 1, p. 27. Hereinafter cited as *OR.* All references are to series I unless otherwise noted.

[2] James H. Lane, "History of Lane's North Carolina Brigade," *Southern Historical Society Papers,* vol. 8 (1880), p. 103.

[3] Joseph E. Johnston to Branch, May 19, 1862; Branch to Johnston, May 22, 1862, Lawrence

Farther north, Brig. Gen. Joseph R. Anderson commanded a small division below Fredericksburg that also began moving south that week. Anderson was at Hanover Junction by May 26. In the event of a serious move toward Richmond by McClellan, Anderson and Branch would be in position to harass the Union flank. They could also observe the erratic wanderings of McDowell. If the Union high command decided to unite McDowell with McClellan, the Confederates were well posted to block the move.

All through his career in Virginia, George McClellan reacted to setbacks in the same way. After consolidating and regrouping as much as he could justify, he would set off on some movement designed to demonstrate to everyone just how furiously he progressed. These little expeditions were, however, usually limited and closely regulated operations. On May 26, for example, McClellan claimed that "We are quietly closing in upon the enemy preparatory to the last struggle." About the same time, however, McClellan felt he had to "take every possible precaution against disaster"[4] and dispatched orders to Fitz John Porter for a demonstration against Confederates in upper Hanover. The commander of the Army of the Potomac saw these Southern troops as a threat to his supply line and thought Porter's expedition necessary to eliminate that threat. Porter gathered a division of three brigades commanded by Brig. Gen. George W. Morell, several batteries, a strong provisional brigade under Col. Gouverneur K. Warren, and a swarm of cavalry. Porter hoped to exterminate Branch's brigade of North Carolinians.

Lawrence O'Bryan Branch owed his rank to his antebellum political skills. In May 1862, he was a 41-year-old ex-congressman with an unsuccessful battle at New Berne, North Carolina, as his sole military credential. Few Confederate generals displayed a more acrimonious disposition than Branch. During his relatively brief Civil War career, Branch engaged in several unseemly public disputes with subordinates

---

O'B Branch Papers, Alderman Library, University of Virginia, Charlottesville, Va. Hereinafter cited as Branch Papers.

[4] *OR* 11, pt. 1, p. 33.

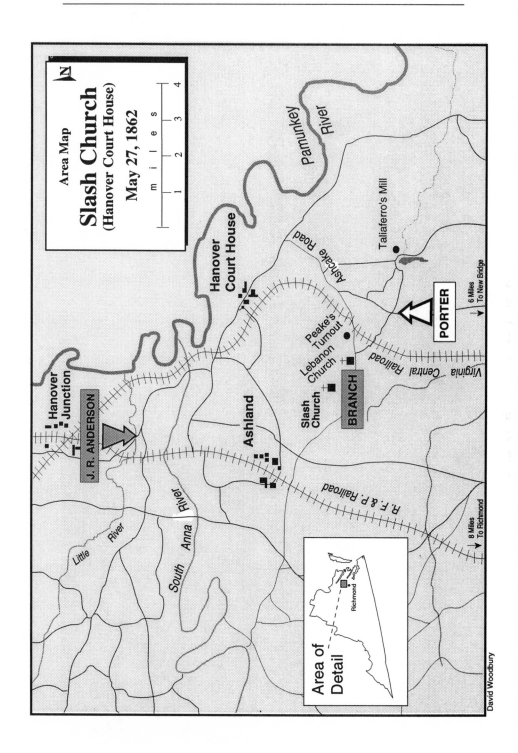

Area Map

Slash Church
(Hanover Court House)
May 27, 1862

David Woodbury

Generals in Gray

Brig. Gen. Lawrence O'Bryan Branch

Carlisle Barracks

Brig. Gen. Fitz John Porter

and other officers, one of which will be documented here. His private letters to his wife reaffirm the notion that he could not endure fools, that they surrounded him and that his military career was a constant struggle against their pernicious influence. The presence of Joseph R. Anderson to the north left the Confederacy in the unsettling position of having a politician and an ironworks magnate commanding thousands of men protecting the approaches to the capital from the north.[5]

General Branch would distinguish himself in the war, but as his second attempt at independent command approached that late May, he was far from confident and seems to have been unready for battle. On May 24, the general wrote hopefully that perhaps General Anderson would arrive the next day: "He ranks me and I would rather be relieved of the responsibility of the chief command."[6] Branch continued to cling to the hope that Anderson would reinforce the North Carolinians around Hanover Court House, but Anderson had other worries.

The morning of May 27, 1862, began earlier for Porter's raiding force than for most other soldiers around Richmond. The troops were awake by 2:30 or 3:00 a.m. in their camps near New Bridge on the Chickahominy. One soldier of the 25th New York recorded that his regiment packed 60 rounds of ammunition per man with two-days' rations. Nearly all accounts agree that the head of the column had started by 4:00.[7] The troops faced a march that tested their soldierly bearing. It rained, a routine discomfort that May, but on this day Porter's men faced the prospect of a long march and possibly a battle. The rain soaked the roads in Hanover County. One Federal recalled that the columns marched through "one broad mass of plastic mud knee deep, while the rain pelted us in torrents." Wrote a man of Brig. Gen. Daniel Butterfield's brigade, "The depth became disgusting."[8]

---

[5] For the best summary of Branch's career, see William C. Davis, ed., *The Confederate General*, 6 vols. (Harrisburg, 1991), vol. 1, pp. 118-119.

[6] Branch to wife, May 24, 1862, Branch Papers.

[7] "W.E.D." to "My Dear Mother" in Rochester (N.Y.) Union and Advertiser, June 9, 1862.

[8] Letter from "Macaulay" (44th New York) in the Rochester *Democrat and American*, June 9,

The other wing of the Union advance, led by Gouverneur K. Warren, moved from lovely Old Church northwest toward Hanover Court
House, nearly 12 miles away. With 2,700 men, Warren's column was
surprisingly powerful. Although the Union high command did not seem
to realize the dimensions of Branch's position in northern Hanover, the
approach of the blue columns from two different directions proved for-
tuitous. Warren was to prevent Confederate movement toward the Pamunkey River and destroy bridges in that area.

*   *   *

Only a few miles southwest of Hanover Court House, General
Branch spent the night of the 26th asleep in his clothes at historic Slash
Church. The old church was built in 1729, and Patrick Henry's uncle
had served as rector for 40 years. Branch's staff slept on the church
pews, while Lt. Col. Edward G. Haywood of the 7th North Carolina lay
on the floor suffering with a toothache.[9]

The nature of Branch's assignment forced him to disperse his units
over a wide area. General Joseph E. Johnston expected Branch to picket
the roads, guard the Virginia Central Railroad tracks, gather intelligence
and provide a legitimate Confederate presence hovering on McClellan's
right flank. For these endless chores Branch had seven regiments of
infantry, miscellaneous cavalry, and one badly equipped battery of artillery under Alexander C. Latham. The two regiments not indigenous to
Branch's Brigade were the 12th North Carolina (still called the 2nd
North Carolina at that early stage of the war), and the 45th Georgia
Infantry. Porter's column outnumbered Branch's defenders three to one.

1862;   John Berry Diary (16th Michigan), May 27, 1862, *Civil War Times, Illustrated*
Collection, United States Army Military History Institute (hereinafter cited as USAMHI), Carlisle,
PA. The rain affected the strategy of the commanders at Seven Pines four days later.

[9] *Bulletin of the Hanover County Historical Society*, (November 1972); Branch to wife, May
26, 1862, Branch Papers.

Several avenues of transportation spread away from Slash Church. Just east of the church, along the same road, lay another, less historic meeting house that bore two names: Lebanon Church or Merry Oaks Church. It is often difficult to distinguish between Lebanon Church and the virtually adjacent Slash Church. Many writers of contemporary dispatches and documents seem to have been unaware of the distinction. A few hundred yards to the east, the Virginia Central Railroad sliced across the road and headed northeastward toward the Court House. The handful of buildings at the intersection of the road and the railroad constituted Peake's Station, more commonly called Peake's Turnout. The road that ran just south of Slash Church past Lebanon Church and across the tracks at Peake's finally entered Hanover Court House some six miles northeast of Slash Church. Most participants who mentioned the road in dispatches or reports called it either the Hanover or the Ashcake Road.

General Branch realized the seriousness of his duties and tried to perform them well. Chief among his tasks was to observe the roads and to protect the Virginia Central Railroad. Although Branch's cavalry was best suited for picketing the roads, the general apparently had little confidence in his horsemen. Only three days earlier he had grumbled that his mounted arm "is limited in numbers and ignorant of the Country."[10] To substitute for the cavalry, Branch dispatched James H. Lane's 28th North Carolina to Taliaferro's Mill. Lane's men were to picket the roads below Hanover Court House and watch the direct approaches to the railroad. Branch had received unconfirmed word that an enemy raiding party was at Taliaferro's Mill as well, making Lane's mission more serious. Once at the mill, strategically located on an arm of Totopotomoy Creek, Lane's strong regiment of more than 900 men and two pieces of artillery from Latham's Battery could sit astride one of the primary roads leading from McClellan's right northward to the railroad.[11]

[10] *Bulletin of the Hanover County Historical Society*, (November 1972); Branch to wife, May 26, 1862, Branch Papers; Branch to Capt. B. B. Douglas (9th Virginia Cavalry), May 24, 1862, Branch Papers.

[11] *OR* 11, pt. 1, p. 743.

Confederate outposts along the New Bridge Road discovered Porter's soggy column shortly before Lane arrived at Taliaferro's Mill, east of the New Bridge Road. Even before he could post his regiment, Lane received word of the intruders and hastened to return north toward Hanover Court House to block the Federal probe. The mere presence of Union troops along the New Bridge Road that morning presented grave problems for Branch and Lane, for the 28th North Carolina constituted the only Confederate defense of the town, and Porter's entire force advanced between the two unbalanced wings of Branch's Brigade.[12]

James Lane later proved to be a reliable general, directing Branch's old brigade with ability on numerous fields. His leadership skills-undeveloped though they may have been in May 1862-probably saved his regiment from destruction in the fields east of Peake's Turnout on May 27. The 28th was a rookie regiment. This first devastating struggle with a determined, dangerous enemy could have ended in disaster.

Lane immediately retraced his route, hoping to reach the Hanover Road before the Yankee raiders. His swarm of skirmishers combed the woods on either side of the Taliaferro's Mill Road. Within a few hundred yards of the intersection with the Ashcake Road, the North Carolinians uncovered most of the 25th New York Infantry, which also had been advancing carefully toward Hanover Court House.

The great landmark on that part of the battlefield, apart from the intersection of the two roads, was the home of Dr. Thomas H. Kinney, which stood (and still stands) on the north side of the intersection. The spacious two story frame house was the centerpiece of several smaller farm buildings, soon to figure prominently in the battle. An enormous field of wheat surrounded the house and its dependencies and was bounded on the south by the road intersection, on the east and west by woods and on the north by a well-defined ravine.[13]

---

[12] Ibid.

[13] Oliver Norton, *Army Letters*, (Dayton, 1990), p. 83. Norton (83rd Pennsylvania) claims the field was clover, but all other sources call it a wheat field.

About noon, the 400 men composing the 25th New York, detached earlier from Brig. Gen. John H. Martindale's brigade to give the advance guard some substance, crashed through the woods on both sides of the Ashcake Road into the fields around Dr. Kinney's.[14] The regiment's right wing collided with Lane's left in the southwest corner of the intersection, and the clash signaled the start of a ferocious fight around the house that raged for nearly an hour.

The two regiments contested the ground virtually alone; Porter and Branch provided little assistance until they had satisfied themselves of the situation. After the event, each side claimed to have been ambushed by the other, but the encounter appears to have been accidental. As the battle warmed, so did the day. The sheets of rain that had irritated Porter's column that morning gave way to a steamy, oppressive afternoon of heat. Farther to the rear, in the ranks of the 83rd Pennsylvania, "officers and men gave out and lay by the roadside together, utterly unable to go any farther without rest."[15]

Most of the immediate advantages in this struggle belonged to Colonel Lane, for his huge regiment possessed superior firepower, even discounting the section of artillery. In addition, the first clash opened with the Carolinians in the woods while half of the 25th New York was caught in the vastness of Dr. Kinney's wheat field across the road. Lane took advantage of this circumstance to drive the New York regiment away from the road. About half of the regiment rallied around the house and outbuildings under the leadership of their colonel, Charles A. Johnson. South of the road, Lane wheeled his cumbersome unit around through the woods with surprisingly little difficulty. The 25th New York seemed a reasonable conquest to Lane, but only because he remained unaware that the better part of a Federal corps was over the hill to the west.

Casualties piled up around Dr. Kinney's house too quickly for the New Yorkers. Their lieutenant colonel fell wounded, several company

---

[14] *OR* 11, pt. 1, p. 702.

[15] Ibid., p. 698; Norton, *Army Letters*, p. 82.

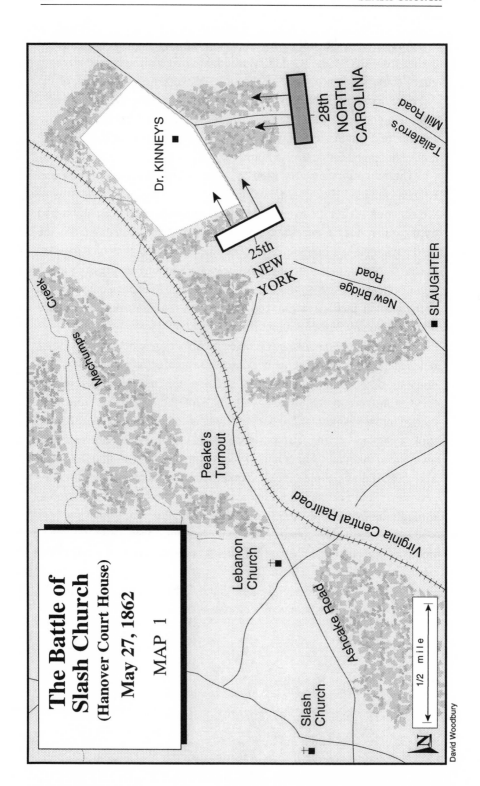

The Battle of
Slash Church
(Hanover Court House)

May 27, 1862

MAP 1

28th
NORTH
CAROLINA

25th
NEW
YORK

Dr. KINNEY'S

Taliaferro's
Mill Road

New Bridge
Road

SLAUGHTER

Mechumps
Creek

Peake's
Turnout

Virginia Central Railroad

Lebanon
Church

Ashcake
Road

Slash
Church

1/2 mile

N

David Woodbury

leaders were killed and wounded, and the regiment teetered on the brink of a serious defeat. Lane's energized unit provided the final shove that pushed the 25th out of the yard and temporarily out of the fight. The North Carolinians boiled out of the woods and charged north across the road. They leaped the roadside ditch, swarmed over the adjacent fence, and took charge of the house and barns, even evicting some of their foe in hand-to-hand fighting. Lane provided leadership from atop his horse, legs crossed on the saddle, helpfully yelling "Charge on the scoundrels, boys!"[16]

This miniature frontal assault secured the wheat field for Lane with few casualties. In addition to shooting large numbers of the 25th New York, Lane's men captured some five dozen wounded and isolated men from that regiment and sent them to Richmond in the care of some similarly disorganized Confederate cavalrymen.

By the time Lane cleared the Kinney wheat field, Fitz John Porter had prepared a strong response in the form of Brig. Gen. Daniel Butterfield's brigade. Porter met the head of that column as it emerged from the New Bridge Road and personally directed the lead regiments into position. Although willing to fight, Butterfield had grave doubts about the effectiveness of his brigade. The rapid march of 15 miles had left the men in such a state that Butterfield "hardly thought it possible for my men to pitch camp and prepare supper. . . ."[17] Nonetheless, Butterfield prepared to resume the contest. Federal artillery already occupied ideal positions south of the Ashcake Road. Four three-inch ordnance rifles under Capt. Henry Benson pounded Dr. Kinney's yard and outbuildings from a knoll across the road. Meanwhile, Dan Butterfield scaled a tree to observe the exact position of Lane's regiment. Satisfied that his arrangements would suffice, Butterfield started the attack.[18]

---

[16] *OR* 11, pt. 1, pp. 716, 743; letter of Maj. E. S. Gilbert (25th New York) published in *Rochester Democrat and American*, June 10, 1862; George B. Johnston Diary, North Carolina Department of Archives and History, Raleigh, NC.

[17] *OR* 11, pt. 1, p. 722.

[18] Ibid., pp. 694, 723.

Across the field to the east, Colonel Lane employed the break in the fight to rearrange his regiment. Discerning the approach of Union reinforcements, Lane shook out a new battle line facing west, at a right angle to his previous alignment. He also called forward the two guns of Latham's Battery under J. R. Potts. The section contained one brass 12-pounder howitzer and one 10-pounder Parrott rifle. These guns occupied part of Dr. Kinney's yard, whence they dueled with the Union artillery across the road.[19]

Once Butterfield started his lines forward, Lane found the situation the unpleasant reverse of his earlier work against the 25th New York. The defenders occupied open fields, making good targets for both Union infantry and artillery. Butterfield's line overlapped Lane's on both flanks even though the first wave of attackers only represented half of Butterfield's Brigade. The front line consisted of the 17th New York and 83rd Pennsylvania-later to earn fame on Little Round Top at Gettysburg-with the 16th Michigan and the 12th New York following along to scoop up stray Carolinians.[20]

The tactical precision and laudable discipline evident in the 28th North Carolina earlier that day evaporated. Lane discovered the 83rd Pennsylvania approaching his right flank through the deep ravine. He refused that flank in an unsuccessful effort to foil the flankers. Faced with too many foes, the regiment crumbled, many companies losing their connection with the body of the regiment. By the time the Federal lines reached Dr. Kinney's, there was no organized defense. The 17th New York laid claim to Potts' 12-pounder, abandoned by the Confederates in their haste to escape. A private named Flood in that regiment shot a valiant Southern artillerist who lingered too long trying to unleash a final shot from the howitzer. The 17th New York suffered no killed or wounded in the entire battle—statistical proof of the feebleness of the

[19] Walter Clark, *Histories of the Several Regiments and Battalions from North Carolina in the Great War*, 5 vols. (Raleigh and Goldsboro, 1901), vol. 2, p. 470; *OR* 11, pt. 1, pp. 744-745.

[20] Ibid., pp. 722-723.

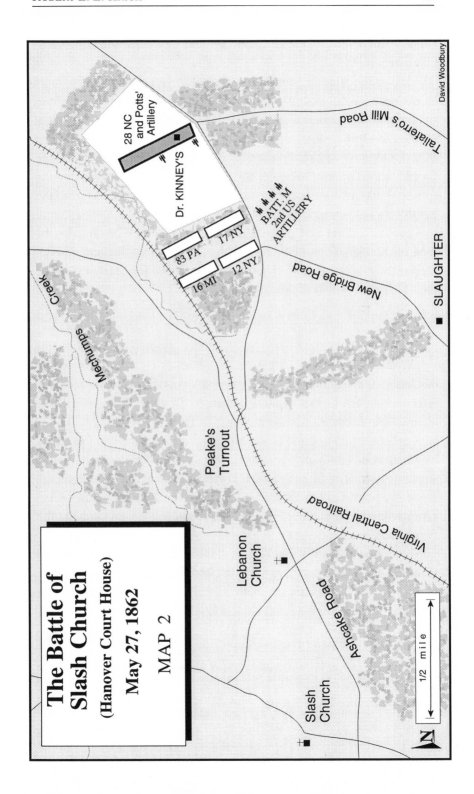

The Battle of
Slash Church
(Hanover Court House)
May 27, 1862
MAP 2

Confederate defense. Colonel Lane admitted, "we were not in a condition to retreat."[21]

The evaporation of Lane's line opened the road to Hanover Court House once again. Butterfield's weary men policed the field, snatching up dozens of disoriented Confederates. Parties of Federal cavalry scouted in all directions, corralling prisoners for the remainder of the day. On May 27, Capt. William B. Royall with part of the 5th U. S. Cavalry captured an entire company of the 28th North Carolina, and the following day two more companies of that regiment surrendered to the cavalry regulars under Brig. Gen. William H. Emory.[22]

Thus ended the first phase of the Battle of Slash Church. For the men of the 28th North Carolina it was a decidedly unpleasant episode, despite their early triumph. Their ordeal continued for nearly two more days before they rejoined the brigade.

*   *   *

While Colonel Lane fought for his regiment's survival, his fellow officers in the brigade's other regiments formed their men for a rescue effort. Although Lane's exploits occurred only three miles from Slash Church, the distance seemed enormous to Branch. Some 12,000 Yankees occupied the road and gentle hills that separated the two Confederate commands. Although Joseph E. Johnston's orders to Branch were vague, they clearly did not prohibit engaging the enemy. Branch recognized his numerical shortcomings, but felt compelled to make some effort at foiling the invaders while trying to rescue the hard-pressed 28th North Carolina.

Like most Civil War battles, the fight at Slash Church did not develop evenly. While crushing the 28th North Carolina, Porter sent a few regiments west to destroy the railroad at Peake's. They posted some

---

[21] Ibid., pp. 726-727, 744.

[22] Ibid., pp. 687, 692. This was the same Captain Royall who killed Capt. William Latané during the most famous episode of Jeb Stuart's celebrated ride around the Union army two weeks later.

artillery in the yard of the Harris House, south of the Ashcake Road. The artillery supported the scattered skirmishers and fought a brief duel with Confederate guns at Peake's. Having destroyed some track and pulled down some telegraph wire, the Union detachment fell back eastward.

Porter mistakenly viewed the 28th North Carolina as his primary enemy. After Lane's survivors fled toward Hanover Court House, Porter's entire column pursued, intent on completing its mission. With two regiments of cavalry in his arsenal, Porter should never have allowed himself to be surprised by the rest of Branch's force just three miles away. This situation offers a graphic example of how Civil War commanders struggled early in the war to use their mounted arm properly.

According to General Martindale, the issue was irrelevant. He maintained in his report that he repeatedly alerted Porter to the presence of Confederates in considerable force around Peake's and beyond, but that Porter "was acting under some great mistake and misinformation." Martindale sent numerous couriers to persuade Porter of the true situation, even dispatching his son as a special envoy.[23]

The first troops to push east against Porter's rear came from the 37th North Carolina. Colonel Charles C. Lee commanded that regiment with skill. He was an 1856 graduate of the U. S. Military Academy, a veteran of Big Bethel, and a promising specimen of Southern leadership. Douglas Southall Freeman identified him as an officer "of particular promise," and a man likely destined for brigade command. When the first Federal shells crashed around Peake's Turnout from the east, Lee hurriedly ordered his regiment to arms. Its camp lay around Lebanon Church, east of the main body of the brigade at Slash Church.[24]

Lee responded well. After notifying General Branch of the situation, Lee ordered up the other section of Latham's Battery. He deployed

---

[23] John O'Connell Memoir (2nd Maine) in Civil War, Miscellaneous Collection, USAMHI, p. 23; *OR* 11, pt. 1, pp. 703-704.

[24] Douglas Southall Freeman, *Lee's Lieutenants*, 3 vols. (New York, 1942), vol. 1, p. 606; Robert K. Krick, *Lee's Colonels* (Dayton, 1992), p. 233; Charles C. Lee to Branch, unpublished official report dated May 29, 1862, Branch Papers.

Modern view of the Kinney House. The 28th North Carolina and 25th New York fought hand-to-hand around this building, scattering casualties through the yard. (photo by Tara Carmichael)

Junction of New Bridge and Ashcake Roads, looking southwest. Martindale's brigade and two guns of Martin's Battery defended this intersection. The 18th North Carolina attacked across the field in front. (Photo by Tara Carmichael)

his regiment as a block across the road while sending the 12th North Carolina Infantry-temporarily attached to Branch-on a flanking mission toward the railroad on Porter's right. However, the Union artillery and infantry stationed just east of Peake's pounded those Confederate dispositions. A well-placed shot exploded one of Latham's caissons, killing two men, wounding seven others, and destroying two horses. This forced the Confederates to temporarily fall back, conveniently misleading Fitz John Porter as to their strength and intentions.

John H. Martindale's brigade arrived at the intersection of the Ashcake and New Bridge Roads in time to be detailed as its defender. While Porter crushed Lane's 28th North Carolina, Martindale's men guarded the intersection, which was Porter's line of retreat. They remained there in reduced numbers when the main body of the column renewed its march to Hanover Court House.

Facing west toward Peake's, Martindale's mixed brigade of soldiers from New York, Maine and Massachusetts formed a line around the intersection, which by then had become the crucial strategic point in Porter's plans. Lieutenant Valentine M. Dunn, commanding a section of A. P. Martin's Battery C, 1st Massachusetts Light Artillery, placed two guns at the crossroads. Dunn's section became the most important tactical point on the battlefield. The guns swept the approach by road well enough, but woods to their left front and right front proved sufficiently dense to shelter Confederate infantry. An open field, bordered north and south by woods, stretched in front nearly to Peake's Station.[25]

Artillery during Civil War battles always drew a crowd. The guns represented a tangible goal for which every man could strive amidst the chaos and disorder of battle. Even General Branch followed that pattern. He conceived a triple-headed attack formation guided on the Yankee guns at the intersection. Although flanking the Union infantry and securing the road junction were desirable prizes, Branch's orders and movements emphasized the artillery.

---

[25] *OR* 11, pt. 1, p. 697.

To that end, he launched the 18th North Carolina straight ahead across the open ground toward the big guns. The 37th North Carolina was to veer north across the Ashcake Road into the woods, bearing toward Martindale's right flank. The 33rd North Carolina and the 12th North Carolina mirrored that move in the other direction, eventually filling the woods on Martindale's left flank. Some of those Carolinians moved so far south that they captured a Federal hospital at the Slaughter House on the main road from New Bridge.[26]

Martindale, with Morell and Porter hovering nearby, labored to assemble his own line. He posted fragments of the freshly thrashed 25th New York immediately on the right of the artillery. The 44th New York of Butterfield's brigade, the column's rearguard in the early fighting, faced the menacing woods opposite the Union left, its right resting on Martin's guns. The 2nd Maine spent the early part of the fight maneuvering around the edge of the woods on the Union right, north of the road.

Although Porter's men were the raiders, the burden of attack clearly lay with the Confederates. The 28th North Carolina remained isolated over the hills toward Hanover Court House. Branch saw it would be bad policy to abandon Lane's Carolinians without testing the obstacles between. According to Colonel Lee of the 37th, he acted as the commander on the field, responsible for both his own unit and the 18th North Carolina. He begged in vain for reinforcements from the start. Finally, General Branch ordered the attack on Martin's guns.[27] The 18th North Carolina bore the horrible brunt of this assault. After arranging their line, the Carolinians stepped out from behind the Harris House. They struggled across about 100 yards of open ground into the face of the assembling Union line. Colonel Robert H. Cowan led the men of the 18th, their bayonets at the ready in anticipation of a grapple around Martin's pair of roaring guns. Federal observers commented on the

[26] Ibid., p. 728.

[27] Charles C. Lee to Branch, unpublished official report of May 29, 1862, Branch Papers.

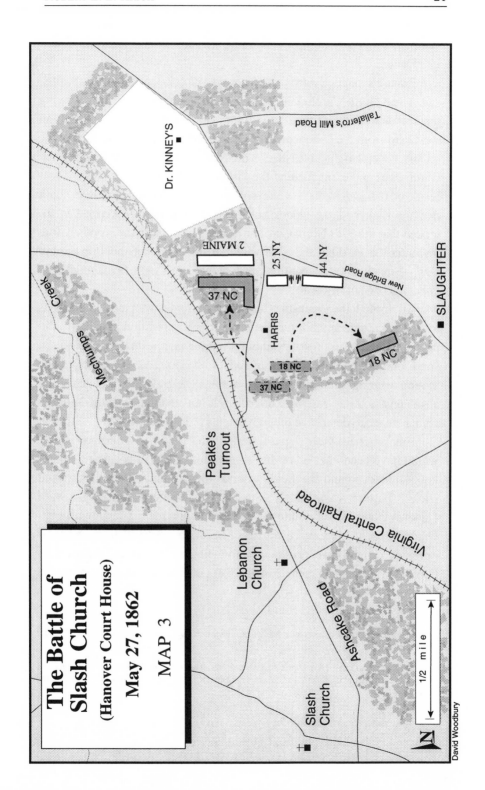

The Battle of
Slash Church
(Hanover Court House)

May 27, 1862

MAP 3

David Woodbury

symmetrical beauty of the Confederate advance, with colorful flags well in advance.

Branch's plan, attractive in concept, developed slowly in reality. The other North Carolinians were unable to support the 18th, leaving that lone unit at the demoralizing mercy of the canister and shell ripping westward from the Union artillery. As the attack faltered, the 2nd Maine on the Federal right unleashed a musketry fire, obliquely flanking the Carolinians and extinguishing the last spark of their attack. As a direct result of the 2nd Maine's volleys, Cowan's Confederates moved south into the shelter of the woods bordering the big field. Branch had intended that the 37th North Carolina assume position in the woods before this attack began, but the 37th was still in support of the 18th farther west. Branch reported that this was Colonel Lee's fault, he having "misconceived one of my orders."[28]

All through the Peninsula Campaign, Federals went aloft in balloons to observe Confederate movements. Porter's expedition apparently did not have a balloon on hand, although more than a dozen miles to the south one of the balloons, prompted by the noise of the battle, made several exciting ascents in the high winds. The balloon's occupants saw absolutely nothing, forcing Porter to rely on traditional methods of reconnaissance to determine the movements of his enemy.[29]

Any aeronaut with a good view of the field that afternoon surely would have been puzzled by his observations. The opposing regiments lay scattered around the fields at crazy angles like randomly dropped sticks. Farthest east, Lane's 28th North Carolina was fleeing toward Hanover Court House. Butterfield's Federal brigade led the pursuit eastward, some of his units using the line of the railroad to speed their progress. Slightly west of them, and facing entirely in the other direction, lay Martindale's men. Finally, parts of Branch's Brigade occupied

---

[28] Endorsement of Branch, June 6, 1862, to Colonel Lee's unpublished report of May 29, 1862, Branch Papers.

[29] *Military Ballooning 1862* (London, 1967), p. 32. This is a reprint of the 1863 original. It consists of a collection of papers read before the Corps of Royal Engineers in England during the Civil War.

various wooded spots farther west. These Confederates presented nothing remotely akin to a solid front. Indeed, the center of their "line"-the open field extending toward Peake's Turnout-contained nothing more than dead and wounded from the 18th and perhaps Latham's two guns. The gap between the 18th and 37th extended for several hundred yards, and was clearly visible to everyone along the Federal line.

This peculiar arrangement bore surprising early dividends for the North Carolinians. From their respective woods, the 18th and 37th North Carolina unleashed a crossfire that shattered most of Martindale's line. Martin's cannoneers abandoned their pieces and ran east, leaving behind only Lieutenant Dunn and three loyal men valiantly trying to serve the pieces.[30]

At about the same time, the abused fragments of the 25th New York joined the artillerymen leaving the field. Colonel Johnson of the 25th had fallen wounded when his horse was struck by four bullets simultaneously. This left only the 44th New York and the 2nd Maine on the line. The 44th had occupied a position parallel to the New Bridge Road and just a few yards west of it when the battle began. The sudden increase in Confederate fire drove the right of the 44th back across the road to the cover of a slight swell. The left of that regiment stayed on the original line, shielded by a hollow that made the men less conspicuous targets.[31]

As the well-directed fire from the 18th North Carolina forced the right wing of the New Yorkers rearward, General Martindale discovered this new problem when he glanced toward his left and noticed that "the smoke was moving toward me. . . ."[32] Only the 2nd Maine and a few men of the 44th New York remained to defend the intersection. Lieutenant Colonel James C. Rice commanded the wing of the 44th New York still on the line, the colonel of the regiment having "retired for the purpose of consulting with the general as to bringing up reinforce-

---

[30] Letter of Lieutenant Dunn paraphrased in George L. Gibbs to "Friend Whittier," June 6, 1862, Lewis Leigh Collection, Book 5, USAMHI.

[31] *OR* 11, pt. 1, p. 728.

[32] Ibid., pp. 705, 717.

ments." Evidence from others in the regiment suggests that Col. Stephen W. Stryker did not perform his whole duty that day. After the war, the regimental historian recorded that Colonel Stryker was discovered by a wounded soldier in the rear "dismounted and seated quietly by a tree, holding his horse."[33]

Four of the 44th's color bearers fell, and a post-battle examination of the flag revealed 42 bullet holes. The survivors, many of whom fought from the road bed, used muskets loaded for them by their wounded comrades. Weapons grew obstinate from excessive use, some discharging while in the process of being loaded. Lieutenant Colonel James C. Rice reported that many men used water from their canteens to cool heated barrels.[34]

All through the fight, men from the 44th performed heroic deeds of resistance. One private fell with two head wounds and a missing finger, yet managed to fire another 20 rounds from his prone position. A bullet broke the arm of the regimental adjutant while he waved his sword. The officer went to the rear, had the arm bandaged, and returned to the front, bearing his sword aloft with the other arm. Most of the surviving officers grabbed weapons and fired toward the Carolinians; even Lieutenant Colonel Rice reported that "I had the pleasure of firing over fifty rounds myself."[35]

A sergeant from the regiment, in his first real battle, mused afterward that "It was hard to see one's brave comrades shot, reel and fall, the life-blood gushing from their wounds. Yet the scene did not effect me as much as I thought it would."[36] It is likely that the right of this regimental fragment fired across the field into the woods occupied by the 37th

---

[33] Eugene A. Nash, *A History of the Forty-fourth Regiment New York Volunteer Infantry* (Chicago, 1911), p. 75; *OR* 11, pt. 1, p. 730.

[34] Frasier Rosenkranz (44th New York) to "Dear Cousin, June 11, 1862, Civil War Miscellaneous Collection, USAMHI; *OR* 11, pt. 1, p. 731.

[35] James C. Rice to Erastus Corning, June 9, 1862, Corning Papers, Albany Institute of History & Art, Box 92, Folder 5.

[36] *OR* 11, pt. 1, p. 733; letter of Sergeant Henry M. Galpin (44th New York), in the Herkimer County (N.Y.) *Journal*, June 12, 1862.

North Carolina, while the left dueled with the 18th North Carolina. The actions of the 12th and 33rd North Carolina regiments during the fight are harder to determine with accuracy. General Branch claimed that after capturing the hospital at the Slaughter House, Col. Robert F. Hoke's 33rd regiment circled into the woods north of the road to support the 37th North Carolina. If Hoke ever arrived he certainly had little impact, for no one mentioned his presence.[37]

The 2nd Maine and the 37th North Carolina engaged in the most desperate fight of the day. After being relieved by the 25th New York, the Maine regiment had moved north of the road to the east side of a fence at the edge of the woods. One Confederate officer described the enemy position as "drawn up along a dirt and cedar fence."[38]

On the other side of the prominent fence lay the 37th, its attention split between the artillery at the crossroads to the right front, and the 2nd Maine a few feet across the fence. The thick undergrowth so typical in Virginia fouled the Confederate advance. The Tarheels crashed through to within 15 yards of the 2nd Maine before discovering the sudden danger to their front. That same irritating mixture of brush and small trees protected them from Martin's artillery, which threw canister into the woods at short range without much effect.[39]

Colonel Charles W. Roberts, commanding the Federals along the fence line, remembered that "through the fence muzzle met muzzle, the fight waxing warm." In the less formal language of one of the foot soldiers, the action was "purty lively for sometime." Because of the varying density of the woods, some companies saw a disproportionate chunk of the fighting.[40]

With Colonel Lee acting as field commander coordinating the attack of the 18th and 37th North Carolina, Lt. Col. William M. Barbour as-

---

[37] *OR* 11, pt. 1, pp. 731, 741.

[38] Charles C. Lee to Branch, unpublished report dated May 29, 1862, Branch Papers.

[39] Ibid.

[40] *OR* 11, pt. 1, p. 709; O'Connell Memoir, p. 24; James H. Mundy, *Second to None: The Story of the 2nd Maine Volunteer Infantry* (Scarborough, 1992), p. 142.

sumed control of the 37th. He barely escaped death when his horse was killed and a spent ball slapped him in the neck. Others shared a similar fate when the regimental major was blown off his horse, but remained unhurt, and the adjutant's horse fell dead in course of the fight.[41]

Union accounts conflict with the main body of sources on two points. A soldier in the 25th New York recorded that the 37th North Carolina attempted to climb over the fence into the field, but was blasted by Martindale's men before it could accomplish anything. Only one account mentions that effort.[42]

Likewise, a man from the 2nd Maine claimed that for a time the Confederates actually were among Martin's abandoned guns. This apparently was a prevalent rumor, as Colonel Roberts of the 2nd took pains in his report to mention that "the pieces were not polluted by rebel hands."[43]

To this juncture of the battle (late in the afternoon) Porter had been badly out-generaled by Branch. He had failed to use his numerical advantage to improve his situation, and he had been whipped twice in separate engagements. He had, however, salvaged the situation against the 28th North Carolina earlier, and it was vital to the success of his expedition that he duplicate that victory against the remainder of Branch's Brigade. An embarrassment in northern Hanover might have a fatal effect on McClellan's already shaky relations with Lincoln and others in Washington.

Porter responded well to the crisis, taking action even before Martindale rode rearward with his grim tale of the collapse of the center of the line. Butterfield's brigade reached Hanover Court House just as Porter realized his peril. As Butterfield's men stacked arms near the court house, they received instructions to return as reinforcements. Other scattered units abounded closer to the Union line. Porter simply

---

[41] Charles C. Lee to Branch, unpublished official report dated May 29, 1862, Branch Papers.

[42] W. E. D. (25th N.Y.) to "My Dear Mother" in Rochester (N.Y.) *Union and Advertiser,* June 9, 1862.

[43] O'Connell Memoir, p. 24; *OR* 11, pt. 1, p. 710.

collared the 9th Massachusetts and the 62nd Pennsylvania from Col. James McQuade's brigade and launched them into the woods north of the 2nd Maine, where they easily flanked the 37th North Carolina. This, as Martindale dryly recorded, "necessarily ended the battle on the right." The fight in the woods had lasted 25 minutes, according to Colonel Lee of the 37th North Carolina.[44]

While those regiments labored through the woods, the 14th New York Infantry wheeled into the field in front of Martin's guns, facing north. This maneuver fixed the 37th North Carolina in position, and ensured the success of the flanking movement by McQuade's two regiments. The valiant 2nd Maine, low on ammunition, greeted the reinforcements with a loud shout and moved wearily rearward.[45] Parts of Butterfield's exhausted brigade moved along the railroad, placing them even farther behind Lee's regiment. The men of the 16th Michigan found themselves too distant to be of great use, so they unleashed a loud trio of cheers for the flag as a substitute for a more active role.[46]

Fresh Federal artillery rolled up to support the attack. Captain Charles Griffin's Battery deployed on a knoll south of the Ashcake Road, near one of the many Harris homes that dotted the field. Good gun positions were rare. The 5th Massachusetts Battery arrived nearby, but could not find room to unlimber. Instead, a cannoneer wrote, "we cooly remained on the field having a fine view of the fight." A member of the battery recorded that he watched the 9th Massachusetts step into the Confederate woods and emerge later with "but few Prisoners when they might have [taken] many."[47]

The ending was disastrous for the 37th North Carolina. The regiment's prolonged duel with the 2nd Maine occupied the full attention of

---

[44] *OR* 11, pt. 1, p. 706; Charles C. Lee to Branch, unpublished report dated May 29, 1862, Branch Papers.

[45] *OR* 11, pt. 1, p. 709

[46] Joseph Stanfield Diary (16th Michigan), May 27, 1862, in Civil War Miscellaneous Collection, USAMHI.

[47] William H. Peacock (Hyde's 5th Massachusetts Battery) to "Dear Sarah," May 31, 1862, in Civil War Miscellaneous Collection, USAMHI.

the Carolinians until they suddenly perceived fresh Union troops on their left flank and even in their rear. Colonel Lee called for a fighting withdrawal, "which was done in only tolerable order," he reported, because "the incessant volleys of musketry at 15 or 20 paces drowned every other sound and no command could be heard."[48] General Branch recognized his increasing peril and ordered each regiment to leave the field. Engineer officer Francis T. Hawks of Branch's staff carried the order into the woods occupied by the 18th regiment. While returning, he met Colonel Lee. When asked how the 37th was faring across the road, Lee replied "Bad sir bad. My regiment has disgraced itself and me."[49]

By most accounts, the rest of the Confederate retreat was a smooth operation. Branch had held the 7th North Carolina out of the battle for such a moment as this. While the individual units disengaged, the 7th formed line of battle across the Ashcake Road and held the Federal pursuit at bay. Although Branch spoke highly of his men for their efforts that day, he especially admired the precision of their retreat, taking an almost McClellanesque pride in a defeat well managed.[50]

By the time Branch began to spread orders for a retreat, dozens of wounded occupied the brigade hospital in the rear, probably near Lebanon Church. Upon receiving orders to evacuate the wounded westward, the brigade surgeon, according to an observer, "most disgracefully mounted his horse, as did two other Surgeons, and left the wounded, ambulances, instruments, and supplies lying unprotected in the yard."[51]

While most of the brigade began its retreat toward Ashland, the 37th North Carolina disintegrated. Colonel Lee still struggled with the problem of noise. Too few of his men heard the retreat order. With McQuade's regiments angling in from the north, the last shreds of

---

[48] Charles C. Lee to Branch, unpublished report dated May 29, 1862, Branch Papers.

[49] Affadavit of Francis T. Hawks, August 2, 1862, Branch Papers.

[50] For evidence of Branch's joy at the orderly retreat, see his report in *OR* 11, pt. 1, p. 742, as well as his unpublished endorsement to Colonel Lee's report and his letter to his wife dated May 30, 1862, both in the Branch Papers.

[51] Louis Shaffner (Surgeon, 33rd North Carolina), "A Civil War Surgeon's Diary," *North Carolina Medical Journal*, vol. 27 (September 1966), p. 410.

regimental unity evaporated. Of the 37th's 219 casualties on May 27, 129 were prisoners of war.[52]

The citizens in the little railroad town of Ashland, northwest of Peake's, braced themselves for occupation with varying degrees of dignity. A stray Georgian in the town remembered that during the afternoon a "scout and itinerate preacher" arrived in town together, spreading the alarm of advancing Federals and announcing a near escape from enemy bullets. Shortly thereafter, a farmer appeared from the same direction. He was quizzed about the progress of the foe. The farmer responded that the enemy was no closer than Hanover Court House. He did recall that just as the scout and preacher had passed him on the road he had shot a squirrel, but that "both he and the squirrel were Confeds, and meant no harm to anyone."[53]

Farther east, Colonel Lane and his regiment found themselves increasingly distant from their comrades. The remaining Parrott commanded by Lieutenant Potts covered the retreat. Near Hanover Court House, Potts made a brief stand in the yard of "Courtland," the home of Philip B. Winston, a Confederate staff officer and future brother-in-law of General Thomas Rosser. According to local lore, the Confederates "were asked to move" so that the house might not be damaged. The retreat also wandered through the estate of future general Williams Wickham, then the colonel of the 4th Virginia Cavalry.[54]

Lane found the direct road to Ashland blocked, forcing him to march north to Taylorsville before curving west to reach Ashland. Upon arriving at Ashland on May 28, Lane's hungry men found the rest of their brigade gone and nothing in Ashland but several overlooked barrels

---

[52] Author's compilation of statistics based on the compiled service records as published in Weymouth T. Jordan, Jr. (comp.) *North Carolina Troops, 1861-1865: A Roster* (Raleigh, 1966-1990), 12 vols.

[53] Unidentified Georgian, "Fagots from the Old Camp Fires," *The Sunny South* (Atlanta), November 5, 1892.

[54] Hanover County Historical Society, *Old Homes of Hanover County* (Hanover, 1983), p. 76; *OR* 11, pt. 1, p. 745.

Men of the 17th New York Infantry proudly display the 12-pounder howitzer they captured from Latham's Battery on May 27, 1862. (courtesy of Seward Osborne)

of whiskey. Colonel Lane allowed a small ration of the stimulant to his willing men, and noted after the war that "I did not have to repeat the order & you can imagine the effect upon empty stomachs. The whole town, male & female, witnessed the performance, & a little before sunset we took leave of them with songs, old rebel yells & a general waving of caps."[55]

Fitz John Porter's exhausted troops held the battlefield. By that measure, and many others, they were the victors. For all of Porter's regiments, and particularly the 25th New York, it had been an uncomfortable day of soldiering. Their pre-dawn awakening preceded a 15-mile march in rain and mud that reached a climax in the hotly contested Battle of Slash Church. The 25th had broken twice, incurred 28 killed and 79 wounded and suffered more than any other Federal unit. The 25th's list of 158 casualties represented 45 percent of Porter's total losses for the expedition.[56] Most of the regiments had fought well. General Martindale was especially happy with the solid work of the 2nd Maine. He made a small speech on the evening of the 27th, promising an extra gill of whiskey to each man as a reward for a good performance. Martindale also commenced wearing a small pine twig in his cap to commemorate the battle, and everyone in the 25th New York followed his example.[57]

Nearby, Lieutenant Colonel Rice of the 44th New York, examining the roadbed near the intersection where his wing of the regiment had fought, found a badly wounded solider of his unit. "I paused, stooped over to hear some dying request to a fond mother or sister, but all he said was this, 'Colonel, is the day ours?' 'Yes,' I replied. 'Then I am willing to die.'"[58]

---

[55] James H. Lane to Thomas T. Munford, January 4, 1893, Munford-Ellis Papers at Perkins Library, Duke University, Durham, N.C.

[56] *OR* 11, pt. 1, p. 685.

[57] John O'Connell Memoir, p. 25; W.E.D. to "My Dear Mother," May 30, 1862, in Rochester *Union and Advertiser*, June 9, 1862.

[58] *OR* 11, pt. 1, pp. 732-733.

While the Federal cavalry chased stray North Carolinians, the infantry fell to burying the dead on the battlefield. They marveled at the size of Branch's sturdy soldiers. One member of the 16th Michigan inspected the woods occupied by the 37th North Carolina. He discovered that most of the dead had been shot in the head, a situation he attributed to the position of the Carolinians "behind the bank of a ditch and a brush fence." In the usual haste of the moment, most of the dead were buried in large pits, three or four feet deep. In some instances, as many as 25 of Branch's men were buried together, "without blanket, shroud or coffin."[59]

Most of the surviving contemporary accounts mention both the appearance of the Confederates, living and dead, and the general disorder of the area around Peake's. One Massachusetts man reported of the Confederates that their area "was strewed with knapsacks, blankets, socks, drawers, shirts, etc., but the men are dressed mean and miserable enough."[60]

Dr. Kinney's house and outbuildings became centers of medical activity. The remnants of the fight between Lane and the 25th New York still littered the yard. Sergeant Clark of the 25th was discovered dead atop a North Carolinian. Lieutenant Fiske of the same regiment lay lifeless under a tree in the yard, a shattered musket by his side. Other graphic evidence of the close-quarters fight scarred the yard. "No man can describe his feelings as he walks over a fresh battle field," wrote Maj. E. S. Gilbert of the 25th. "It is terrible, and the sight haunts one for many days. The Lord deliver me from another such a sight."[61]

Most of Branch's wounded fell into Porter's hands, where they received treatment by Federal surgeons. One "very robust, large, muscular" Tarheel was prepared for a thigh amputation with the usual

---

[59] Joseph Stanfield Diary, May 28, 1862; Daniel G. Macnamara, *The History of the Ninth Regiment Massachusetts Volunteer Infantry* (Boston, 1899), p. 96.

[60] Joseph Simonds (22nd Massachusetts) to "Dear Sister Susie," May 28, 1862, in Lewis Leigh Collection, Book 49, USAMHI.

[61] Major E. S. Gilbert letter of May 31, 1862, in Rochester (N.Y.) *Democrat and American*, June 10, 1862.

chloroform. He seemed remarkably immune to the effects of it, until the surgeon of the 16th Michigan "forced him to large and free inspirations," whereupon he died. This episode received official attention as an extreme example of the widely differing responses to anesthetic.[62]

To the west, Branch's North Carolinians stopped to assess their damage. Roll call revealed severely depleted ranks. The 18th North Carolina's fight directly before Martindale's line translated into substantial casualties. Colonel Cowan counted 22 killed and 22 mortally wounded among other losses. The 37th North Carolina lost 219 men. Lane's 28th North Carolina losses numbered 288, of which 265 were captured. In contrast to Branch's 746 casualties, Porter recorded only 355. His figures, however, show that more Northern troops were shot that day than North Carolinians. The huge number of prisoners accounts for the disparity in numbers. One of the oft-cited tragedies of this battle occurred in Company G of the 37th North Carolina. The four Robinett brothers served together in that company; three of the four were killed outright on the field in the afternoon of May 27.[63]

Among his men, Lawrence Branch emerged from the fight with a mottled reputation. Many in his brigade blamed him directly for the defeat, one declaring ungrammatically that, "We was defeated through General Branch's Bad Management."[64] Branch justified the fight by commenting that he "had no orders against fighting, and thought it proper to fight some before retreating." He also hoped the noise of the

---

[62] *The Medical and Surgical History of the War of the Rebellion, (1861-65)*, 12 vols., (Washington, D.C., 1870), vol. 2, p. 72.

[63] Jordan, *North Carolina Troops*. 7th N.C. = 0 killed, 2 mortally wounded, 4 wounded, 15 prisoners, 2 wounded & prisoner. Total = 23; 12th N.C. = 1 killed, 6 mortally wounded, 3 wounded, 12 prisoners, 6 wounded & prisoner. Total = 28; 18th N.C. = 22 killed, 22 mortally wounded, 32 wounded, 62 prisoners, 26 wounded & prisoner. Total = 164; 28th N.C. = 8 killed, 6 mortally wounded, 1 wounded, 265 prisoners, 8 wounded & prisoner. Total = 288; 33rd N.C. = 0 killed, 0 mortally wounded, 2 wounded, 21 prisoners, 1 wounded & prisoner. Total = 24; 37th N.C. = 26 killed, 20 mortally wounded, 28 wounded, 129 prisoners, 16 wounded & prisoner. Total = 219; Casualties for Latham's Battery not examined; Grand total for Branch's force = 746 casualties. These statistics are derived from data in several volumes in this excellent series. Colonel Lee of the 37th North Carolina was killed June 30th at the Battle of Glendale.

[64] William Graves Morris to Louisa Morris, May 30, 1862, Morris Papers, Southern Historical Collection, University of North Carolina, Chapel Hill.

fight "would attract to me some re-enforcements." Joseph R. Anderson had several brigades about 10 miles distant at Hanover Junction. Sometime during the afternoon, Branch received a dispatch from Brig. Gen. Charles W. Field of that force, offering two brigades of reinforcements because "I hear cannonading in your direction." Branch's response is not on record, but help never arrived from that direction.[65]

Others took the criticism a step further. William T. Nicholson, adjutant of the 37th North Carolina, wrote a lengthy, anonymous letter to the Richmond Examiner describing the battle from his perspective. General Branch took issue with the tenor of the "grossly slandering" piece, erupted in rage, and scoured his command for the culprit. The style of the letter reminded Branch of Colonel Lee's official report so much that he summoned Lee and demanded an explanation. Under that pressure, Lee finally admitted that Adjutant Nicholson was the guilty party.[66]

Having identified Nicholson, Branch set about ruining the adjutant. He "felt it due to myself" to prefer lengthy charges, citing seven specific untruths in the newspaper article. Branch professed distaste for such acrimony, although the historical record is replete with examples of the general ripping into colleagues and subordinates. Despite his hesitancy, Branch pushed on because "every sensible person must be satisfied that longer submission in silence under these monstrous and abominable slanders would be equivalent to admitting their truthfulness."[67]

These "monstrous and abominable slanders" consisted of several remarkably petty points concerning the development of the battle. Nicholson wrote that Branch's headquarters when the battle began were distant more than a mile. In fact, they were at Slash Church, which is two-thirds of a mile away by air, and almost exactly one mile by road. Branch also officially complained that Nicholson's article did not credit Branch with as timely an arrival on the field as the general thought

---

[65] Branch to *Richmond Examiner*, May 29, 1862; C. W. Field to Branch, May 27, 1862, Branch Papers; *OR* 11, pt. 1, p. 742.

[66] Branch to wife, June 1, 1862, Branch Papers.

[67] Branch to Governor Clark, June 8, 1862, Branch Papers.

proper. The two officers also argued about whether Branch or Colonel Lee commanded the field at the start of the fight. Only three of Branch's charges had any substance, the most important being a refutation of Nicholson's claims that Branch hoarded reinforcements at the expense of the 37th and 18th regiments. Although Branch held back only the 7th North Carolina, the sentiment among many of the men was that he did not manage his force well.[68]

Branch was an early devotee of the conspiracy theory of human affairs. His papers reveal an almost constant fixation on his conniving political enemies back in North Carolina. To them went the responsibility for Nicholson's attitude. He feared that they might "ruin my reputation." To block their machinations, Branch resorted to three counterattacks. He made a public example of Adjutant Nicholson; he urged all his correspondents at home to publish his letters; and he sought approbation from his new chief, Robert E. Lee. On June 9, an outraged Branch wrote Lee asking for a court of inquiry. The court's duty would be two-fold. In addition to examining the battle and revealing the true facts of the case, the court was to announce its findings on Branch's competence.[69]

This was clearly going too far. Faced with the first of what proved to be many cases of aggrieved subordinates, the new commander of the Army of Northern Virginia unveiled his tactful pen in responding to Branch. While sympathizing with Branch, Lee did "not see how it would be possible to have the thorough investigation," especially at a time of national crisis when "every one is or ought to be at his post." Branch viewed this as sufficient to salve his feelings, though a close reading of Lee's words yields a faint whiff of rebuke.[70]

The Battle of Slash Church was the first heavy fighting of the battles around Richmond. Four days later, Joseph Johnston launched his jum-

---

[68] "Charges and Specifications preferred against William T. Nicholson. . . . ," n.d., Branch Papers.

[69] Branch to R. E. Lee, June 9, 1862, Branch Papers.

[70] R. E. Lee to Branch, June 11, 1862, Branch Papers.

bled attacks at Seven Pines. Two weeks after that, Jeb Stuart performed his mounted circumnavigation of the Army of the Potomac. Finally, two more weeks later, Lee opened his historic campaign to relieve Richmond of its burdensome besiegers.

Porter's sortie into upper Hanover achieved one item of lasting importance. On May 28 and 29, his troopers destroyed both railroad bridges over the South Anna River. They also hovered around Ashland, annoying other Confederate railroad operations. The loss of those bridges and their accompanying rail lines haunted Confederate efforts well into the Seven Days Battles one month later. Porter's avowed goal of stranding Joseph R. Anderson's force well north of Richmond could not be met, however, as those Southerners were already near Richmond by the time Porter sealed off the northern approaches. The victory did provide McClellan with a convincing weapon to brandish in the direction of his political tormentors. Although Porter returned to his camps along the Chickahominy almost immediately, the victory perpetuated the illusion that the Army of the Potomac still possessed the initiative.

The long awaited meeting between McClellan's right and McDowell from Fredericksburg never materialized. The Union flank still dangled in mid-June, permitting Stuart's cavalry excursion. Remarkably, it still floated in late June, inviting Lee's stunning attacks in the Seven Days Battles. McClellan surely did not extract any lasting lessons from the affair at Slash Church.

The most significant result of the battle was accidental. One month later, the same Union troops who had weathered the fight on May 27 bore the brunt of Confederate assaults in two much larger engagements. The men of Morell's division repelled several spirited attacks on June 27 at Gaines' Mill, a feat facilitated by their recent experiences in close combat. The most serious Confederate penetration at Malvern Hill on July 1, due largely to the contours of that battlefield near the Crew House, again tested Morell's troops. Their experiences at Slash Church surely contributed to their sturdy performance under such trying circumstances.

Branch's defeated North Carolinians gained valuable experience as well. With the exceptions of shooting Stonewall Jackson accidentally in 1863, and breaking briefly at the Battle of North Anna in 1864, that brigade carved a reputation for valor equal to that of most brigades in the Army of Northern Virginia. As evidence trickled in after the engagement near Slash Church and after the war, the truth of Branch's predicament (both geographically and statistically) became clear. The success of his fight became apparent in light of the potential for disaster.

* * *

The Battle of Slash Church will never appear as part of a television mini-series. Nor is it likely that a book devoted solely to the battle will emerge. Still, the evolutions of the action, the precise surviving maps and the numerous personal accounts provide a lucid view of a Civil War battle. Slash Church magnified many times is Sharpsburg, Gettysburg, or Gaines' Mill. While those encounters consumed thousands of men, featured vast hordes of combatants, and produced far reaching strategic ramifications, they were not much different from Slash Church to the farmers and factory workers doing the shooting. A Civil War battle for most participants consisted of what they could see and reach, which usually limited their observations to the division level at the very broadest. The fight at Slash Church provides the student with a chance to understand clearly the mechanics of a Civil War battle. That alone is a compelling reason to appreciate the engagement of May 27, 1862. The thousands of men who grappled over a grim battlefield that long afternoon in upper Hanover County were more concerned with the shared catastrophe that enveloped them than with the educational opportunities the little battle offered. From either perspective, the action at Slash Church warrants study and respect.

* * *

The following list of sources is intended as a supplement to the material cited above in the main essay. Although the author examined these important items, he did not find graceful opportunities to insert them into the text. As any thoughtful historian realizes, many years hence his subjective conclusions will be less useful to his successors than will his bibliography. So these references are included as an aid to future Slash Church scholars:

- Apted, Alfred. Reminiscences, in the Civil War Miscellaneous Collection at USAMHI. Apted served in the 16th Michigan.

- Fowler, Frederick. Letters in Civil War Miscellaneous Collection at USAMHI. Fowler served in the 5th New York Zouaves.

- Furst, Luther C. Diary, in Harrisburg CWRT Collection at USAMHI. Furst was a signalman during the raid.

- Harper's Weekly, June 21, 1862. There is a statement by an unidentified eyewitness in this issue.

- Porter, Fitz John, "Hanover Court House and Gaines's Mill," in Robert U. Johnson and Clarence C. Buel, eds., *Battles and Leaders of the Civil War*, 4 vols. (New York, 1884-89), vol. 2, pp. 319 ff. Queens County (N.Y.) *Sentinel*, October 2, 1862. This issue includes a letter from Charles Stewart Brooks of the 5th U. S. Cavalry.

- Rochester (N.Y.) *Democrat and American*, June 12, 1862, letter of a member of the 12th New York named Furman.

- Rochester (N.Y.) *Union and Advertiser*, June 7, 1862, letter of Capt. A. C. Preston of the 25th New York; July 2, 1862, letter of Maj. E. S. Gilbert of the 25th New York.

- Simonds, Joseph. Letters in the Lewis Leigh Collection, Book 49, USAMHI. Simonds served in the 22nd Massachusetts.

- Stone, Edwin W., *Rhode Island in the Rebellion,* (Providence 1864), pp. 92-96. Good material on Weeden's Battery.

Terry L. Jones

Dr. Jones, author of the award-winning *Lee's Tigers: The Louisiana Infantry in the Army of Northern Virginia* (Baton Rouge, 1987), and *Capt. William Seymour's Diary: The Civil War Reminiscences of a Louisiana Tiger* (Baton Rouge, 1991), is an assistant professor of history at Northeast Louisiana University. He has written many articles on Civil War subjects and is completing a book on Campbell Brown.

Down the Peninsula with Richard Ewell

Captain Campbell Brown's Memoirs of the Seven Days Battles

By June 1862, events seemed to move rapidly outside Richmond, Virginia. Union Maj. Gen. George B. McClellan's huge Army of the Potomac stood within five miles of the besieged capital, and Confederate Gen. Robert E. Lee searched for a plan to stave off the onslaught. On June 23, he met with Maj. Gen. Thomas J. "Stonewall" Jackson and other generals to form a plan by which to exploit the weakness in McClellan's position. The Federal army was divided by the Chickahominy River. Major General Fitz John Porter's corps lay on the north bank of the swampy stream, isolated from the rest of McClellan's army. Lee planned to bring Jackson's force from the Shenandoah Valley and mass the bulk of the Confederate army near the village of Mechanicsville. Jackson, fresh from his victorious Valley Campaign, was to swing in from the north on June 26 to out-flank Porter's strong position. His arrival on the field would be the signal for the divisions of A. P. Hill, James Longstreet and D. H. Hill to cross the Chickahominy and move on to attack Porter's front from the west. The plan was complicated and dangerous but held the promise of the destruction of McClellan's largest corps and engendered the hope that the Federals might be sent reeling back down the Peninsula.

After the meeting, Jackson headed back to rejoin his column on its way from Charlottesville, Virginia. Accompanying his army was 21-year-old Capt. Campbell Brown, assistant adjutant general to Maj. Gen. Richard S. Ewell, commander of a division in Jackson's small army. Brown belonged to a prominent Spring Hill, Tennessee, family; his mother, Lizinka Campbell Brown, was a first cousin to Ewell. Having joined Ewell's staff the day before the First Battle of Manassas, Brown had seen much hard service and had been slightly wounded in the shoulder at the Battle of Cross Keys two weeks earlier. Keenly observant, highly educated at schools both in the United States and Europe, Brown was well aware of the historic events swirling around him. He frequently kept notes on the army's activities during the war and in 1867 began writing a detailed memoir of his war service. Following is

Captain Campbell Brown

Brown's account of the Seven Days Battles. The narrative's original spelling and punctuation is left intact, although some excessively long paragraphs have been broken up for easier reading. Brown begins with Jackson having just left for his meeting with Lee, while Ewell pushes the column towards Richmond.[1]

*   *   *

We encamped the first day near Charlottesville, the next between Walker's Church (Rives' farm) and Gordonsville—the next we were scattered along the R.R.d. [railroad] from Gordonsville to Beaver Dam. At Walker's Church, the people of the neighborhood had prepared what they hoped would be lunch for the Army, and begged that the troops might be allowed to stop and eat it. Gen'l E. compromised on halting each Reg't. for a short time. The day was very hot & dusty—the men quite tired & of course dirty. We rode, as usual, at the head of the column, or rather in advance of it—and as we came in sight of the Church, I thought I had never seen anything more beautiful than the collection of ladies in their cool, fresh-looking dresses, scattered in groups about the green churchyard, under the shade, busied in their labor of love. As the troops were not yet in sight, we dismounted and entered the gate. I was soon introduced to one or two gentlemen & as many married ladies—but Turner[2] and I fixed our attention on two very pretty girls whom we determined to know. As soon as the first Reg't. came up abreast of the Church, it was halted and the work of feeding began. The

[1] The editor would like to express his great appreciation to the Tennessee State Library and Archives for permission to publish Brown's memoirs and for the gracious assistance offered him on this project.

[2] Thomas T. Turner, an 18-year-old Baltimorean, joined Ewell's staff in the fall of 1861, probably as a volunteer aide. Appointed first lieutenant on April 29, 1862, he served Ewell as an aide-de-camp. In October 1865, he married Campbell's sister, Harriet. Record Group 109 (RG 109), Compiled Service Records of Confederate General and Staff Officers, and Nonregimental Enlisted Men, Microcopy 331, Roll 252, National Archives, Washington, D. C.; Percy Gatling Hamlin, *"Old Bald Head" (General R. S. Ewell): The Portrait of a Soldier* (Strasburg, Va., 1940), p. 72.

girls were to stand inside of the fence and pass the provisions over it, to prevent their being overwhelmed in the rush Gen'l E. knew would take place. My first attention had been to move a bucket of buttermilk close to the fence for my charmer, who acknowledged the service with a nod and a blush and I now stood a yard or two away watching her hand glasses of it to the men. I saw one big fellow of an enterprising turn, come up boldly & get one glass—then stood so as to look very small & get another—then appear in another disguise as candidate for a third. Flesh & blood couldn't stand it, & I had to tell her that others must go without if he got so much. She looked rather surprised & indignant at my speech—but didn't answer—and I thought I had ruined my chance, when just as a fresh stream of candidates came up, the buttermilk gave out. She then rewarded my patience by acknowledging with a smile that I was right—and as the troops moved off (the first two Reg'ts having taken in what was meant to supply over thirty) we struck up quite a lively conversation. I soon found out who she was, got a regular intro-duction to strengthen my position, presented Turner and Greene,[3] and after a talk of two hours or more walked home with Miss Mary Meri-wether[4] & her friend, whose name I forget. Miss M. was the handsom-est woman I ever met—tall, straight, graceful, natural, with beautiful dark eyes & hair, regular features & the gait & air of a Juno rather than a Venus. I made love desperately for the time I had—returned some months later & yet a third time in 1864—& having only seen her on those three occasions. Consequently I could not tell whether her mind was a fit companion for so perfect a body—If it be, she is a prodigy.

[3] B. H. Greene, of Mississippi, joined Ewell's staff as a volunteer aide a few months after the First Battle of Manassas. He rose to the rank of major and served as the division's commissary of subsistence. By late 1864 he was still serving with Ewell as an engineer. Brown-Ewell Papers, Tennessee State Library and Archives, Nashville, Tennessee, Campbell Brown memoirs, p. 13; U.S. War Department, *The War of the Rebellion: The Official Records of the Union and Confederate Armies*, 128 vols. (Washington, D.C., 1890-1901), series I, vol. 12, pt. 1, p. 782. Hereinafter cited as *OR*. All references are to series I unless otherwise noted. Ibid., 36, pt. 1, p. 1074.

[4] Mr. T. W. Meriweather, a wealthy 57-year-old Albemarle County farmer, listed a female, M. G. Meriweather, as living in his household in the 1860 Census Population Schedule. This girl, however, would have been only 14 years old in 1862. She is the only female Meriweather–of any spelling—listed in the county census records. 1860 Census Population Schedules, Albemarle County, Virginia, Microcopy T-7, Roll 291, pp. 52-53, National Archives, Washington, D. C.

Next day by noon we reached Gordonsville. Before getting there Gen'l Ewell sent me to direct our wagons to that point. I gave the order as usual to Maj. Snodgrass,[5] A.Q.M., and then by the Gen'l's special advice paid a short visit to Mr. Wm. C. Rives'[6] family, who treated me very kindly. On reaching Gordonsville about 1 or 2 p.m., I found that the wagons had not come up, & was interrogated by Gen'l Ewell as to the cause. I told him that I had found them five miles from the place, four hours before, and given plain orders. He insisted I must have made a mistake in my orders, & sent me in all haste to turn them back. I rode at a gallop for thirteen or fourteen miles through hundreds of wagons on the Louisa C.H. road—then finding my horse about used up, persuaded a young wagonmaster whom I knew to lend me his, which was stone-blind & fell four or five times in the three miles to the C.H.—which I reached covered with dust and completely exhausted, to find from Maj. Harman[7] that the change of direction was in consequence of his orders, & all right—and that Gen'l E. had probably heard of the change of programme in fifteen minutes after I left him. This was slightly trying to the temper, but it was at least a consolation that I did not have to retrace my steps. I went to the telegraph-office, sent a message to Gordonsville, & I spent the night with Snodgrass. I had made the sixteen miles in about two hours—which was a pretty severe finish to the twenty three or four miles previously travelled.

At Beaver Dam I recollect Turner & I, who had ridden ahead, were waiting to meet Gen'l E. who was coming by rail. A fearfully hard rain

---

[5] Major C. E. Snodgrass was Ewell's acting quartermaster. He was dropped from the army roles on August 30, 1862. RG 109, Compiled Service Records of Confederate General and Staff Officers, Microcopy 331, Roll 233, National Archives, Washington, D.C.

[6] William Cabell Rives, a leading citizen of Albemarle County, had studied law under Thomas Jefferson and served in the United States House of Representatives, Senate and as minister to France. Although he originally opposed secession, Rives supported Virginia and served briefly in the Confederate Congress early in the war. He died in 1868. Dumas Malone, ed., *Dictionary of American Biography*, 10 vols. (New York, 1935-1936), vol. 8, pp. 635-636; William H. B. Thomas, *Gordonsville, Virginia: Historic Crossroads Town* (Verona, Va., 1971), p. 13.

[7] Major John A. Harman was Jackson's chief quartermaster. *OR* 11, pt. 2, p. 559.

came up—& the india-rubber blanket, under which we were sleeping in a skirt of woods not far from the depot, became so full of water in the hollow made by its sinking down between us, that I woke thinking Turner was pulling the cover off me. The rain had not fairly waked us, our heads being covered, and we were much surprised to find a gallon or more of water in the blanket. Both of us drank out of it, & then emptied it & went to sleep again. About midnight the train came & Turner went to join Gen'l E., leaving me according to previous orders with a courier, to wait til morning in case any thing should turn up. Turner gave afterwards an amusing account of Gen'l E.'s & Maj. Nelson's[8] adventure with a belligerent wagon driver into whose team they stumbled, in the dark. Near Ashland we again saw Gen'l Jackson & found ourselves in communication with Lee's army. We had known our destination from the time we reached Gordonsville—and the men were in high spirits at the chance of catching McClellan. The march thro' the "Slashes of Hanover"[9] began before day [June 26] & was a strange & dreary one—simply on account of the flat, swampy, dense nature of the country—with no extended views, almost no population. Skirmishing a little towards afternoon & hearing heavy fighting away to our right, we camped at Hundley's Corner, where a lively skirmish took place between our picket Regiment (the 1st Maryland) & a party of the enemy who were probably watching us—but were soon driven out of sight. A ludicrous incident happened about midnight. A horse got loose & tore about the bivouac of Taylor's Brigade,[10] treading on several men &

[8] Hugh M. Nelson had served as a captain in both the 1st Virginia and 6th Virginia Cavalry regiments. He may have lost his position during the army's reorganization during the spring of 1862, for he was on Ewell's staff as a volunteer aide during the Valley Campaign. During the Seven Days, he was an aide-de-camp to Ewell and held the rank of first lieutenant. Nelson was slightly wounded at the Battle of Malvern Hill and died from typhoid fever a few weeks after the Seven Days Battles. RG 109, Compiled Service Records of Confederate General and Staff Officers, Microcopy 331, Roll 186, National Archives, Washington, D.C.; *OR* 11, pt. 2, p. 607; Ibid., 12, pt. 1, p. 782.

[9] The "Slashes of Hanover" was a poor area of cut-over land in Hanover County. Occupied largely by poor white farmers, it was the birthplace of Henry Clay. Bernard Mayo, *Henry Clay: Spokesman of the New West* (Boston, 1937), p. 6.

[10] Richard Taylor was the son of former president Zachary Taylor and former brother-in-law of

raising a false alarm of a night attack, over which Taylor &c were a good deal exercised for a few minutes. Luckily nobody was shot, & the brute only trod on two or three before he was caught—didn't put anybody "hors du combat."[11]

Next morning [June 27] we moved, our Divn leading, with a guide, in the direction I believe of "Old Coal Harbor." Our line of march was at right angles, or nearly so, to that of the evening before—and as it turned out, two or three miles wrong—for Jackson after riding with us for two hours directing the march, suddenly changed its direction so much that we came into the proper road with the rear of our line leading, if I am not mistaken.[12] I was sent to recall some of the skirmishers, who

---

Jefferson Davis. Originally colonel of the 9th Louisiana, he was promoted to brigadier general in October 1861 and given command of the Louisiana Brigade. He rose to the rank of lieutenant general and emerged from the war as one of the South's most respected officers. William C. Davis, ed., *The Confederate General*, 6 vols. (n.p., 1991), vol. 6, pp. 29-31; See also T. Michael Parrish, *Richard Taylor: Soldier Prince of Dixie* (Chapel Hill, 1992) and Richard Taylor, *Destruction and Reconstruction: Personal Experiences of the Late War* (New York, 1879).

[11] June 26 had not gone well for the Confederates. Lee expected Jackson to be in position on the flank of Fitz John Porter's Union corps that morning, but Jackson was slow. He issued orders to move out by 2 a.m., but his men did not depart camp until after daylight and never seemed to hurry during the day's march. Jackson did not reach his assigned position on time. A. P. Hill grew impatient and opened the attack on his own that afternoon. His men engaged in an unsuccessful slugfest with the well entrenched enemy at Beaver Dam Creek-this was the heavy firing Brown refers to. As darkness fell, the Federals repulsed the Confederates, and Jackson was still not in position. Historians still debate whether fatigue, poor staff work or even a reluctance for his men to do all the fighting caused Jackson's slowness that day. "Stonewall" only reported that his march was impeded by felled trees and destroyed bridges. *OR* 11, pt. 2, pp. 553-555; Douglas Southall Freeman, *Lee's Lieutenants: A Study in Command*, 3 vols. (New York, 1942-1944), vol. 1, pp. 506-511, 656-659.

[12] Porter retreated from his Mechanicsville-Beaver Dam Creek line during the night to near Gaines' Mill, four miles to the southeast. The Federals dug in behind Boatswain's Swamp with strong artillery support. But on this day Jackson again mismanaged his march. He left Hundley's Corner and moved south to Walnut Grove Church, where he met Lee. Lee ordered Jackson to stay on the far left of the army and turn Porter's right flank, with D. H. Hill supporting him. To do so, Jackson was to turn east at the church and follow a circuitous but generally eastward course toward Old Cold Harbor, thereby outflanking any Federals north of the Chickahominy aligned to oppose A. P. Hill's advance. But Jackson's famous secretiveness backfired. He told his guide to take the column to Old Cold Harbor and the guide naturally took the shortest route. After leaving Walnut Grove Church, the guide took a road that went to Old Cold Harbor by way of Gaines' Mill, where Porter's entire force was entrenched. Jackson was on this road when he heard A. P. Hill's attack begin at Gaines' Mill in mid-afternoon. *OR* 11, pt. 2, pp. 553-555; Stephen W. Sears, *To the Gates of Richmond: The Peninsula Campaign* (New York, 1992), pp. 227-228; Freeman, *Lee's Lieutenants*, 1, pp. 523-524.

had to hurry in order to catch up with the
column. This second change was made by
turning square to our left—so that the march
was thus The head of our column had passed
the turning off point at A—so we moved off
to the left by the rear. The immediate cause I
think of Jackson's finding out his mistake
was the appearance on our right, & marching
straight towards us, of Branch's Brigade,

Facsimile of sketch from Brown's memoirs.

which was in column of regiments, moving across the open field with
colors flying—and presented as fine a sight as one often see's.[13] It was
the first & only time I ever saw troops moving in such an order except
on parade—and it struck me as a good formation for crossing a country
that was at all open. There was very little variety in our movements in
action or on the march. We marched by the flank & fought almost
invariably in a single line—often with a second near enough to fill any
gaps made in the first—but very seldom using more than one line in a
charge or attack—and sometimes attempting to throw in a second &
failing—sometimes succeeding.

When we turned to the left, we were, as I was informed, about two
and a half miles from Mechanicsville, on the line between it and Coal
Harbor—thus having gotten too far to our right and rendering a detour to
the left necessary to put us in position. We passed thro various deserted
Federal camps, and after a long tramp, made more trying by our frequent
halts and the suspense of our situation (the troops, officers & men, not
knowing when we would begin fighting, but looking for it every moment & feeling that there was hard work cut out for us), we came up

---

[13] Jackson first realized his error when he heard the firing from Hill's attack and questioned his
guide about the road they were on. Brown must have observed Lawrence Branch's North Carolina
brigade (A.P. Hill's Division) moving forward at about the same time. His map is confusing and
does not correctly depict Jackson's movements, but his description is accurate. When Jackson
realized he was on the wrong road, he halted the column and had the men about face. The end then
became the head, and the dusty troops turned to their right, not left, to cut across country to the
proper road. Sears, *To the Gates of Richmond*, pp. 220, 227-228; Freeman, *Lee's Lieutenants*, 1,
pp. 523-524; Maj. George B. Davis, *The Official Military Atlas of the Civil War* (New York, 1983),
plate 63-8.

with D. H. Hill's Divn.[14] When we did so, heavy firing was going on and I suppose we had marched ten miles or more and that it was two o'clock.

Our troops were halted just before the head of the column emerged from the woods into an open field—and I recollect Gen'l Jackson was standing near a battery (one of Hill's) located on the side of the lane along which we were moving and just in front of a farmhouse. Whether I was sent forward to find him or went there with him to carry back a message, I am uncertain—but we lay for some time in the road—then moved the head of our column back a few hundred yards, passed off to our right in the woods & formed along the edge of a field, facing a wood of perhaps a quarter to half a mile long on the opposite side of the field, which was six hundred yards wide.[15] Gen'l Jackson in person rode along with Gen'l Ewell forming the troops & told him the wood just mentioned was full of the enemy. I recollect feeling great surprise at their forbearance in letting us approach so near unmolested, and especially in allowing Carrington's battery[16] to be located on a knoll about fifty or sixty yards in front of the wood we held. Jackson instructed us to send forward a strong skirmish line into the wood. At this time very heavy firing was going on just beyond it & not more than a mile from us. Our skirmishers moved cautiously across the field & disappeared in

[14] Major General Daniel Harvey Hill, a 40-year-old West Point graduate and Mexican War veteran, was Jackson's brother-in-law. A portion of his division had seen heavy action the previous day at Mechanicsville. Although Hill was often critical of others, he served Lee well until he left the Army of Northern Virginia in 1863. Hill became a corps commander in the Army of Tennessee and served in other posts in South Carolina, Georgia and Virginia. He died in 1889 of cancer. Davis, *Confederate General*, 3, pp. 102-105.

[15] By the time Jackson's column turned around and headed back the correct way, D. H. Hill had moved ahead and was in front of Jackson at Old Cold Harbor. Not knowing the terrain, Jackson worried about moving toward the firing on A. P. Hill's front for fear of being mistaken for an enemy column. Therefore, he stopped, hoping Hill would drive the enemy past his position where he could ambush them. *OR* 11, pt. 2, pp. 553-555; Sears, *To the Gates of Richmond*, pp. 227-228; Freeman, *Lee's Lieutenants*, 1, pp. 523-234.

[16] Major James McDowell Carrington's battery was attached to Taylor's Louisiana Brigade. It was also called the Charlottesville Battery. Jennings Cropper Wise, *The Long Arm of Lee or The History of the Artillery of the Army of Northern Virginia*, 2 vols. (Lynchburg, Va., 1915), vol. 2, p. 988; Freeman, *Lee's Lieutenants*, 1, p. 440.

the wood. Everybody seemed holding their breath—waiting for the crash—but all was silent. In a few minutes, an officer appeared to report the skirmishers beyond the wood & no enemy.

The firing beyond grew heavier—Gen'l. Ewell sent me to Jackson for orders. They were to move forward, inclining to the left of the wood—that he had been misled as to the position of the enemy. When I returned, the troops were already moving in the direction indicated—& I found Gen'l. E. had received direct orders from Gen'l Lee.[17] Trimble[18] had gone to the right of the wood so often mentioned—having a talent for mistakes. I had seen him going thus as I rode up, & Gen'l E. sent me to turn him in the right direction. I found him already beyond the wood & turned him along its farther edge towards Coal Harbor (as I afterwards found). We soon got in range of a heavy fire—and old Trimble deviated still further from his course, in spite of me, to avoid it—not unfortunately as it turned out. As we passed thro' the edge of an orchard, poor Wood McDonald[19] of Elzey's[20] Staff rode up to Trimble, his face flushed, his sword drawn, in the wildest excitement, begging him to come and support Elzey. Trimble was perfectly cool and quiet—and told him he would do so, but must take advantage of the ground

---

[17] A. P. Hill, on Jackson's right, was unable to drive Porter's men from their position, so, at about 3:30 p.m., Lee ordered Ewell to attack on his front across Boatswain's Swamp to relieve some of the pressure on Hill. Ewell responded by sending in Richard Taylor's Louisiana Brigade. *OR* 11, pt. 2, pp. 553-555; Freeman, *Lee's Lieutenants*, 1, pp. 523-524; Sears, *To the Gates of Richmond*, pp. 227-230.

[18] Isaac Ridgeway Trimble, a crusty and aggressive 59-year-old West Point graduate, commanded a brigade of Virginia infantry under Ewell. He would receive a terrible leg wound at Second Manassas and be promoted to major general in January 1863. During Pickett's Charge at Gettysburg, Trimble was wounded again and captured. Surgeons amputated his leg as a result of this second wound. He died in 1888. Davis, *Confederate General*, 6, pp. 60-61; Stewart Sifakis, *Who Was Who in the Civil War* (New York, 1988), p. 661.

[19] Lieutenant C. Wood McDonald was Brig. Gen. Arnold Elzey's inspector general. *OR* 11, pt. 2, p. 985.

[20] Brigadier General Arnold Elzey, of Maryland, was a West Pointer and Mexican War veteran. He commanded one of Ewell's brigades. During this day's fighting he was wounded in the face. Late in 1862, Elzey was promoted to major general and spent most of the remaining war years on duty in Richmond. Elzey died in 1871. Davis, *Confederate General*, 2, pp. 98-103.

&c—and continued his march. Wood, poor fellow, in too great exalta-
tion to stand Trimble's slow speech & motion rode away with a reproach
for his inertness. As he went back to his command, he was killed just on
the edge of the road. It seems even now uncharitable to write it, but it is
true—he was drunk—the first time I ever saw him so!

Just as he rode off, I went in search of Gen'l. E.—found him putting
some troops into action just to the right of the main road up the hill to
the enemy's works—and when that was done, we rode together to Trimble. He then sent me back, by order of Gen'l. Lee, to find Whiting[21] &
Lawton[22] & hurry them up to this point. I did so—Lawton having pretty
much followed Trimble—and Whiting, Lawton.

As I returned with Lawton, I saw Gen'l. Lee for the first time. He
was sitting quietly on his horse (the same famous iron-gray)[23] at the
forks of the road at Coal Harbor, talking to (I think) A. P. Hill).[24] He
ordered these troops to take a sheltered position in reserve—and I rode
on to find Gen'l. Ewell. As I went down the road from Coal Harbor
towards the swamp, men came rushing out of the bushes on the right. I
had seen troops of other commands coming out of these as we came up,

---

[21] Brigadier General William Chase Whiting was a 38-year-old West Pointer from Mississippi.
He commanded his own brigade and John Bell Hood's Texas brigade during the campaign and
performed his duties well. Despite clashing with Jefferson Davis, he later rose to major general but
was mortally wounded on January 15, 1865, at Fort Fisher, North Carolina, and died in Federal
hands on March 10. Ibid., 6, pp. 132-133.

[22] Brigadier General Alexander Robert Lawton was a West Pointer from South Carolina and a
graduate of Harvard Law School. He commanded a brigade of Georgians in Jackson's old division
and later took charge of Ewell's division when Ewell was wounded at Groveton. Seriously
wounded himself at Antietam, Lawton was unable to retake the field and was appointed
quartermaster general of the Confederate States Army by President Davis in 1863. He survived the
war and became the American minister to Austria in 1887. Lawton died on July 2, 1896. Ibid., 4,
pp. 27-28.

[23] Brown refers to Lee's famous horse, Traveller.

[24] Major General Ambrose Powell Hill was one of Lee's best division commanders. A
36-year-old Virginian and West Pointer, Hill was forging a reputation as the hard-hitting
commander of the "Light Division." Promoted to lieutenant general and command of the Third
Corps in 1863, he suffered from poor health later in the war. Hill was killed on April 2, 1865,
while trying to rally a defense when the Federals broke through the Petersburg defenses. Davis,
Confederate General, 3, pp. 96-98; See also James I. Robertson, Jr., *General A. P. Hill: The Story
of a Confederate Warrior* (New York, 1987).

but these I knew to be Louisianians and to leave a gap in our line.[25] Col.
Cantey[26] of the 15th Alabama with two of his companies also came
out—but they as well as Col. Stafford's[27] 9th La. and parts of the 8th La.
and 7th La. were in some sort of order & soon came under the control of
their officers. I concluded that my first duty was to rally these men and
as Seymour[28] had been killed, to get some one to take command of the
Brigade. This took 3/4 of an hour of hard work. We formed just behind
a little crest—on the flank of Trimble's two Reg'ts. and when the line
was in some sort of order I reported to him the condition of affairs and
set off to find Gen'l. Ewell. Trimble ordered the officer in command
(Stafford I believe, Hays[29] being wounded at Port Republic) to go back

[25] As Jackson got into position across the swamp from Porter, A.P. Hill was fully engaged on
the Confederate right. To relieve some of the pressure on Hill, Lee ordered Ewell to send his
brigades forward. Colonel Isaac G. Seymour temporarily commanded the Louisiana Brigade
because Taylor was ill. He led his men into the swamp but was hit hard by the stubborn Union
defenders and was repulsed in some confusion. *OR* 11, pt. 2, pp. 553-555; Terry L. Jones, *Lee's
Tigers: The Louisiana Infantry in the Army of Northern Virginia* (Baton Rouge, 1987), pp.
103-104.

[26] James Cantey, originally from South Carolina, was a former lawyer and legislator and a
Mexican War veteran. After the Seven Days he left his regiment to return to Alabama to take
command of an infantry brigade. Promoted to brigadier general in January 1863, he commanded
part of the Department of the Gulf and participated in the Atlanta Campaign. One officer accused
him of hiding during the Battle of Resaca on May 9, 1864, and he was absent on sick leave during
much of the campaign. Cantey died in 1874. Davis, *Confederate General*, 1, pp. 160-161.

[27] Leroy A. Stafford, a wealthy, educated Louisiana planter, opposed secession but formed a
company of volunteers when it came. His men elected him lieutenant colonel of the 9th Louisiana,
and he became colonel when Richard Taylor was promoted to brigadier general in late 1861.
Stafford temporarily commanded the Louisiana Brigade during parts of the Seven Days, Second
Manassas and Antietam Campaigns. His excellent record earned him a promotion to brigadier
general in October 1863 and command of the Second Louisiana Brigade. Stafford was mortally
wounded on May 5, 1864, at the Wilderness. Ibid., 5, pp. 194-195.

[28] Isaac G. Seymour was a 57-year-old Yale University graduate and Mexican War veteran.
After serving as the first mayor of Macon, Georgia, he moved to New Orleans and became
prominent as a newspaper editor. The men of the 6th Louisiana Volunteers elected Seymour their
colonel, and he was in temporary command of the Louisiana Brigade when killed. Jones, *Lee's
Tigers*, pp. 6, 103.

[29] Harry T. Hays was a 41-year-old Mexican War veteran and New Orleans lawyer. As colonel
of the 7th Louisiana, he performed well at First Manassas and in Jackson's Valley Campaign. Hays
was the brigade's senior colonel but was absent during the Seven Days Battles recuperating from a
severe wound suffered at the Battle of Port Republic on June 9. Upon General Taylor's
recommendation, he was promoted to brigadier general in July 1862 and was given command of
the Louisiana Brigade when Taylor transferred west. After being severely wounded again at

out of fire across the road, as he found his men somewhat nervous where they were, & to let them be quite till needed.

As I rode up the hill towards the enemy's works, a mounted man half-wild with fright or excitement dashed up and informed me that Gen'l E. had sent him for a Reg't. to form on the right of Lawton's troops or the left of the Texas Brigade (I forget which & it is quite immaterial) and charge with them-that if he had that, he could take the position. While he was yet talking, Jno. M. Jones[30] came down the road at his usual sober trot, and on my telling what the man reported, & asking for Gen'l Ewell, he said he had been all along the line on the left of the road & the Gen'l wasn't there. So we rode together to find the 13th Ga. Regt. of Lawton's Brig., which had been left in reserve when the Brig. advanced to charge, because they had no bayonets—being armed with Miss. Rifles. Col. Douglas[31] expressed a perfect willingness to advance, if we could find the precise point where he was needed—and riding to do so, I met Gen'l Ewell on foot, his splendid chestnut sorrel mare "Maggie" having just been killed under him. He was limping slightly from a spent ball which had entered his boot & glanced round his leg. By this time the fight was over, the final charge having taken place just as we left Col. Douglas, and I found Gen'l E. had sent no such order as the courier delivered to me. I never saw the fellow after, to my knowledge & never knew his exact motive in telling the tale.

Spotsylvania on May 9, 1864, Hays served in the west for the remainder of the war. He was active in Louisiana White Democratic politics during Reconstruction and died in 1876. Davis, *Confederate General*, 3, pp. 78-80.

[30] Lieutenant Colonel John Marshall Jones served Ewell as an assistant adjutant general and acting inspector general. A West Point graduate, he later served as inspector general and assistant adjutant general for Gen. Jubal Early. In May 1863, Jones was promoted to brigadier general and given command of the Stonewall Brigade. Wounded at Gettysburg and Payne's Farm in 1863, he was killed on May 5, 1864, at the Wilderness. Ibid., 3, pp. 203-205; *OR* 11, pt. 2, p. 607.

[31] Colonel Marcellus Douglas rose from a company captain to command of the 13th Georgia. He was killed on September 17, 1862, at Antietam. Robert K. Krick, *Lee's Colonels: A Biographical Register of the Field Officers of the Army of Northern Virginia* (Dayton, 1979), p. 109.

When I caught up with the Gen'l, he was just pulling off his boot &
emptying out the bullet, which had flattened against a tree before striking him. We went on together as far as the top of the hill, where we
could see that the field was entirely in possession of our troops and the
fighting over—then he sent me to find young Champion[32] & send his
saddle to the point where we started in—to find Gen'l Lee or Gen'l
Jackson & get leave to withdraw his troops to rest at the same spot &
collect stragglers—and to try to find his spare horse. About midnight we
met again, but I had not found his horse—tho' the other commissions
were executed. We sat down & ate a part of our lunch—but before we
finished it, up came Gen'l Ripley[33] of Charleston and was of course
asked to join us. I had been interrupted in eating my share by attending
to my horse—So Ripley ate it & I went without till next day.

Next morning [June 28] we moved to Bottom's Bridge.[34] I was
ordered to tell Trimble, who was astray as usual, to follow the rest of the
Brigade[s]. Not finding him with his troops, I gave the order to W.
Carvel Hall[35] who was at the head of the column—his A.A.G.—desig-

[32] Private Frank Champion, of the 15th Alabama, apparently was one of Ewell's couriers.
Ewell praised him in his after-action report for helping rally the men. *OR* 11, pt. 2, p. 606.

[33] Roswell Sabine Ripley was a Northerner by birth who married into a Charleston, South
Carolina, family. A West Pointer and Mexican War veteran, he was promoted to brigadier general
after participating in the bombardment of Fort Sumter. He commanded the Department of South
Carolina before getting an infantry brigade in D.H. Hill's division during the Seven Days Battles.
Lee had doubts about Ripley's combat ability, however, so, after Ripley was wounded in the throat
at Antietam, the war department sent the brigadier back to command the Department of South
Carolina. Ripley died in 1887. Davis, *Confederate General*, 5, pp. 89-90.

[34] After hours of intense fighting, John Bell Hood's Texas Brigade finally broke through
Porter's lines at Gaines' Mill. Other Confederate units reinforced the breakthrough and forced a
Federal retreat across the Chickahominy. Not sure what McClellan would do next, Lee had
Jackson send Ewell on June 28 with some cavalry down the north bank of the river to guard the
lower crossings should McClellan try to retreat to Yorktown or Fort Monroe. *OR* 11, pt. 2, p. 607;
Sears, *To the Gates of Richmond*, pp. 255-256; Frank E. Vandiver, *Mighty Stonewall* (1957; rpt.
College Station, Texas, 1989), p. 310.

[35] Captain William Carvel Hall was Trimble's assistant adjutant general. He later served in the
same capacity on the divisional level for Trimble and Gen. Raleigh Colston. Rising to the rank of
major, he was captured with Trimble at Gettysburg and held in Fort McHenry before being
exchanged. Hall served the remainder of the war with the inspector general's office. *OR* 11, pt. 2,
p. 616; Ibid., 25, pt. 1, p. 1008; Ibid., pt. 2, p. 837; Ibid., series II, vol. 6, p. 103; Ibid., 7, p. 1001.

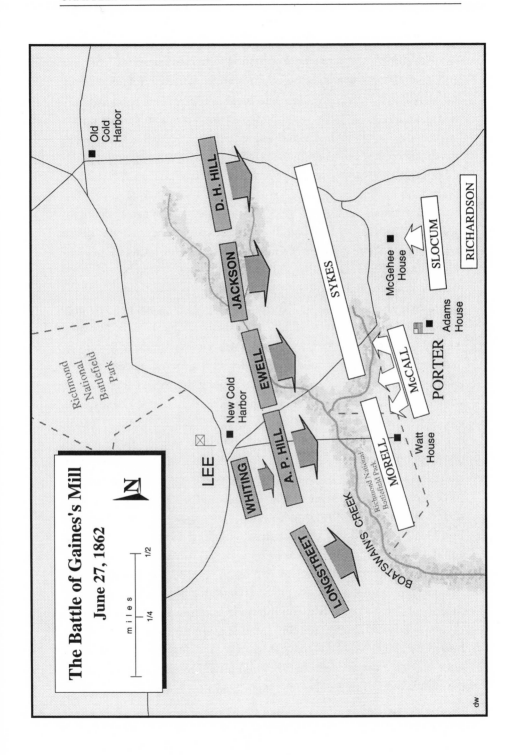

The Battle of Gaines's Mill
June 27, 1862

N

miles

1/4   1/2

LEE

Old Cold Harbor

D. H. HILL

JACKSON

SYKES

McGehee House

SLOCUM

RICHARDSON

EWELL

Richmond National Battlefield Park

New Cold Harbor

Adams House

PORTER

McCALL

A. P. HILL

WHITING

MORELL

Watt House

Richmond National Battlefield Park

LONGSTREET

BOATSWAIN'S CREEK

dw

nating to him the road to take. Soon as I was out of sight, up came old Trimble, turned off to the right & halted. Before getting to Bottom's Bridge, Gen'l E. sent me back for Trimble, whom I found placidly self-satisfied at his position-and had some difficulty in persuading into the right way. It was only when he found there was a somewhat uncertain cross-road that he might take, that he became reconciled to it. Luckily we came out all right-& much to the old fellow's disappointment did not even strike a Yankee picket-post or stray Regim't.

About noon we reached a point opposite the immense depot of stores that McClellan had had at Savage Station, and saw the dense column of smoke rising from their burning. Soon afterwards the head of our Column reached & crossed the R.Rd. at the Bottom's Bridge road—and we halted, throwing out a company or two of the M'd. Line [1st Maryland] as skirmishers. They soon became engaged in a skirmish with a small party of Cav'y who held the Bridge. The R.Rd. bridge over the Chickahominy (York River R.R'd.) was already destroyed, so as to indicate plainly that McClellan had given up that line of retreat. While our troops lay here, mostly in the woods along the road, I was sent off with an order & Turner soon after with another, for Trimble (I think). At any rate we met in search of the same party just as the most fearful explosion took place that I ever heard, sounding like the simultaneous discharge of many guns—and the woods between us & the river were filled with falling shells. Our first idea was that the enemy intended to force a passage of the river and had concentrated batteries and opened fire for that purpose. Turner rode on with his message while I started to find Gen'l E. & tell him of the batteries' falling short. But I met him coming full gallop & in a minute saw a dense white column of smoke unlike that from guns, showing an explosion. Pretty soon, just as we had got out into the open in sight of the bridge, we heard a roaring in the direction of Savage Station, growing momentarily louder & clearer—then an Engine & train came full speed towards the bridge, loaded with bursting shells, powder barrels &c. The troops on the road were hurried away for fear that the train might possibly leap the gap in the bridge—but instead of doing so it went down with a grand crash, thirty miles an hour, into the river. It was one of the grandest sights I ever looked at.

It is hard to realize the value of all the stores destroyed by McClellan. As I passed a house that day, I asked for a drink of water. The man brought it to me, but said I had better not drink as the Yankees had somehow poisoned his spring—though he couldn't find anything in it. I tasted the water—it was not poisoned, but impregnated with two or three different medicines. I saw the Spring—a bold, clear stream. Riding a mile further & crossing a good-sized branch, or small creek, I came to a Federal Hospl & a well down which they had emptied an immense quantity of drugs and hospl stores—and the mystery of the Spring was at once explained. I saw the owner afterwards & learned that in less than two days the water was good again.

At Bottom's Bridge we remained some hours, tore up a mile of track, burnt the ties & bent the rails—& then by Gen'l Jackson's order marched back to Grapevine Bridge, a long, narrow, rough causeway, crossed the Chickahominy & rejoined the Army, after marching all night. Next day (29th June) we followed the rest of Jackson's command to White Oak Swamp and on towards Malvern Hills, without other event than the engagement of some of our Artillery at the Swamp.[36]

The night of the 29th [June 30] we encamped short of White Oak Swamp, and happened to make Hd.Qrs. at a house where Gen'l Sickles[37] had been, two days previous, & to buy of the owner two or three

---

[36] June 29 was another frustrating day for Lee. McClellan was falling back to the James River, so Lee issued orders for his divisions to converge on Savage's Station to try and interdict the Union retreat. While Ewell guarded Bottom's Bridge, the rest of Jackson's force was to cross over the Chickahominy to join the attack on Savage's Station. But Jackson failed to rebuild needed bridges in time and may have misunderstood Lee's orders. Late on June 29, an intense but indecisive fight broke out at Savage's Station between John Bankhead Magruder's division and the Federal rear guard. Brown is in error on the dates. Ewell tore up the Richmond & York River Railroad at Dispatch Station on June 28 and remained at Bottom's Bridge on June 29 to guard against a possible Union crossing. At 6 p.m., June 29, he received orders to join Jackson at Grapevine Bridge. On June 30, not June 29, the division rejoined Jackson at Grapevine Bridge and followed him to White Oak Swamp. Ibid., series I, vol. 11, pt. 2, pp. 494-495, 556-557, 607; Campbell Brown notes on the Seven Days Campaign in Folder 6, Box 2, Brown-Ewell Papers; Vandiver, *Mighty Stonewall*, pp. 310-312; Sears, *To the Gates of Richmond*, pp. 261-269.

[37] Brigadier General Daniel Sickles, a former U.S. Congressman from New York, seems to have because the young man was having an affair with Sickles' wife. A jury found the congressman not

dozen 1/2 pint bottles of Champagne brought on by Sickles for the convenient brewing of cocktails. Next day (30th) in the cannonade at the Swamp, Capt. (now Col.) Carter[38] vigorously shelled a house behind which the enemy were sheltered—and on getting over the Swamp found a half-dozen holes in the building & two of his female cousins hid in the cellar![39]

The enemy had held their ground well for awhile, but suddenly taken a panic and abandoned even their knapsacks, their tents standing, their ammunition wagons, &c. I never heard of any adequate cause for their fright, which was beyond any I ever saw. At a spring near the house above mentioned, I found seven canteens in a pile, where a soldier had gone to fill them, but run away too frightened to carry them. The horses had been cut from the wagons, the knapsacks left where they were piled, in rear of the Regts.

---

guilty due to temporary insanity–the first successful use of that plea in the United States. Because of his political clout, Sickles became commander of a brigade—which would earn fame as the Excelsior Brigade—in Joseph Hooker's division. In command of the III Corps at Gettysburg, Sickles was again in the midst of controversy when he changed the position of his line contrary to army commander George G. Meade's wishes. Sickles behaved bravely during the engagement and won the Medal of Honor for his performance at Gettysburg, but lost a leg there as well. He retired from the army in 1869, and then served as minister to Spain and again in Congress. Sifakis, *Who Was Who in the Civil War*, pp. 594-595; see also W. A. Swanberg, *Sickles the Incredible* (New York, 1956).

[38] Johnston B. Carter served on Elzey's staff as an ordnance officer. He rose to the rank of lieutenant colonel of artillery and became the brigade's chief ordnance officer. RG 109, Compiled Service Records of Confederate General and Staff Officers, Microcopy 331, Roll 50, National Archives, Washington, D.C.

[39] Lee continued the pursuit of McClellan on June 30. On that day the enemy would have to cross White Oak Swamp and funnel through the crossroads of Glendale. Lee planned to concentrate the bulk of his army and push from the west to smash McClellan's strung-out columns, while Jackson pressured the Union rearguard at the swamp crossings from the north. Jackson approached the swamp and saw Federal artillery and infantry deployed on high ground on the other side. He brought up 28 artillery pieces and opened fire on them at 1:45 p.m. After a lengthy artillery duel and a probe across the swamp, Jackson decided the crossings were too well guarded to push his men across. For the remainder of the day he did nothing while Longstreet and A. P. Hill fought furiously not far away at Glendale. *OR* 11, pt. 2, pp. 556-557; Vandiver, *Mighty Stonewall*, pp. 315-316; Sears, *To the Gates of Richmond*, pp. 286-287.

On the 1st July we passed thro' the battle ground of Frazier's Farm, which already smelt horribly.[40] The weather was very dusty & oppressive, & the unburied dead putrefied at once. This morning Gen'l Early joined & took command of Elzey's brigade. Early was so disabled by his wound rec'd. at Wmsburg, that I had to help him mount his horse by pushing him up.[41]

At Willis's Church we found a field hospital filled with wounded—and opposite it some twenty or thirty Yankee dead, awaiting burial, laid side by side—a ghastly row. All the morning we had been hearing guns & by this time the fire was quite heavy—an occasional shell flew over our heads, dense columns of troops, ambulances with wounded, stragglers streaming to the rear, filled the road ahead—the air was stifling and the clouds of dust rose over the tops of the pines & indicated to the Federal artillery the points at which to fire. We heard vague rumors of heavy fighting on the right, of a strong position to be assailed, of the repulse of D. H. Hill, &c. The situation seemed more serious than on the 27th, & it was apparent that for the first time both armies were concentrated, face to face.[42] We avoided the road & moved

---

[40] On June 30 at 4 p.m., Longstreet and A.P. Hill finally attacked the enemy around Frayser's Farm (Glendale) in a vain attempt to sever McClellan's retreating column. In the vicious fight, the Federals were battered but held their positions until they were able to withdraw after dark. McClellan lost more than 3,700 men in the fight, while the Confederates suffered more than 3,600 casualties. *OR* 11, pt. 2, pp. 495, 759, 837-838; Sears, *To the Gates of Richmond*, pp. 279-307.

[41] Brigadier General Jubal A. Early was a cantankerous 44-year-old West Point graduate from Virginia and veteran of the Seminole and Mexican Wars. Although he opposed secession, Early became colonel of the 24th Virginia Infantry and eventually one of Lee's more famous lieutenants. Rheumatic, irritable and witty, Early was a fighter and rose through the ranks from colonel to lieutenant general and command of the Second Corps of the Army of Northern Virginia in 1864. On July 1, 1862, he assumed command of Elzey's brigade because that officer had been shot through the face at Gaines' Mill. Early had been severely wounded in the shoulder at Williamsburg in May 1862, and Ewell wrote in his Seven Days report that Early was "so disabled. . .as to be unable to mount his horse without assistance." After the war, Early wrote prolifically and was president of the Southern Historical Society. He died in 1894. *OR* 11, pt. 2, p. 607; Freeman, *Lee's Lieutenants*, 1, p. 185; Davis, *Confederate General*, 2, pp. 89-90.

[42] By July 1, McClellan was well entrenched on Malvern Hill, a prominent height above on the James River. Lee, frustrated over his failure to crush McClellan during the retreat, believed one large assault would break the Federals and push them into the river. Lee prepared his lines and ordered Jackson to attack the Federal right, while his other divisions assaulted the left. Poorly executed against the Union defenses, the subsequent attack was a bloody failure. *OR* 11, pt. 2, pp. 495-496; Sears, *To the Gates of Richmond*, pp. 313-315.

forward parallel to it thro' the pines, till near the famous "gate-posts" & "cross-road,"[43] the point on which from 3 p.m. till 9 at night the heaviest of the enemy's fire was concentrated. About 100 yards in rear of this, slightly sheltered by the ground, Early's & the La. Brigade (now under Stafford of the 9th La.) lay down in line.

Whiting's Divn had only been partially engaged on the 27th, & it was Jackson's intention to attack the enemy's right with it this day. He therefore ordered it to our left, where it lay in echelon some 300 yards to our rear, while Whitin [sic] rode forward & examined the ground, after which he called on Gen'l Jn for another Brigade to put on his extreme left. Trimble's of our Divn was sent, and Gen'l Trimble, who always was very active in finding out the ground in his front, soon came back to report a favorable opportunity to attack an exposed flank there. Whether he was correct or not I never knew—but he always maintained that that was the true point of attack.[44] Whiting then moved his troops further forward—found a gap between his right & D. H. Hill's left & asked a brigade to fill it. Stafford was sent forward. About 5 p.m. D. H. Hill's attack was made & failed—or perhaps it was made before—at any rate it had failed by that hour.[45]

Soon after an order was given by Gen'l Jn to Gen'l Ewell to be ready to send a brigade by the best route to Hill's support. Turner, Greene & I were sent to find out the route—& when we returned found the troops ready to move over under a second order. The only brigade

---

[43] These gateposts were located where the road to the Poindexter House left the Quaker Road. Brown's notes on Seven Days, Folder 6, Box 2, Brown-Ewell Papers.

[44] Trimble wrote that he asked Jackson's permission to launch a surprise attack against the Federal right flank at 3 p.m., but that Jackson refused. Jackson did not mention the incident in his report. *OR* 11, pt. 2, p. 618.

[45] D. H. Hill felt strongly that an attack against the formidable Union line would not succeed, but Lee was adamant and ordered artillery deployed to knock out the Federal guns. After the Confederate artillery had weakened the Federal defenses, Brigadier General Lewis Armistead's brigade was to lead the infantry attack with a shout, which would be the signal for the other brigades to follow. The artillery fire, however, was ineffective and Hill informed Jackson of his misgivings. While discussing the situation with his brigade commanders, Hill heard Armistead's advance begin between 4 p.m. and 5 p.m. and had no choice but to send his division forward. Hill suffered heavily, losing 1,746 men in the bloody repulse. Ibid., pp. 559, 627-628, 819.

left was Early's & therefore Gen'l E. went with it in person, taking Turner & Greene & leaving Maj. Nelson & me to wait his return at the x-roads, & to report to him any new developments. Bradley T. Johnson[46] & the Md. Line were also left here—some 400 men—not more. They lay on the right of the road—the opposite side from that recently occupied by Early—and tho' somewhat sheltered by the ground, were under very heavy shelling for several hours. The gun boats were shelling the woods, pretty much at random, killing few or none, but frightening many. We were unused to them—had vague ideas of their powers, but were led by their recent achievements on Western rivers & against forts, to respect them highly—tho' this day's work destroyed their prestige with us. About 5 p.m. they sent a shell thro' the centre of the Md. flag, which exploded just in rear of the line, hurting no one. The 10-pdr. & 20-pdr. Parrots[47] on Malvern Hill annoyed us more & did more harm. I saw a man's body lying against a large pine tree, 18 inches to 2 feet thro'. A rifle shell had come thro' the tree & carried off his head.

Gen'l Jackson had two narrow escapes, which I happened to see. About 10 or 11 a.m. he rode out with Gen'l Ewell to our left to meet Gen'l Whiting, & just as they emerged from the woods into the wheat-field, a piece of artillery passed to the rear, making quite a dust & drawing a heavy fire. One or two shells struck just in front of the party, at the moment of emerging from the woods, just as Gen'l Whiting joined them. They rode on quietly, when one or two more pitched viciously down just at the head of Gen'l. Jn's horse, which kept on at its shambling gait, Jackson talking earnestly to Gen'l E. took no notice, but the

---

[46] Bradley Tyler Johnson was a prominent Maryland politician who helped raise the 1st Maryland (Maryland Line) in 1861. By the spring of 1862, he was in command of the regiment, serving in George H. Steuart's brigade. Well respected as an officer, he was promoted to brigadier general in 1864. After the war, Johnson served in the Virginia senate and died in 1903. Davis, *Confederate General*, 3, pp. 173-178.

[47] The Parrott gun was an accurate and powerful rifled cannon with a reinforced breech. It was named for its inventor, Robert Parker Parrott. Patricia L. Faust, ed., *Historical Times Illustrated Encyclopedia of the Civil War* (New York, 1986), p. 558.

latter quickly stooping caught his horse by the bridle & stopped him, a second or two before the shell exploded. They were near enough to it to be covered with dust. Gen'l E. made some remark that appeared to irritate Whiting—I think it was to the effect that he should like to be with the larger part of his Divn if agreeable or practicable. He answered sharply & got a reply hardly calculated to soothe—but Jn interfered with the remark—"Come, gentlemen, don't let us have any quarreling," and the matter ended. There was no personal feeling in it at any time. I heard Whiting say to Gen'l Jn that if he were to make the attack, he would move by a flank up one or more of the ravines that set off from the creek in our front, & not form line until as near as he could get to the enemy's position under shelter. Whose nerve failed, I never knew—nor whether the attack was countermanded by Gen'l Lee, who rode over about 1 or 2 p.m. & looked at the ground. None was made—& I never saw Whiting's idea put into operation during the war—tho' I have heard it approved by good authority.

About 3 p.m. Gen'l E. rode over to the right to become acquainted with the ground, leaving Turner, Maj. Nelson & me near the gate-posts. Jackson was there with Maj. Dabney[48] & two or three couriers. A courier sitting on the fence near the gate-post, had his horse struck in the head by a fragment of a shell which had struck one of the gate-posts & exploded with a tremendous report. The poor creature had part of the head blown away between the brain & the nostrils, making it blind & frantic. Three or four horses much frightened were struggling to get away from their riders—& Gen'l Jn.'s old sorrel partaking the general alarm dashed off, pulling him down on his hands & knees. Turner, Maj. Nelson & I ran to him, fearing he was hurt—but he had recovered his

---

[48] Major Robert Lewis Dabney was a Presbyterian minister who rose from chaplain of the 18th Virginia to a brief three-month term as Jackson's assistant adjutant general and chief of staff. He was a rather poor staff officer, however, and quickly returned to the ministry. After the war, Dabney wrote a popular biography of Jackson *Life and Campaigns of Lieut. Gen. Thomas J. Jackson, (Stonewall Jackson)*. Dabney died in 1898. Sifakis, *Who Was Who in the Civil War*, p. 165; Henry Kyd Douglas, *I Rode With Stonewall* (Chapel Hill, 1948), pp. 101, 365; Freeman, *Lee's Lieutenants*, 1, p. 372.

feet & his horse kept pulling him along. After 20 or 30 yards of this, he managed to stop it, mounted & at once rode to the rear. I saw him once or twice again, but he very properly established his Hd.Qrs. in a less exposed place, 100 yards back.

The road by constant use became so dusty that one caisson or a single hurrying horseman would raise a cloud of dust & cause their batteries to open on it—and having set guns to enfilade the road down which we advanced & knowing the range of the x-roads, they annoyed & impeded us considerably. Col. Crutchfield,[49] Genl Jns' Chf. of Art'y., a competent but lazy officer, made this day a very poor use of his artillery. The enemy had in front of our wing about 30 pieces of Artillery, many 20-pdr. Parrott's—beautifully posted along a ridge that completely overlooked our position. Crutchfield had 40 pieces at least, under his command—never more than 6 opposed at once to these odds. It was subject of remark then & afterwards—never explained to me, tho' I several times asked Jackson's Staff about it. During the day some 20 pieces were brought up & put in position—a few at a time. They had to go into battery under fire, to be silenced in a half hour or less—& to come up & withdraw by the road already mentioned, so as to be exposed for a mile to an artillery fire said by every one to be as heavy with perhaps one exception as they experienced during the war.[50] No great

[49] Colonel Stapleton Crutchfield was graduated first in the Virginia Military Institute (VMI) class of 1855 and served as an officer in several Virginia infantry regiments before becoming Jackson's chief of artillery in May 1862. After losing a leg at Chancellorsville, he served in Richmond. On April 6, 1865, three days before the surrender at Appomattox, a shell killed Crutchfield at Sayler's Creek. Others held a much higher opinion of his abilities than did Brown. General Edward Porter Alexander described him as being "a most excellent officer." Crutchfield was being considered for promotion to brigadier general when wounded at Chancellorsville. Edward Porter Alexander, *Fighting for the Confederacy*, edited by Gary W. Gallagher (Chapel Hill, 1989), pp. 201, 581; Freeman, *Lee's Lieutenants*, 1, p. 372; Sifakis, *Who Was Who in the Civil War*, p. 156; see also Wise, *Long Arm of Lee*, for details of Crutchfield's career.

[50] Longstreet, D. H. Hill and William Nelson Pendleton, commander of the army's reserve artillery, all criticized the poor use of Confederate artillery at Malvern Hill. One reason for the failure appears to be that Crutchfield became ill during the day and left the field without appointing anyone to replace him. As a result, the artillery came up in driblets instead of in force and was knocked to pieces by the Federal cannoneers. Jackson got only 18 guns into action during the battle. *OR* 11, pt. 2, pp. 536, 628; Freeman, *Lee's Lieutenants*, 1, pp. 595-596.

loss resulted from these tactics-but much unnecessary confusion & discouragement to the troops. The truth is that while our actual loss on the left was small, the moral effect of the day was decidedly that of a defeat.[51]

As the troops moved forward into position, along the same narrow road, the shells came crashing thro' the pines, their noise & terror greatly exaggerated by the falling limbs—the sound of large guns on the boats was rendered additionally deep & solemn by the closeness & heat of the day—all the litter-bearers with wounded, the frightened stragglers & the broken caissons or ambulances met them in their advance—that by the time they were in position in reserve, they had been exposed to all the discouraging influences usually encountered by troops brought forward in the crisis of an action. As they lay for hours in reserve they were exposed to a cannonade the violence of which rendered rest impossible—and every now & then one of their number was stricken down. About 1 p.m. Gen'l Early, Col. J. A. Walker[52] & his volunteer A.D.C., Willy Field, son of Judge Field and as fine & brave as possible, were lying together on the grass eating dinner, when a shell after passing through the body of a soldier struck just under Field's side (he was leaning on his left elbow with his back towards the enemy) and without actually touching him raised him a few inches from the ground. It stopped, fortunately without bursting, under Walker's very backbone. At first he thought Field was unhurt, but on examination found him

---

[51] Brown puts the Battle of Malvern Hill in a much better light than it deserves. Lee's assaults were piecemeal and uncoordinated, and losses were heavy. On the left Jackson suffered 2,162 casualties out of Lee's total of 5,650. Malvern Hill, in fact, was a disaster for the Confederates. *OR* 11, pt. 2, p. 559; Sears, *To the Gates of Richmond*, p. 335.

[52] Cadet James A. Walker, a Virginian, was dismissed from the VMI in 1852 by then Professor Thomas J. Jackson. In 1861 he organized a company of volunteers in the 4th Virginia and was promoted to lieutenant colonel of the 13th Virginia in May 1861. Walker rose to command the regiment in the spring of 1862 and upon the recommendations of a number of general officers, was appointed brigadier general in May 1863. He took command of the Stonewall Brigade and led it through the rest of the war, receiving a serious wound at Spotsylvania in 1864. Davis, *Confederate General*, 6, pp. 86-87.

dead—tho' his skin was unbroken & not even his clothing torn. The concussion had killed him.[53]

About 4 or 5 p.m. a heavy fire opened just in front of us, where Stafford was posted. We at first supposed the enemy attacking, but soon found Stafford had advanced on them—a movement we could not explain, as Whiting's line, with which he was to co-operate, was stationary. In half an hour or less he was repulsed and then came the reason. A staff officer apparently of Gen'l Whiting's had in an excited manner ridden up to one or two of the left reg'ts. & inquired why they didn't charge with the troops on the left—& had ordered them to charge. Expecting such an order, they had obeyed it & the command passed from reg't. to reg't. along the whole brigade. The result of their isolated attack was a sharp, short fight & a speedy repulse—not till they had silenced & very nearly captured a battery that stood in advance of the enemy's main line. The whole affair was over so soon & the uselessness of the attack so evident at once, that fewer lives were lost than might have been expected. This was partly owing to the nature of the ground they went over—a dense marshy bottom & points of sandy ground running into it from the enemy's position. Hence the enemy's fire was uncertain, as they were unseen, & plunging instead of sweeping, so that most of it went over their heads.[54]

About nightfall the crowd of stragglers from the front grew quite dense. Col. Jno. M. Jones, Maj. Nelson, Turner & I were now together without orders. Jones having just returned from Gen'l Ewell & report-

---

[53] Private Willy Field, of the 44th Virginia, was the son of Orange County Circuit Judge Richard H. Field. Early reported that young Field was the only casualty suffered when the brigade was caught between Confederate and Union artillery fire. William H. B. Thomas, *Orange, Virginia: Story of a Courthouse Town* (Verona, Va., 1972), p. 33; *OR* 11, pt. 2, p. 611.

[54] Colonel Leroy A. Stafford was in command of the Louisiana Brigade after Seymour's death. Stafford also claimed that at dusk, while in support of Whiting's division, an unknown officer brought orders for Stafford to attack a Federal battery. The 6th, 7th and 8th Louisiana advanced, but the 9th Louisiana did not because those in command of the regiment either did not hear the order or did not understand it. Stafford claimed the brigade lost 116 men in the twilight assault but did not mention any near success as claimed by Brown. *OR* 11, pt. 2, p. 620.

ing no need of anyone there—and with nothing special to do. So having communicated with Bradley Johnson, who approved of the idea & agreed to use his reg't. where it stood to stop all stragglers on that side of the road, we organized an impromptu provost-guard to stop stragglers & turn them back. Two only of our couriers out of eight detailed were with us—the rest having slipped off to the rear. These two were Sgt. Barrett & Sgt. or Corp'l Wright[55] of Loudoun Co. Sometimes on foot, but mostly on horseback, we formed a little cordon across the road & started many men back for the front. How far they went, whether they sneaked round us in the dark or lay down behind trees or logs or (improbable) returned to their reg'ts., we had no means of telling. Most were from D. H. Hill's Divn & must have been lying some hours in the woods, as his troops had left our front early in the evening. One poor fellow, nearly scared to death, felt a great oppression on his chest when stopped & assured me he could hardly breathe, so badly had he been "stung with a bung"—shaken or contused by a shell. This excuse of "shocked by a bomb" became familiar to me that evening. One man had had a shell to burst "right in his face"—a cunning Irishman walked lame &c, &c. Amid all the noise I happened, being unoccupied at the instant, to hear Col. Jones about six feet from me in a sharp altercation with a straggler trying to pass him—all at once Col. J. fired on him at not more than six feet off & the man disappeared in a rapid trot towards Malvern Hill, as if bent on taking it single-handed. I called to Jones, "Great heavens Colonel, weren't you afraid of hitting him." "Oh no, I aimed a foot over his head—but it wouldn't have mattered much if I had killed him."

Soon after 9 p.m. Gen'l E. returned & I rode with him to find Gen'l Jn. About 12 p.m. we met D. H. Hill who had been on the same errand, was out of patience, & was returning to his command. They rode together till 3 a.m. without success, when the moon having gone down &

---

[55] Sergeant Barrett was probably Campbell Boyd Barrett of White's Battalion of Virginia Cavalry, which served as Ewell's escort. The identification of Wright is unclear. RG 109, Compiled Service Records of Confederate Soldiers Who Served in Organizations from Virginia, Microcopy 324, Roll 190, National Archives, Washington, D.C.

it being useless to search further, Hill went back & Gen'l. E. & I lay down in a wood till dawn. About 6 a.m. we found Gen'l Jn two miles back at his wagons, eating breakfast. So strongly had Hill represented the shattered condition of his command & so precisely was it corroborated by what Gen'l E. had seen, that he represented to Gen'l Jn. in strong terms the danger to us of McClellan's showing a little enterprise & making even a slight counter-attack. Jn listened quietly & then assured him there was no danger of such an event.[56]

So impressed was Gen'l E. with the disorganized state of the centre, that he sent me back to have the 30 or 40 captured ammunition wagons at White Oak Swamp moved back to the Richmond side of it, so as to be safe in event of our retreat. It soon came up a very hard rain—and by the time I got all the wagons across, the bridge, or corduroy rather, across the swamp was under water. But by noon I was back with Gen'l E. whom I found in a little farm house in front of the position held by Stafford, the day before. On the 1st we had only one brigade (Stafford's) actively engaged—but Early's was under fire for ten hours or more—and Trimble's with the bulk of Whiting's Divn was so far detached on our left that in case of an attack on our centre or right, they would have been utterly useless. There was no open ground on which we could form—no position for artillery, no roads behind the flanks by which to retire, if necessary. How much McClellan was used up, I do not know—nor how capable our right would have been of effective resistance—but unless they were more concentrated & better posted than we, a strong column, penetrating the left centre, where D. H. Hill's repulse had left a gap, could have forced us back at least a mile or two. But as it turned out Jackson correctly appreciated McClellan's character.

---

[56] Although Brown states Ewell and Hill could not find Jackson that night, Major Dabney remembered differently. He recalled that Jackson's divisional commanders found the general about 1 a.m. and woke him to report. Dabney claimed they expressed a belief that the enemy would attack in the morning, but that Jackson dismissed the idea and said McClellan would have withdrawn by then. Robert Lewis Dabney, *Life and Campaigns of Lieut. Gen. Thomas J. Jackson, (Stonewall Jackson)* (1865; rpt. Harrisonburg, Va., 1983), p. 473.

He had not the vigor to make an effort to redeem the campaign, tho' he knew we were badly repulsed.[57]

We lay still most of the 2d, resting & getting rations. Then finding that McC.n had gone towards Westover, Jn's corps was ordered down there by a circuitous route. We arrived in front of it about 10 a.m. of the_____[sic][58] & were at once drawn up to attack. Not one piece of Arty was along—and our Divn, the strongest in the Corps numbered by a field report made next day less than 3000 effectives—i.e. 2965 or 2970. About the first of May before the Valley Campaign, we had been 8,500 strong, & since then Ed. Johnson's[59] 2 brigades of 3 Reg'ts. each had been given us. The loss in killed, wounded & captured bore no great proportion to this falling off—most of the men absent being broken down by the continued, severe marching & rejoining us in a few days. But for the present purpose they were useless.

Our Div'n had orders to be ready to advance—the skirmishers had been ordered forward & were already engaged. I rode down the lines with the order & as I came back a Colonel (I think [James A.] Walker of the 13th [Virginia]) of known efficiency, stopped me & said that he heard we were to attack. I told him I understood so. "Well, said he, I don't like to say it, but you must tell Gen'l Ewell the men won't fight much—they are too tired & they don't like those gunboats that we hear." I was shocked but felt the same way myself & could understand it. We were completely exhausted & the knowledge that the enemy had a strong

---

[57] Both armies were in poor shape after Malvern Hill and in no condition to continue the contest. By July 2, McClellan had lost almost 16,000 men, while Lee had suffered more than 20,000 casualties. On that day McClellan withdrew from Malvern Hill to Harrison's Landing, eight miles to the southeast on the James River, where he would be protected by gunboats and have a secure supply line. *OR* 11, pt. 2, pp. 37, 973-984; Stephen W. Sears, *George B. McClellan: The Young Napoleon* (New York, 1988), p. 223.

[58] Ewell arrived at Westover on Friday, July 4, 1862. *OR* 11, pt. 2, p. 607.

[59] Edward Johnson was graduated from West Point in 1838 and served in the Mexican and Seminole Wars. An accomplished swearer, he often led his men into battle brandishing a cane or club. Johnson had been promoted to brigadier general in December 1861 but was badly wounded in the foot at the Battle of McDowell in May 1862. Unable to accompany his brigades, they joined Jackson for the Seven Days Battles without him. Johnson eventually recovered and was promoted to major general and command of Jackson's old division. He was captured on May 12, 1864, at Spotsylvania. Ibid., 12, pt. 1, pp. 470-471; Davis, *Confederate General*, 3, pp. 186-187.

position & plenty of artillery, while we must cross a narrow strip of ground to attack them, was by no means reassuring. Just at the critical moment when we were about to advance an order came from Jackson to halt where we were. It was rumored at the time that Jn was anxious to push on, but Longstreet[60] had come up & taken command—& that he had twice given a positive order to J'n before the latter would agree to halt. This story was generally believed at the time & I never heard it contradicted. Yet it had not one word of truth in it. Last winter Col. C. S. Venable,[61] Gen'l Lee's former A.D.C., told me positively as of his own knowledge that the order to advance had been given to Jackson by Gen'l Lee—that Jn finding the worn-out & depressed condition of his troops had represented it so strongly to Gen'l Lee that the latter had countermanded the order! I told Venable the common rumor. He had heard of it before, but said it contained no truth—that he knew it was Jn who had prevented the advance—& I may, here add had saved us from a stinging repulse if not more.[62] We staid here a day & a half, then marched back to the vicinity of Richmond & encamped near

[60] Major General James Longstreet grew up in Alabama and Georgia, was a West Point classmate of Ewell and had served bravely in Mexico. He fought well throughout the Seven Days Battles and earned Lee's respect, later becoming known as "Lee's War Horse." After Antietam, Longstreet became a lieutenant general and led the army's First Corps for the remainder of the war. Some officers thought he was prone to moving too slowly, but he was known to be ferocious in combat. Longstreet was criticized for being too slow at Gettysburg, was praised for helping win the Battle of Chickamauga, Georgia, and survived a serious wound in the Wilderness. After the war he joined the Republican Party and sometimes wrote critically of Lee's wartime tactics. The controversial Longstreet died in 1904. Davis, *Confederate General*, 4, pp. 91-95. See also Jeffry D. Wert, *General James Longstreet: The Confederacy's Most Controversial Soldier* (New York, 1993).

[61] Charles Scott Venable was educated in Virginia and Europe, and taught mathematics before the war. After seeing action at Fort Sumter and First Manassas, he joined Lee's staff while the general was President Davis' military advisor in Richmond. During the Seven Days Battles, Venable was a major and Lee's aide-de-camp. He was later promoted to lieutenant colonel and served Lee faithfully throughout the war. Venable resumed teaching after the surrender and died in 1900. Sifakis, *Who Was Who in the Civil War*, p. 675; *OR* 11, pt. 2, pp. 498, 502.

[62] The bulk of Lee's army arrived near Harrison's Landing on July 3. An earlier skirmish with Jeb Stuart's cavalry had alerted the Federals to the approaching enemy and pointed out vulnerabilities in their defenses. When Lee arrived, he found Longstreet and Jackson arguing about the propriety of an attack against such a well fortified position. Longstreet argued in favor of the assault, while Jackson, remembering the slaughter at Malvern Hill, was against it. After hearing them out, Lee sided with Jackson and canceled Longstreet's proposed attack. Douglas, *I Rode With Stonewall*, p. 112; Vandiver, *Mighty Stonewall*, p. 325.

the Chickahominy, with Hd.Qrs. of our Divn at Strawberry Hill, & so
ended for us the "Seven Days Battle." The loss of our Divn in killed &
wounded was 985—mostly at Cold Harbor.[63] But the seeds of disease
sown by the malaria of the swamps carried off a good many more.

At Westover when the order came to halt our line, Gen'l E. took
advantage of the leisure to ride out to our skirmishers & reconnoitre the
ground in front. We came to a small house on a knoll some 150 yards
behind the skirmish line, which was here considerably thrown forward—and as it commanded a wide view in front, got off our horses to
use our glasses & sat down in the shade to await events. An occasional
shot was whistling by but no danger expected, so Gen'l E. presently sat
down on a large box with his feet drawn upon it, his back against a tree
& his head on his hands & went to sleep. I sat on the ground with my
back against the same box. All at once four or five shots whistled past at
us, & Gen'l E. got up with his hat in his hand & began examining the
box where a ball had struck within an inch of his heel & passed *between*
his foot & thigh. As he was doing so, he found a couple of holes in his
cap—which it was barely possible could have been made while on his
head, without killing him! Yet he had gone to sleep with the cap on &
pulled it off in waking. The ball which missed his heel had passed
within less than six inches of my head before striking there. We moved
behind the knoll & were no more molested. Just before this Turner's
horse had wandered off into the valley behind the knoll. He went to
catch it & as he stooped to take the rein a ball struck just below his hand.
It was one of those fired at us & must have barely grazed the top of the
little hill & then descended rapidly in order to reach the ground so soon.

*   *   *

---

[63] Ewell's casualties during the Seven Days came to 987. Of these, 764 were lost on June 27 at
Gaines' Mill, what Brown refers to as Cold Harbor. *OR* 11, pt. 2, pp. 610, 616.

Brown's account of the Seven Days ends abruptly as he next describes Jackson's advance towards Cedar Mountain. Captain Brown continued to serve with Ewell for most of the war and rose to the rank of major. In 1863, his mother, Lizinka, married the general and the two soldiers were thus bound even closer. On April 6, 1865, Federals captured both Brown and Ewell at Sayler's Creek during Lee's withdrawal from Petersburg. The two Southerners lived as prisoners in Boston's Fort Warren for several months before being paroled. Returning to Spring Hill, Tennessee, the two went into business together and developed the family estate—eventually called "Ewell Farm"—into a prosperous dairy and stock farm. Tragically, in January 1872 both Lizinka and Ewell died from pneumonia. By that time, however, Brown was a prominent Tennessee farmer and businessman, and continued to prosper. He had married Susan Rebecca Polk of Columbia, Tennessee, in 1866 and eventually fathered five children. By 1893, Brown had served one term in the Tennessee House of Representatives and sat on the board of trustees for both the University of Tennessee and Spring Hill Male College. But the Panic of 1893 proved devastating. Brown, who suffered from bouts of depression, was already burdened with family responsibilities and mistakenly believed he had lost his family's fortune in the economic collapse. On August 30, overwhelmed by anxiety, Major Campbell Brown walked into a field outside Grand Rapids, Michigan, and committed suicide.

Carmen Brissette Grayson

Carmon Grayson holds degrees from Georgetown University
and Johns Hopkins University, and a doctorate from the University of Virginia. Dr. Grayson is a professor of history at Hampton
University, Hampton, Virginia, and resides in Willimsburg on the
Virginia peninsula.

Military Advisor to Stanton and Lincoln:

Quartermaster General Montgomery C. Meigs and the Peninsula Campaign, January-August 1862

Throughout the winter of 1861 and into the spring of 1862, President Abraham Lincoln struggled to find professional military advice. His general-in-chief, the young, energetic and charismatic Maj. Gen. George B. McClellan, built a formidable army and designed a comprehensive plan he thought could end the war, but Lincoln and the general communicated poorly, and the Federal secretary of war, Edwin M. Stanton, came to dislike McClellan personally. The two politicians and the general often felt themselves working at cross purposes. Lincoln, facing unprecedented military and strategic questions for which his background as a country lawyer did not prepare him, needed professional assistance.

Lincoln admitted to Maj. Gen. Ethan Allen Hitchcock, whom he sought to recruit as an adviser, that he "had no military knowledge" though he held the presidential powers of commander-in-chief.[1] Stanton, conceding that he "was not a military man," likewise felt it "very

---

[1] Ethan Allen Hitchcock, *Fifty Years in Camp and Field: Diary of Major-General Ethan Allen Hitchcock, U. S.A.*, edited by W. A. Croffut (New York, 1909), pp. 439, 437-448. Article II, Section 2, Paragraph 3 of the United States Constitution grants to the president the supreme military power in just 35 words: "The President shall be commander in chief of the Army and the Navy of the United States, and of the militia of the several states, when called into the actual service of the United States. . . ."

extraordinary" that he could find "no military man to give opinions" on military subjects.[2] The commander-in-chief, however, did not lead the troops into battle nor did the secretary of war, who acted as the president's deputy in directing the war. The man who did take the field did so as general-in-chief but without clear legal authority. General Winfield Scott filled the position until November 1, 1861, when General McClellan replaced him.

Lincoln bowed to intense Republican pressure and relieved McClellan, a Democrat, as general-in-chief on March 11, 1862, restricting his authority to the Army of the Potomac. The president and Stanton tried to function as their own high command, and this attempt by two lawyers to assume the duties of general-in-chief caused much of the disarray in Union policy from March to July 1862-the crucial period during which McClellan waged his Peninsula Campaign. The problems of the president and the secretary of war left them "hungry for competent military leaders."[3] Eventually, their search led them to a professional military man of intelligence who was willing to freely offer advice: Brig. Gen. Montgomery Cunningham Meigs, quartermaster general of the U.S. Army.

Maj. Gen. Carl Schurz, a Republican, once accused Lincoln of contributing to their party's electoral losses because he had appointed Democratic generals. The president retorted: "It so happened that very few of our friends had a military education or were of the profession of arms." He concluded by reminding Schurz that the question at issue seemed to be ". . .whether the war should be conducted on military knowledge, or on political affinity, only that our own friends . . . seemed to think that such a question was inadmissible."[4]

[2] George C. Gorham, *Life and Public Services of Edwin M. Stanton*, 2 vols. (Boston, 1899), vol. 2, p. 429. Hitchcock, *Fifty Years in Camp and Field*, p. 442.

[3] Herman Hattaway and Archer Jones, "The War Board, the Basis of the United States First General Staff," *Military Affairs*, vol. 1 (February 1982), p. 1.

[4] Roy P. Basler, ed. *The Collected Works of Abraham Lincoln*, 8 vols. (New Brunswick, 1953), vol. 5, pp. 494-495.

Perceived both as one of the administration's "friends" and "of the profession of arms," Meigs proved to be an exception to the president's generalization. The quartermaster general, an 1836 West Point graduate, had spent his entire career as an army construction engineer and was highly regarded for his building of the Washington aqueduct and the extension of the United States Capitol. A protégé of Sen. (later Secretary of State) William H. Seward, Meigs enjoyed a reputation for competence and probity. Indeed, Lincoln's secretary of the navy, Gideon Welles, thought that Seward relied more heavily on Meigs than he did on Lincoln in military matters.[5] Meigs, for his part, considered the secretary of state as the only "man of worth" in Lincoln's cabinet.[6] Meigs did not bring battlefield or command experience to his role of adviser, but his intelligence and political loyalty led Lincoln and Stanton to depend on his military advice with its West Point imprimatur. From the crisis over protecting the Federal forts in the Confederacy in March-April 1861 to the withdrawal of the Army of the Potomac from near Richmond in August 1862, the 45-year-old army captain-of-engineers-cum-brigadier moved in Washington's highest military councils and exerted influence disproportionate to his experience and training.

Army regulations required the quartermaster general's department to provide: the quarters and transportation of the army; storage and transportation for all army supplies; army clothing; camp and garrison equipage; cavalry and artillery horses; fuel; forage; straw; material for bedding, and stationery.[7]

---

[5] "[Seward] had great confidence in Meigs on all occasions, and deferred to him more than to his superior, in all matters of a military nature." Gideon Welles, *The Diary of Gideon Welles*, 3 vols. (New York, 1911), vol. 1, p. 62.

[6] Meigs to father, Dr. Charles Meigs, August 10, 1861, in Montgomery Cunningham Meigs Papers, Library of Congress Manuscript Division, Washington, D.C., Addendum, container 22, microfilm reel 4. Hereinafter cited as Meigs Papers. All Meigs' letters to his father are in containers 22 and 23, reels 4 and 5 by date, unless otherwise noted.

[7] *Revised Regulations for the Army of the United States, 1861* (Philadelphia, 1861), p. 159, cited in Russell F. Weigley, *Quartermaster General of the Union Army: A Biography of M.C. Meigs* (New York, 1959), pp. 218-219.

A job description of the duties Meigs actually performed would have showed that he frequently acted outside the sphere of his responsibilities as quartermaster general. For example, Meigs: directed the Union war department's first responses to Maj. Gen. Thomas J. "Stonewall" Jackson's campaign initiated on May 23 in the Shenandoah Valley; drew up and signed the secretary of war's name to orders without the secretary's knowledge; drafted military orders to Maj. Gen. Irvin McDowell and McClellan for the president and secretary of war; advised the chief executive on the disposition of the Army of the Potomac in July; analyzed the military consequences of the emancipation of the slaves for the secretary of war's annual report; and sent secret instructions to a corps commander for launching a surprise attack on Richmond.[8]

Probably at no other time in the war did Meigs wield as much power at the White House as during the Peninsula Campaign, and the extent of his influence during that period is best illustrated by his roles in three events: the deployment of McDowell's 35,000-man corps in April and May; the response to the first reports of Jackson's Valley Campaign in May; and the removal of the Army of the Potomac from its base on the James River in July. In terms of influence at the White House and war department, the quartermaster general enjoyed unchallenged preeminence among the army bureau chiefs in Washington.

---

[8] Draft of Meigs' *Annual Report of the Quartermaster General for the Year 1862*, a portion of the *Annual Report of the Secretary of War* (November 28, 1862) in Meigs Papers, container 30, "Correspondence, Military Orders" file "August-December, 1864 and Undated." All items are in container 30 unless otherwise noted. "Report of the Secretary of War," December 1, 1862 in *Message of the President of the United States to the Two Houses of Congress at the Commencement of the Third Session of the Thirty-Seventh Congress, IV* (Washington, 1862), pp. 3-19. Meigs' personal views were sometimes too strong for the administration. On freeing slaves, he wrote, "Emancipation to the black man & slavery to his white master-It will be after all but a righteous retribution when this is brought about. . . ." Meigs to "Sister Nannie," September 22, 1862, Meigs Papers. In his draft, Meigs had called for the "permanent occupation and cultivation of the [Confederacy]," noted the administration's intention to "reduce the [Confederate] leaders to poverty," and to arm freed blacks. These views were omitted in the report. Meigs' portion begins on page 17 from "Rightly ordered. . . ." to page 19, "By striking down this system. . . ." See also Meigs to Erasmus D. Keyes, November 18, 1862, Meigs Papers.

1861 Prelude: From the Federal Forts to Bull Run

Two events indicate how quickly Meigs rose to influence. In August 1860, President James Buchanan reprimanded the captain for a breach in military discipline. The captain of engineers had by-passed his superior, Secretary of War John B. Floyd, complaining of some matter directly to the president, who scolded Meigs and reminded him that military procedures "separated subaltern and the commander-in-chief." Only eight months later, Meigs had gained the confidence and trust of the new president of the United States. In April 1861, Abraham Lincoln chose Meigs to draft orders-for the president's signature-for an expedition to relieve Fort Pickens, off Pensacola Bay, Florida.[9]

Disagreement over what to do about Fort Sumter in South Carolina and Fort Pickens divided Lincoln's Cabinet. Both garrisons needed reinforcements and supplies, but Union attempts to deliver the men and matériel risked war. Ready to take that chance, Postmaster General Montgomery Blair supported an expedition to Sumter. Secretary of State Seward, averse to rescuing Sumter, pressed instead for an expedition to Fort Pickens. After a late-night cabinet meeting on March 28, the administration resolved to resupply both forts.

The following day, Seward brought Meigs to the White House to reassure the commander-in-chief. "The President talked freely with me," wrote Meigs, and when Lincoln asked if Fort Pickens could be held, Meigs answered: "certainly."[10] At a second conference on March 31, Lincoln gave him command of the Fort Pickens relief effort, and by April 23 Meigs' expedition succeeded in delivering to the Federal fort 1,100 troops and supplies enough for six months. Fort Sumter, however,

---

[9] President James Buchanan bluntly warned Meigs that the latter's dispute with Secretary of War John B. Floyd over public works contracts did not justify violating military discipline. The president did not want to find himself in "a direct and sometimes an unbecoming and angry correspondence with any subaltern in the Army who might feel himself aggrieved by one of his superiors." Buchanan to Meigs, August 13, 1860, Meigs Papers.

[10] Montgomery C. Meigs, "The Relations of President Lincoln and Secretary Stanton to the Military Commanders in the Civil War," *American Historical Review*, 26(1920-1921), p. 299.

fell April 13, and, as Meigs steamed back to Washington, the Civil War had entered its second week.

Meigs had predicted to Lt. Col. Erasmus D. Keyes, his partner in the Pickens enterprise, that they could expect a "reward" if they rescued Pickens. Meigs later noted that in this "first expedition against the Rebellion," he and Keyes had been "successful in saving that fort for the United States."[11] Meigs seemed ambivalent about suggestions that he might command an army: "Too much rests upon success & I might fail," he acknowledged. "If I succeeded I should do good to my country[,] if I failed I might ruin it. Such things should be forced upon men not sought."[12] But Meigs was quite willing to offer advice, and the president seemed to be always anxious for it. Lincoln asked opinions of Meigs that spring, and the soldier made a positive impression upon those who heard him. "All member of cabinet received me kindly and cordially," Meigs wrote to his father in early May, "[they] seem pleased at the result & ask of me advice even on subjects upon which I have to tell them I am ignorant-Calling on the President I find myself talking to nearly a full cabinet."[13] The administration promoted Meigs to brigadier general and appointed him quartermaster general of the Union army on June 13, just five weeks before the North's confrontation with Confederate forces at the Battle of First Manassas.[14]

Meigs estimated that his new position as quartermaster general carried real power in the army and influence on the war even if it did not

[11] Meigs Journal, April 1, 1861, longhand copy in John G. Nicolay Papers, Library of Congress Manuscript Division, Washington, D.C. Keyes to Meigs, May 3, 1861, Meigs Papers; Meigs Pocket Diary, April 6, 1863, microfilm reels 1 and 2, Meigs Papers.

[12] Meigs to father, October 8, 1862, Meigs Papers.

[13] Meigs to father, May 6, 1861, Meigs Papers.

[14] According to Meigs, "[T]he Pred't & several cabinet ministers wished me there [in the quartermaster post] but there has been much opposition." Lincoln sent for the captain after dinner on June 12 "to say that he had been for some time trying to make me Q. M. Genl. That he did not know whether I knew this or not." Meigs to father, June 12, 1861, Meigs Papers. As late as August 7, Keyes awaited promotion. "It will mortify me to death to be set back below some of the new brigadiers," he confided to Meigs. Later in the month, he was made a brigadier general of volunteers. Keyes to Meigs, August 7, 1861; Ezra Warner, *Generals in Blue*, (Baton Rouge, 1964), p. 264.

Quartermaster General Montgomery C. Meigs

entail the highest military rank. Major generals commanded army corps, the lieutenant general commanded the whole army, he noted, but he would provide the means by which to supply and move those armies. The quartermaster general's command, he wrote, "extends from the Atlantic to the Pacific[,] the Lakes to the Gulf."[15]

Reflecting profound optimism about Union strength, Meigs prophesied a month before the Battle of First Manassas: "[O]ne good battle & the back of the rebellion is broken."[16] Lincoln called war councils on June 25 and 29 to plan the Union offensive against the South and the quartermaster general had a significant voice in these plans. On July 21, Confederate forces routed the Union army. A relationship of ease and trust had developed between Lincoln and Meigs since their first meeting the previous March, so at 3 a.m. on July 22, the quartermaster general, having just returned from observing the Manassas battlefield, went to the White House for a "long talk" with the president.[17]

First Manassas precipitated personnel changes in the high command and in the administration. Later on the same day that Meigs had had his "long talk" with Lincoln, the president ordered McClellan, who had won two victories in western Virginia, to take command of the Department of the Potomac and organize a Union army to move against the Confederates in Virginia. McClellan arrived on July 26 and by November 1, when he replaced the aging Scott as general-in-chief, he had molded unorganized regiments into the formidable Army of the Potomac. On January 13, 1862, Lincoln named Stanton to replace the incompetent secretary of war, Simon Cameron, with whom Meigs had worked harmoniously.[18] Meigs believed that he had Cameron's "confidence &

---

[15] Meigs to father, June 12, 1861, Meigs Papers.

[16] Ibid., July 18, 1861, Meigs Papers.

[17] Meigs Journal, July 22, 1861, Nicolay Papers.

[18] Cameron opposed Meigs' promotion to QM Gen. "I did not want Meigs in the QM Gen Dept.," he confessed, "but now he is there I can't spare him." Meigs to father, July 30, 1861, Meigs Papers. Meigs–even as a colonel–also drew up orders for the secretary's signature and in at least one case authored an extensive letter to Sec. of the Navy Gideon Welles from Cameron. Cameron, "Secret and Confidential" letter to Gideon Welles, May 29, 1861; Cameron order to Meigs, May 30, 1862, Addendum, container 29, microfilm reel 12, Meigs Papers.

affection," but concluded that his superior "wishes to do right but he is not up to his high assignment."[19] Stanton, by contrast, quickly mastered his post. Meigs' relations with the new secretary, and with Lincoln and McClellan, formed a significant part of the complex situation in the Union's high command between March and August 1862.

Meigs and the High Command

Meigs had the confidence of Seward and Lincoln and would form a strong working relationship with Stanton, but he found little common ground with fellow West Pointer McClellan. One of their early encounters began cordially enough, when, within a week of the commanding general's arrival, the quartermaster general told McClellan that "he stood where Washington stood when he was first in command of the revolutionary armies & that if he will do his part as well he will make as great a name."[20] By winter, relations had cooled. On December 27, 1861, the quartermaster general went to the halls of Congress to testify before the Joint Committee on the Conduct of the War that he had had little to do with commander of the Army of the Potomac. He knew nothing of the general-in-chief's intentions. "My opinion has not been asked, and I have not been consulted," he said. "I do not complain." McClellan had once invited Meigs to come and talk over the commander's plans. "I went to his house one evening," Meigs later explained, "but he was out. I have not gone again, for I supposed that when he wanted me he would send for me. That time, I suppose, has not come yet."[21]

Nevertheless, two months later, the two generals met on friendly terms in Stanton's office where Meigs found himself, "always talking confidentially" with McClellan, and he was pleased to discover that "we

[19] Meigs to father, July 30, 1861, Meigs Papers.

[20] Meigs to father, July 30, 1861, Meigs Papers.

[21] Meigs' testimony before the Joint Committee on the Conduct of the War on December 27, 1861, *Report of the Joint Committee on the Conduct of the War*, Part 1: Army of the Potomac (Washington, D.C., 1863), p. 154.

seem always to agree upon most points as I propose and discuss with him."[22] The meeting left a generally positive impression on the quarter-master general: "It is pleasant to see him . . .selfconfident, cheerful & pleasant. This confidence in himself is so evident, so simple & natural without any appearance of conceit. . .that I must believe as my wishes & hopes are that it is well founded. He does not consult."[23]

In contrast, Lincoln did seek Meigs for advice.[24] On Friday, January 10 a "much depressed" Lincoln came to him, Meigs wrote later, and "in great distress" pleaded: "General, what shall I do? The people are impatient; Chase[25] has no money and he tells me he can raise no more; the General of the Army has typhoid fever.[26] The bottom is out of the tub. What shall I do?"[27] Meigs suggested that the president call a council of military advisers, which Lincoln did that same day. This session was followed by a White House meeting the next Sunday, which McClellan and Meigs both attended. Also present were Seward, Secretary of the Treasury Salmon P. Chase, Blair, McDowell, Brig. Gen. William B. Franklin and Lincoln.[28]

The same group reconvened at the White House Monday afternoon, January 13. Although the quartermaster general had secretly testified before a congressional committee 16 days earlier that a coolness existed between him and McClellan, at this meeting Meigs assumed an almost avuncular role, moving his chair alongside the younger man, urging him

---

[22] Meigs to father, February 11, 1862, Meigs Papers.

[23] Ibid.

[24] The quartermaster general maintained that the president had consulted only him during the difficult time of early January 1862, but that statement is patently incorrect. Meigs, "The Relations of President Lincoln," p. 239.

[25] Secretary of the Treasury Salmon P. Chase.

[26] Typhoid had immobilized McClellan since December 20.

[27] Meigs, "The Relations of President Lincoln," pp. 302, 292.

[28] Six months earlier, Meigs had characterized McDowell stringently: "McDowell appointed. . .through the influence of Mr. Chase is not a great man. No one in the army would have selected him as the first officer to be made a general. A good, brave, commonplace, fat man." Meigs to father, July 30, 1861, Meigs Papers.

to reveal his strategy to those assembled. McClellan, who had earlier outlined his plans to Chase and who on the previous day had explained his intentions to Lincoln "in a general and casual way," worried that further discussion would compromise the strategy.[29] He offered to reveal his aims to those assembled if the president would commit his request to writing and if Lincoln "assumed the responsibility of the results."[30] This Lincoln did not do and, according to Meigs, the president "yielded in despair to his wilful [sic] General."[31]

Lincoln showed his willingness to listen to Meigs again on March 1, 1862 when the quartermaster showed up unexpectedly at the White House to deliver a memo. The president was in conference with Welles when an aide announced Meigs. The messenger returned to the general with the Lincoln's reply: "General Meigs is it? He never comes without he has something to say worth hearing. I will see him surely." Meigs asked his father: "That's a desired reputation to have at headquarters, is it not?"[32]

Eight days later, Meigs again found himself conferring with Lincoln and other administration officials. The ironclad *C.S.S. Virginia* had sunk two U. S. ships in Hampton Roads and seemed invulnerable against the Federal Navy's return fire. Seward summoned Meigs out of church to the White House. The quartermaster arrived to find secretaries Seward, Stanton and Welles and the superintendent of telegraph already gathered. Lincoln soon entered with Cmdr. John A. Dahlgren, commander of the Washington Navy Yard. Meigs later recorded his views of the council, which corroborated Welles' account. Both described Stanton's state of extreme anxiety and used almost the same words to record Stanton's remarks. In Welles' judgment, the quartermaster was "in full sympathy with Stanton in all his fears and predictions." Meigs, wrote

[29] Ibid., 292-293. George B. McClellan, *McClellan's Own Story* (New York, 1887), p. 156.

[30] Ibid., p. 158.

[31] Meigs, "The Relations of President Lincoln," p. 293.

[32] Meigs to father, March 2, 1862, Meigs Papers.

Welles, did not have information on which to base a judgment so that he was unable "to allay panic or tranquilize the government officials."[33]

Meigs' resonance to Stanton's outlook increased in the months leading up to operations on the Peninsula.

The close personal and professional relationship between the two men began as early as Monday, February 10, 1862, at a time when Stanton kept a punishing schedule. Meigs arrived in Stanton's office shortly after the secretary had returned from a conference with Lincoln, who had conducted little other business that day because his son, Willie, lay seriously ill.[34] At the start of what turned out to be a four-hour visit, the secretary of war lay collapsed on his sofa, too sick to discuss business with the quartermaster, who urged him to go home. Stanton confessed that he was not physically able to do so. Meigs summoned a Dr. Wheeler "of the Navy" who happened to be near. The doctor administered ammonia and valinium to the prostrate secretary, and put ice to his head and hot bricks to his feet. For two or three hours after these ministrations, the secretary remained in his office, "coughing violently" and convulsively and thanking Meigs for his attention. Three hours into the visit, Stanton told Meigs that only "at this moment" did he see Meigs' face and recognize him. "Yet," Meigs observed, Stanton "seemed not to know that he had done so" throughout the visit.[35]

Stanton's collapse did not puzzle Meigs. The new secretary had had a "narrow escape" because he kept an exhausting schedule. Even during his four-hour ordeal, the secretary of war signed a paper for Lincoln's private secretary and tried to talk briefly with Vice President Hannibal Hamlin, Seward and McClellan. Whenever Stanton tried to speak, he found he could not, and "the ammonia & valinium were again administered." Two days earlier, the secretary had received members of Con-

---

[33] Meigs to father, March 9, 1862, Meigs Papers; Welles, *Diary*, p. 64, 62.

[34] C. Percy Powell, *Lincoln Day by Day: A Chronology, 1809-1865*, 3 vols. (Washington, D.C., 1960), vol. 3, p. 94.

[35] Meigs to father, February 11, 1862, Meigs Papers. Meigs' phrasing is awkward. He apparently means that Stanton *had* recognized Meigs throughout the visit but later seemed not to realize that he had known all along who was nursing him.

gress all day, worked through Sunday and gone to bed at 3 a.m. Monday. For an hour or two later that morning, he had seen "this crowd of citizens who each had his special object to gain." Such a schedule, said Meigs "is exhausting to the brain[,] to the life force—I find it so with myself and I have had a pretty long trial of it—I need more sleep than ever before." Stanton first came to the office with "explosive energy so conspicuous" and indulged in many "fulminations," Meigs noted, but "though full of energy & pluck & art & keenness—he may overwork himself & with fatal results."[36]

One of the projects to which Stanton would devote prodigious labor was replacing McClellan. The president's War Order No. 3, which the Cabinet approved and the president endorsed on the evening of March 11, removed McClellan as general-in-chief. Stanton's frantic search for military guidance had begun earlier that day when he had visited the hotel room of 63-year-old General Hitchcock, who was retired and ill. Stanton begged him to accept a position as military adviser to the administration. He promised Hitchcock "any legislation" the general might want if he would accept the post. Stanton went so far as to offer command of the Army of the Potomac to Hitchcock.[37] Hitchcock declined, and the secretary of war turned to Meigs for military counsel.

With the spring offensive about to begin and still lacking a general-in-chief, Lincoln and Stanton became the Union's *de facto* high command. The two lawyers sought confidence in drawing closer to Meigs. On March 12, the secretary of war "surprised" the quartermaster general by summoning him to his office "immediately." The meeting produced three significant results: (1) the formation of the War Board—a military council made up of army bureau chiefs; (2) the strengthening of close ties between the two men, neither of whom supported McClellan's strat-

---

[36] Ibid; Meigs to father, July 29, 1862, Meigs Papers.

[37] Hitchcock, *Fifty Years in Camp and Field*, p. 438-439. Just, 48 hours after Stanton's attempt to lure the reluctant Hitchcock to serve as military adviser, Confederate President Jefferson Davis, likewise in need of military guidance, charged Gen. Robert E. Lee with conduct of military affairs in the armies of the Confederacy. Frank J. Welcher, *The Union Army, 1861-1865* (Bloomington, 1989), p. 797.

egy; and (3) the assignment to Meigs of special responsibility for the army's move to the Peninsula.[38]

When Meigs arrived in Stanton's office, he found Brig. Gen. James W. Ripley, the Army's chief of ordnance, with the secretary. According to Meigs, Stanton "informed us that he desired to have a council every day at 11 a.m. of the chiefs of Bureaux in which the general conduct of the war and of the War Dept should be discussed."[39] Later, after Ripley had left the room, the conversation turned immediately to army politics and the fate of General McClellan:

> Stanton: General you saw an order in the *Intelligencer*.
> Meigs: Yes sir.
> Stanton: What do you think of it?
> Meigs: I think it is right. Gen. McClellan at the head of 200,000 men actively operating in the field is not physically able to attend to, to think even of this operation & requirements of other commands. . . .No man away from headquarters with 200,000 men under his immediate direction can do this & Gen. McClellan ought not to have such respon-sibility & should I think be glad to be relieved of it.[40]

The secretary of war approved of Meigs' observations and sought much closer ties with him. Stanton:

> replied in substance that he wished to place himself fully in communi-cation with me, that he had the fullest confidence in my ability in my patriotism & that he said this to show me that he wished as far as one man could to another to place himselfalong side of me to ask my counsel and assistance in carrying out the great work to which he knows we are both devoted. He was also pleased to say that he had

---

[38] Meigs, "Memorandum," March 12, 1862, pp. 1-4, Meigs Papers.

[39] Ibid., p. 1.

[40] Ibid., pp. 1-2. The order relieving McClellan as general-in-chief had been printed in newspapers, which is how McClellan himself learned of his fate.

observed all & that he had more confidence in me in these regards than in any other man in the army.[41]

Stanton's strong endorsement heartened Meigs to petition the secretary for an increase in the quartermaster general's staff to relieve him from the pressure of time-consuming details. The secretary agreed and went even further, telling Meigs that he was to consider the assistant secretary of war, shipping executive John Tucker, under his orders and, if necessary, to assign him a room in the quartermaster general's office, then in the Winder Building, a block away from the war department.

Though Tucker, who had assumed his post on January 29, did an excellent job of gathering transports for the Peninsula, Stanton held a low opinion of his office work. The quartermaster general knew as well as he did, confided Stanton, "that the most trusted agents needed attendance." Meigs, thus, must consider the Peninsula "expeditions" as "particularly" under his "watch & supervision."[42]

An early Stanton biographer judged that Meigs acted as "Stanton's main support" in certain respects.[43] Meigs, one of the secretary's "faithful lieutenants," acted closely with Stanton as a political ally, professional colleague and personal friend.[44] The relationship survived confrontations during which the professional soldier disagreed on military points with the notoriously intimidating Stanton. At least three times during War Board meetings Meigs challenged the secretary's simplistic judgments. Stanton once stated that "If our men would only be cool, and watch their chance" they could disable the *C.S.S. Virginia* just by hitting the ironclad in a vulnerable part. Meigs quickly pointed to the difficulty of "looking out of a blind port-hole, to aim the gun so as to strike the vessel the moment her side should be exposed, and it would

[41] Ibid., p. 2.

[42] Ibid., pp. 3-4. The quartermaster general concluded his account of the meeting with Stanton thus: "I think I have precisely given in this memorandum the full measure of his confidence in my ability as expressed by him."

[43] Frank A. Flower, *Edwin McMasters Stanton* (New York, 1905), p. 294.

[44] Ibid., p. 293.

only be for an instant."[45]   In a second incident Stanton dismissed a request from Maj. Gen. Henry W. Halleck for more engineers with a statement betraying obvious ignorance of their functions. Meigs immediately rejoined with a short lecture on the military role of engineers as "the eyes of a General."[46] Finally, Meigs did not yield when an irascible Stanton scolded him in front of the War Board for bothering the secretary of war with requests for permission to buy horses. "You do not understand why I bring these matters before you," Meigs insisted, "If you will give me the authority which I had in this matter. . .I will not trouble you with these questions."[47] Despite such diagreements, Stanton, Meigs and Lincoln usually found themselves in accord on larger matters of strategy.

No military adviser in the spring of 1862 stood closer to Lincoln and Stanton than did Meigs. He was assigned, or himself assumed, duties outside the purview of his role as quartermaster general. Some of these duties Meigs himself once characterized as matters that would "naturally be intrusted to the Commanding General."[48] The proximity of Meigs' office to those of Lincoln and Stanton facilitated the daily and even hourly contact with the president and secretary of war. Meigs represented a professional military sanction reinforcing the judgments of his civilian superiors. Thus, he acted as a military counterpoint in Washington to field commanders, like McClellan and McDowell, who dissented from some of the administration's decisions.

May 17, 1862: McDowell's Troops to Richmond

With the embarkation of Brig. Gen. Charles S. Hamilton's division (III Corps) at Alexandria on March 17, the Army of the Potomac began

---

[45] *Proceedings of the War Board*, March 14, 1862, in Edwin M. Stanton Papers, Library of Congress Manuscript Division, Washington D.C. Hereinafter cited as *War Board*.

[46] Ibid., March 19, 1862.

[47] Ibid., March 25, 1862.

[48] Meigs, "The Relations of President Lincoln," p. 288.

its move to the Virginia Peninsula. McClellan sought to capture Richmond from the east, thus avoiding a 100-mile direct assault overland and obviating the need to cross several large rivers between Washington and the Confederate capital. The strategy, of which Meigs had always disapproved, made Lincoln anxious from the outset. Both feared an attack on Washington from the Shenandoah Valley.

Confederate Gen. Joseph E. Johnston worked Lincoln's fears to the South's advantage. He ordered "Stonewall" Jackson to move against elements of Maj. Gen. Nathaniel Banks' army that were preparing to leave the Valley to join the Army of the Potomac. On March 23, Jackson attacked Brig. Gen. James Shields' division at Kernstown, just south of Winchester. Despite a tactical defeat, Jackson succeeded strategically by frightening Washington into keeping troops in the Valley, where they posed little danger to Richmond and could not materially aid McClellan.

Renewed concern for the Federal capital's safety a week later prompted the administration again to withhold troops from the army on the Peninsula, an action that profoundly affected the evolution of McClellan's campaign. Meigs, Stanton and Hitchcock visited the White House on April 12 and informed Lincoln that McClellan had left the capital with almost 20,000 fewer troops than the president had demanded be retained.[49] The three men were concerned by a report brought to Stanton the day after the commander of the Army of the Potomac had sailed to the Peninsula. The military governor of the District of Columbia, Brig. Gen. James S. Wadsworth, who had assumed the duties of the newly-created position only 16 days earlier, determined that McClellan had left behind only about 19,000 troops to defend the capital.[50] Not a professional soldier, Wadsworth frankly acknowledged his

---

[49] Benjamin P. Thomas and Harold M. Hyman, *Stanton: The Life and Times of Lincoln's Secretary of War* (New York, 1962), p.188. U. S. War Department, *The War of the Rebellion: The Official Records of the Union and Confederate Armies*, 128 vols. (Washington, D.C., 1890-1901), series I, vol. 11, pt. 3, pp. 57-62. Hereinafter cited as *OR*. All references are to series I unless otherwise noted.

[50] James S. Wadsworth, "Summary of Responsibilities," n.d., series 1-a, container 5, Wadsworth Family Papers, Library of Congress Manuscript Division, Washington D.C. See also McClellan, *Own Story*, p. 226. Wadsworth claimed that his orders never clearly defined his duties, the boundaries of his jurisdiction or whether he commanded a department or a district. Although

lack of military acumen and carried his figures to Stanton, who then asked Adj. Gen. Lorenzo Thomas and Hitchcock if McClellan had violated the president's order to leave the capital secure. The War Board found that, given Wadsworth's figures, McClellan had not met the president's stipulations. The next day, April 13, the administration acted to secure Washington by withholding McDowell's I Corps from McClellan.[51] This satisfied Meigs, who even six days earlier had warned Stanton and the War Board of the capital's vulnerability.[52]

Not until May 17 would the administration feel Washington secure enough to release McDowell's force to join McClellan on the Peninsula. Meigs drew up for Stanton's signature the May 17 orders to both McDowell at Falmouth, near Fredericksburg, and McClellan outside Richmond. McDowell was to proceed overland toward Richmond and position himself so as to always cover Washington.[53] McClellan had asked that all reinforcements be sent by water. Stanton acknowledged Meigs' preparation of these orders and signed them "on consultation" with the president, Col. Joseph G. Totten, chief of the corps of engineers, ordnance chief Ripley and Col. Joseph P. Taylor, commissary general of subsistence.[54] McDowell's orders and the circumstances surrounding their composition provide two indications of Meigs' influential position. Stanton made no substantive changes in the Meigs draft and

---

Stanton told him to exercise "in many respects" the functions of a departmental commander, Wadsworth had reported to McClellan until April 4, when he came under McDowell's jurisdiction. Henry Greenleaf Pearson, *James S. Wadsworth of Geneseo* (New York, 1913), p. 81; "Extracts from the Journal of Henry J. Raymond, II," edited by his son, *Scribner's Monthly*, vol. 19 (January 1880), p. 420.

[51] *OR* 11, pt. 3, pp. 57-62.

[52] *War Board*, March 27, 1862.

[53] Meigs draft of orders to Maj. Gen. Irvin McDowell, mistakenly filed in "Correspondence, Military Orders, May-June 1861," Meigs Papers; *OR* 11, pt. 1, p. 28; McDowell's testimony before the Joint Committee on the Conduct of the War on June 30, 1862, *Report of the Joint Committee*, p. 272.

[54] *OR* 11, pt. 1, p. 28.

though Lincoln proposed additions to McDowell's orders, Meigs persuaded the president to omit them. Lincoln had suggested that McDowell's orders include the following:

> You will retain the separate command of the forces taken with you; but while co-operating with General McClellan you will obey his orders except that you are to judge, and are not to allow your force to be disposed otherwise than so as to give the greatest protection to this capital which may be possible from that distance.[55]

Meigs thought it "dangerous" to instruct a military subordinate that in some cases he need not obey the orders of a superior. As another route to the same goal he suggested that the chief executive incorporate these stipulations into McClellan's orders, a copy of which would be sent to McDowell. Lincoln agreed.[56]

Meigs wrote two drafts of McClellan's May 17 orders. At the bottom of the second draft, the version ultimately sent, he inscribed: "As sent to the President & approved by him."[57] These orders informed McClellan that McDowell was joining him by land and that McDowell's specific task was to protect the capital. McClellan was to extend his right wing to join with McDowell's left. Finally, McDowell was to retain command of the Department of the Rappahannock and of the forces with which he moved.[58]

Two revealing differences emerge between Meigs' original draft and his second, the approved version. The initial draft mentioned the security of the capital only once, though forcefully, at the outset, but in the process of incorporating McDowell's instructions into McClellan's orders Meigs made five explicit references to the safety of Washing-

---

[55] *OR* 11, pt. 3, pp. 176-177.

[56] Ibid., p. 177.

[57] *OR* 11, pt. 1, p. 27; Meigs, "For Major-Gen McClellan before Richmond," May 17, 1862; first draft, "Major Gen McClellan," May 17, 1862, Meigs Papers.

[58] *OR* 11, pt. 1, p. 27.

ton.[59] A second shift in emphasis between the two versions was the addition, in the approved text, of the assurance, insisted on by Lincoln, that McDowell would retain command of the troops with which he moved.[60]

This interaction between Lincoln and Meigs as the latter drafted orders provides an insight into the kind of advice the quartermaster general offered the president. A note written at the bottom of the original draft of McClellan's May 17 orders also underscores how far Meigs' activities transcended the ordinary duties of his post. He advised the president that the secretary of the navy "should be requested" to station one or two gun boats at Fredericksburg to allow McDowell to leave a smaller guard force there. Less than a week later, Meigs' advisory role escalated. Lincoln turned to him for guidance in devising the Union response to Robert E. Lee's strategy of using Jackson to create a diversion in the Shenandoah Valley to keep McDowell's forces from joining McClellan's army on the Peninsula.

Not surprisingly, to the end of his life Meigs defended the wording of May 17 order, pointing out that it did not initially "detach" McDowell from McClellan's command but only required that he approach Richmond overland to shield Washington. He dismissed McClellan's demand that McDowell's troops come on his left, "between him and the deep sea," and concluded that his protests showed that "he was not competent to alter his plans to suit his orders."[61]

May 24, 1862: McDowell's Troops to the Valley

---

[59] Ibid.

[60] Ibid. Unlike the official version, Meigs' initial draft made no mention of McClellan's "earnest call for reinforcements." This omission did not change the substance of the orders but it did soften the tone of Meigs' first draft.

[61] Meigs, "The Relations of President Lincoln," p. 296.

Between 1 p.m. and 2 p.m. on Friday, May 23, Jackson's forces attacked Col. John R. Kenly's 1st Maryland Infantry Regiment at Front Royal, Virginia. Nine hours later, the first alarm reached the war department with Gen. John W. Geary's three dispatches from Rectortown, Virginia: Fighting had erupted around Front Royal, he wrote, and he feared a movement against the railroad at Thoroughfare Gap. Geary requested strong reinforcements.[62]

Lincoln and Stanton, however, were not in Washington to read and respond to Geary's dispatches. The president and the secretary were on a steamer in the Potomac, returning from a consultation with McDowell at Fredericksburg, and they remained out of contact with the war department for seven hours after news of the attack on Front Royal reached the capital.[63] In the absence of the commander-in-chief and the secretary of war, three men worked at the war department interpreting the incoming dispatches and making decisions: Assistant Secretary of War Peter H. Watson, Wadsworth and Meigs. Watson, Stanton's former law partner in Ohio, received Geary's first dispatches at the war department. At 11 p.m., a dire communiqué from Banks arrived, and Watson sent a message to Meigs, who lived on nearby H Street: "Have you any suggestion to make," he asked.[64]

Meigs took charge and gave orders to people over whom his authority was legally unclear. In at least two cases, he felt secure enough about Stanton's reactions to send out orders in the secretary's name without his knowledge. Banks' dispatch telling of the Front Royal attack and the threat to his escape route at Middletown reached the war department at 11 p.m.[65] Meigs wrote a summary for Stanton of another communication from the Valley: "Banks thinks that Jackson & Ewell having driven

[62] *OR* 12, pt. 3, p. 215; *OR* 51, pt. 1, p. 628.

[63] Lincoln and Stanton had departed Washington the night before, May 22, and reembarked at the landing at Aquia, Virginia, for the capital at 10 p.m. Friday night, May 23. They reached the Washington Navy Yard at 5 a.m. Saturday morning, the 24th. C. Percy Powell, *Lincoln Day by Day: A Chronology, 1809-1865*, 3 vols. (Washington, D.C., 1960), vol. 3, pp. 114-115.

[64] *OR* 51, pt. 1, p. 628.

[65] *OR* 12, pt. 1, p. 525.

back Frémont arrived in front of him reinforced by Anderson & 20,000 & they with 16,000 effective men & he calls for reinforcements." Meigs added that Anderson had been in front of McDowell and "is not known to have moved."[66] Meigs, above Stanton's name, then ordered Maj. Gen. John Dix in Baltimore to prepare to move all the railroad transportation he could spare and to report what force he could mobilize to assist Banks.[67] At 11:30 p.m., again in Stanton's name, Meigs ordered Brig. Gen. Abram Duryée at Catlett Station to collect the necessary transportation to move a regiment to Thoroughfare Gap in the morning.[68]

Although Meigs directed the Union response in those first few hours outside his authority as quartermaster general, he did not order the movement of any troops, only their preparation. The pivotal question arose late the afternoon on the 24th by which time Lincoln and Stanton had resumed active control of military policy: What should be done with McDowell's forces scheduled to join McClellan in front of Richmond? Meigs bore significant responsibility for crafting of the momentous orders.

The administration suspended but did not rescind McDowell's orders to join McClellan. Lincoln ordered that most of the I Corps go to the Valley to chase down Jackson. In 1888, Meigs would insist that this decision had been made because Jackson's troops had driven Banks in confusion across the Potomac and "spread terror in Maryland, and doubt in Washington. Then, and not till then, did the president order McDowell to march to the Shenandoah."[69] Lincoln's actions and Meigs' observations within 72 hours of those events, however, raise doubts about the

---

[66] Meigs was referring to Maj. Gen. Richard S. Ewell, Maj. Gen. John C. Frémont and Brig. Gen. Joseph Reid Anderson. Meigs, "Summary of Activities, 11 to 12 p.m., May 23, 1862," Meigs Papers.

[67] *OR* 12, pt. 1, p. 523; *OR* 12, pt. 3, p. 216; Meigs, "Summary of Activities."

[68] Ibid. Watson had already instructed Col. Daniel C. McCallum, military director and superintendent of railroads, to collect transportation for the regiment at Catlett so a brigade could be moved on a single train to Front Royal if needed. *OR* 51, pt. 1, p. 628.

[69] Meigs, "The Relations of President Lincoln," p. 296.

quartermaster's attempts at justification 26 years later. The president sent troops out of Washington to Banks on the afternoon of the 24th, before Banks crossed the Potomac, and Vice President Hannibal Hamlin, denied that there had been serious concern about Washington's safety.[70] Meigs himself showed no great anxiety about the city. His choice of words for the instructions deliberately avoided language that suggested a threat to the capital. He minimized the campaign itself as "the late flurry," which need not be a discouragement because "it is one of the accidents of war."[71]

The quartermaster general's response to developments in the Valley revealed two significant facts: (1) He strongly disapproved of McClellan's campaign plan and condemned it as the cause of Jackson's attack; and, (2) The aim of his initial orders and those of the administration-including those to McDowell-were to destroy Jackson's force not merely to protect a vulnerable capital. McClellan's strategy on the Peninsula "invited" Jackson's attempt, Meigs insisted, and the attack would never have occurred if "a reasonable plan of campaign had been adopted. . . ."[72] After Lincoln and Stanton directed the Union response to Jackson's moves, Meigs explicitly stated the objectives: "I hope it will result yet in capturing a part of Jackson's force at least-certainly we shall clear the Shenandoah Valley of his troops in a few days."[73] And a few days later: "Jackson's army is being gradually surrounded. I pray that the movement may be successfully carried out & that he may be caught in the web we have woven with care and labor in the last week."[74]

---

[70] Robert G. Tanner, *Stonewall in the Valley: Thomas J. "Stonewall" Jackson's Campaign Spring 1862* (Garden City, 1976), pp. 239-240. Hannibal Hamlin wrote to Ellen Emery Hamlin: "I do not imagine there was any more fear of Washington than of Bangor, from the rebels. I am sure I felt none, & all cool men were amused or provoked at the fright exhibited here." June 1, 1862. Hamlin Collection, Raymond N. Fogler Library, Special Collections Department, University of Maine, Orono, Me.

[71] Meigs to father, May 26, 1862.

[72] Ibid.

[73] Ibid.

[74] Meigs to father, May 30, 1862, Meigs Papers.

Meigs drafted the order to divert McDowell with all its fateful consequences. Lincoln accepted Meigs' changes, signed the order and delivered the stroke at 5 p.m. "At that moment, 5 p.m.," concluded one historian, "the Valley Army won its Valley Campaign."[75] McDowell felt it as a "crushing blow."

Meigs could not accurately assess the impact on McClellan's situation of the redirection of troops because he did not know the size of the of Confederate force at Richmond. "[I]t may be possible," he admitted, "that they are as numerous or more numerous than the Army of McClellan," but he took comfort in the Union's qualitative superiority.[76] Meigs had played an important role in diverting troops from the Union's major campaign of which he strongly disapproved toward the effort to chase down Jackson in the Valley, and he did so without a clear idea of the effect such diversions would have on the North's main thrust towards Richmond. In defending this action, Meigs wrote, "It failed of success," but the effort to destroy Jackson's "power for mischief" was correct because Jackson inflicted "infinite damage" and even escaped to do more.[77] On June 17, having achieved his objective of weakening McClellan in front of Richmond, General Robert E. Lee ordered Jackson from the Valley to join the Confederate forces facing McClellan outside Richmond.

The Army of the Potomac advanced to within a half-dozen miles of Richmond, but was thrown back in a series of battles in late June 1862. The Federal victory at Malvern Hill on July 1 nevertheless left McClellan on the defensive, and he withdrew to Harrison's Landing on the

---

[75] Tanner, *Stonewall in the Valley*, p. 239. The administration changed McDowell's orders four times between May 17 and June 17-to Richmond, to the Valley, again to Richmond and a final cancellation of those orders. McDowell's full corps never joined McClellan's army in front of the Confederate capital. Historian Kenneth P. Williams thought the instructions displayed the president's stylistic "charm" of expression and noted that the command said "not a thing" about relieving a threat to Washington. More important, the order did not increase McClellan's force before Richmond-precisely the point where Union strength should have been concentrated. *OR* 12, pt. 3, pp. 219-220. Kenneth Powers Williams, *Lincoln Finds a General: A Military Study of the Civil War*, 5 vols. (New York, 1949), vol. 1, p. 175.

[76] Meigs to father, May 26, 1862, Meigs Papers.

[77] Meigs, "The Relations of President Lincoln," p. 296.

James River, about 17 miles from the Confederate capital. The outcome of these clashes-now known as the Seven Days Battles-spurred the quartermaster general to a startling admission. He carried the responsibility for supplying a campaign and for providing military advice for an operation that he thought from the outset would lead to defeat. "[A] terrible reverse on the Peninsula. One which I have foreseen from the moment I believed that it was determined to move the army to that cul de sac."[78] Early in the campaign on the Peninsula, Meigs had written to his father, "I regret that our army ever went there."[79] We do not know how his conviction that the campaign would result in ultimate defeat affected Meigs' decisions or the informal advice he gave to Lincoln and Stanton in 1862. Meigs' statements do reveal, however, his belief that neither Lincoln nor Stanton (and by extension, himself) bore real responsibility for developments on the Peninsula. He placed the entire burden on McClellan and his strategy: "Believe nothing you hear against the President and Secretary as responsible for these disasters," he told his father. "The true cause is the false military move which placed an army in a narrow peninsula where it was easily checked by inferior forces until the gathering hordes of a barbarous people advanced in greatly superior numbers to overwhelm our gallant freemen."[80] If the administration made any mistake, Meigs insisted, it was only in "permitting Gen. McClellan to adopt a false line of operations & by not appreciating the enormous waste of men allowing such operations as we have carried on during this campaign."[81]

The quartermaster general expressed his interpretation of the result of the Seven Days Battles clearly: "We have certainly had a reverse. The natural result of an improper line of operations, an improper division of our army & I fear it would be just to add of bad inefficient leadership on the Peninsula." Meigs thought that a "great leader" would

---

[78] Meigs to father, July 8, 1862, Meigs Papers.

[79] Meigs to father, April 29, 1862, Meigs Papers.

[80] Meigs to father, July 8, 1862, Meigs Papers.

[81] Ibid.

not have put the army in its "false position," and even if such a general had risen to command the army just before the opening attacks on 26 June he still would have managed the subsequent battles better than had McClellan and "would have crushed the rebels."[82]

The Peninsula Campaign
The Army of Harrison's Landing

The Meigs and Stanton families had planned a boating party on the Potomac River to celebrate the Fourth of July. Instead, the quartermaster general spent the holiday evening trying to persuade Lincoln to withdraw the army from its new position at Harrison's Landing. Lincoln resisted Meigs' vehement arguments. "President thinks I tried to stampede him," Meigs observed in his diary the next day. "How long before he comes to my opinion to withdraw the army from a dangerous and useless position."[83]

Meigs' opinion had three salient points: (1) that the strategic foundation of the campaign on the Peninsula was weak, (2) that the army had suffered serious defeats that left it in desperate condition, and (3) that McClellan's popularity with the troops threatened the government.

Strategically, while McClellan saw opportunity in basing the army at Harrison's Landing on the James River, Meigs perceived only danger. If the army "did not go into Richmond from a position only 5 miles distant from the city I don't think it is likely to do so from one 20 miles distant to which it has retreated," Meigs deduced.[84] On July 14, Meigs appeared before the Committee on the Conduct of the War and declared that the army blundered strategically because by approaching Richmond by the Chesapeake Bay and the James River it weakened Washington's

---

[82] Meigs to father, July 8, 1862, Meigs Papers.

[83] Thomas and Hyman, *Stanton*, p. 207. Powell, *Lincoln Day by Day*, p. 125. Meigs Pocket Diary, July 5, 1862, Meigs Papers.

[84] Meigs to Nannie Rodgers, July 13, 1862, Rodgers Family Papers, Library of Congress Manuscript Division, Washington, D.C., series 1, container 9. Hereinafter cited as Rodgers Family Papers. All citations are in series 1, container 9 unless otherwise noted.

security. It should have moved overland, he said, keeping in position between the Confederate capital and Washington. "My individual opinion is, and always has been, that it was an unwise movement," he stated. The army should have been moved forward en masse from Washington to Richmond. "I have never for a moment seen any reason to doubt that that view was correct," he insisted.[85] Now that the army was on the Peninsula, Meigs imagined an additional strategic threat. The Confederate forces might, from behind fortifications with only 20,000 men, give the impression of great strength. This would "idle" the Union army and thereby free remaining rebel troops "for other expeditions."[86]

Meigs later claimed that the first dispatches received from Harrison's Landing persuaded him that McClellan's was "a defeated army," even though Lincoln himself came to read the incoming messages from the army quite differently.[87] "Affairs at Richmond are in a very critical condition, and the president is deeply anxious," wrote Lincoln's close friend, Sen. Orville Hickman Browning of Illinois, the day after the Battle of Malvern Hill.[88] Two days later, however, on July 4, the day that Lincoln challenged Meigs' effort to "stampede" him into redeploying the army, a more hopeful reading of affairs emerged: "The fight at Richmond has been a terrible one-the advantages I think, being decidedly with us," related Browning, after he and the president had looked over McClellan's messages.[89] On July 5, the two men read together McClellan's dispatches summarizing the combat between June 25 and July 1. "The result is much more satisfactory to us than was previously supposed," Browning wrote.[90]

---

[85] Meigs' testimony before the Joint Committee on the Conduct of the War on July 14, 1862, *Report of the Joint Committee*, pp. 296-297.

[86] Meigs to Nannie Rodgers, July 13, 1862, Rodgers Family Papers.

[87] Meigs, "The Relations of President Lincoln," p. 296; Meigs to Nannie Rodgers, July 13, 1862, Rodgers Family Papers.

[88] Theodore Calvin Pease and James G Randall, eds., *The Diary of Orville Hickman Browning*, 2 vols. (Springfield, Ill., 1927-1933), vol. 1, p. 556.

[89] Ibid., p. 556.

[90] Ibid., p. 557.

Despite Lincoln's more optimistic reading of events, the quarter-master general detected signs that perhaps Lincoln was "[c]oming to my opinion." The president went to visit McClellan at Harrison's Landing early in July. Enroute, while at Fort Monroe, Lincoln admitted to Maj. Gen. Ambrose E. Burnside that he had come to find out "whether it would not be advisable to remove the army from the Peninsula to an-other line of operations."[91] During his two-day visit to the army, Lin-coln polled McClellan and his five corps commanders. Four of the six officers argued against removing the army from outside Richmond, stat-ing the army's health was "good," "very good," "better" or "excel-lent."[92] Only VI Corps commander, Franklin, and Meigs' close friend IV Corps commander Keyes, dissented. The latter claimed that the health of the army was "getting worse" and that the president should not lose a day in moving it.[93] Later, again at Fort Monroe, the president told Burnside that nothing would be decided until Halleck, the new general-in-chief arrived in Washington.[94] The day after his return from the Peninsula, July 11, Lincoln thought the army in "good condition," and in "better condition and more of it than he expected."[95]

Meigs' pessimism deepened as the chief executive's optimism in-creased. The quartermaster general recorded extreme visions of destruc-tion and defeat unchanged from his judgment of 11 days earlier:

> The first news from Richmond-The dispatches from the chief
> officers were so gloomy gave so bad so hopeless a picture of
> defeat demoralization destruction & decay-such ascription of
> overwhelming numbers to the rebel army that I think I am

---

[91] Burnside's testimony before the Joint Committee on the Conduct of the War on March 19, 1863, *Report of the Joint Committee*, p. 637.

[92] Basler, *Collected Works*, vol. 5, pp. 309-312.

[93] Ibid., p. 311; Keyes to Meigs, August 14, 1862, Meigs Papers.

[94] Burnside's testimony before the Joint Committee on the Conduct of the War on March 19, 1863, *Report of the Joint Committee*, p. 638.

[95] Pease, *Diary of Orville Hickman Browning*, p. 557; Helen Nicolay, *Lincoln's Secretary*, (Westport, Conn., 1949), p. 148.

> much more distressed than I was by the disaster of Bull Run-
> 'The sad remnants of our brave troops' an expression used in
> all of the dispatches conveys such a picture of calamity & de-
> struction.[96]

The army's quartermaster on the Peninsula, Lt. Col. Rufus Ingalls, challenged Meigs' views with a fundamentally different evaluation on July 18:

> The army is a magnificent one to-day. All we require now is
> more men and generals full of health and desire to go into
> Richmond. We must and soon can go forward. This army
> must not go back one foot.[97]

Responding to Meigs' mid-July request for information about the situation in the army, Capt. James Brisbin of the quartermaster department replied with similar enthusiasm, stressing the strategic advantages of the army's base. "Our position is impregnable," began the captain, never in his military career had he seen "so strong a natural position for a large army. The hand of Providence has fortified it." He continued with a detailed appraisal of the terrain at Harrison's Landing, all pointing to its tremendous military strength.[98]

But if Lincoln and others thought the condition and position of the army good, doubts about its commander persisted. The quartermaster general wanted the army recalled from Richmond not only because of its strategic vulnerability but also because he feared that McClellan's power over the Army of the Potomac might pose a danger "to our state. . . .He might be too strong for our imperilled government."[99] Four veterans of the Seven Days Battles wrote Meigs agreeing on one major point:

---

[96] Meigs to Nannie Rodgers, July 13, 1862, Rodgers Family Papers.

[97] *OR* 11, pt. 3, p. 327.

[98] Brisbin to Meigs, July 17, 1862, Meigs Papers.

[99] Meigs to Nannie Rodgers, July 31, 1862, and September 5, 1862, Rodgers Family Papers.

McClellan was enormously popular with the troops. Three of the four also suggested that if the popular commander were removed for some reason, the quartermaster general himself could lead the force.

On July 12, Burnside told Brig. Gen. Stewart Van Vliet that the administration was about to remove McClellan.[100] Burnside had just hours earlier heard this news from Lincoln. Van Vliet had been McClellan's chief quartermaster on the Peninsula, but had been relieved at his own request on July 10. Van Vliet knew the army and its commander well, and within 48 hours of hearing the news from Burnside, he warned Meigs from New York that the administration risked trouble in taking this step.

Van Vliet explained that he knew "most of the Wadsworth men" in New York, and they expected McClellan's removal, but while the "thinking portion of the people" (by which he seems to have meant New York Republicans in general and supporters of Gen. James S. Wadsworth's gubernatorial aspirations in particular) did not sympathize with the commander of the Army of the Potomac, "the masses are much attached to him." To disregard that fact, cautioned Van Vliet, would

> do immense harm both to the masses and to the Army of the Poto-
> mac. . .I speak knowingly. . .I know the temper of the Potomac Army.
> . . As you are one of the powers behind the throne, I trust that you
> will give the foregoing due consideration if you have not already
> done so-McClellan must not be relieved and virtually retired. . . .[101]

Van Vliet suggested that in any case, the country needed McClellan's services "to chalk out the movements of all our armies." As to who else might possibly head the Army of the Potomac, Van Vliet insisted on only four possibilities: Don Carlos Buell, Fitz John Porter, Franklin or Meigs. "If any other man is put there," wrote Van Vliet, "there will be

---

[100] Van Vliet to Meigs, July 14, 1862, Meigs Papers.

[101] Ibid.

no improvement. See if this is not prophecy."[102] Brisbin echoed Van
Vliet's assessment of McClellan's popularity in more rhapsodic terms:

> [McClellan's] mere appearance along the front sets the sol-
> diers wild[.] I am confident that Napoleon nor any other genl
> that ever lived had so universally the love and confidence of
> an Army-He is in fact an idol and his removal would inevita-
> bly ruin the Army of the Potomac. I do believe if Genl
> McClellan were to be superceeded [sic] over half the officers
> in this Army would resign-I am not a hero worshiper but I do
> think Genl McClellan is the greatest genl of the age. . .Little
> Mac as they call him is certainly the man for the place-True
> he may not be so great a genl. as he is esteemed[,] but he has
> the confidence of the Army and that is the half in a fight.

Only one man could compete in Brisbin's judgment: "I would not
fight *here* under any other man-except yourself-and would rather be
under you than any officer in the Army."[103]

Ingalls, who replaced Van Vliet as quartermaster of the Army of the
Potomac, sang McClellan's praises as well: "The commanding general
is in excellent health and full of confidence, and is the 'pride and boast'
of his men."[104] The only partisan criticism came from Meigs' friend
Keyes, who grumbled that McClellan only rewarded favorites who
"cussed Congress, damned the Republicans and been of that type of
Breckinridge Democrat who don't seem able to imagine we are at war."
Keyes pressed Meigs about the reliability of rumors circulating at Harrison's Landing that "you are to command the army."[105]

The rumors of a change in command had reached McClellan as
well. The general wrote his wife on July 30 that Burnside had been

---

[102] Ibid.

[103] Brisbin to Meigs, July 17, 1862, Meigs Papers.

[104] *OR* 11, pt. 3, p. 327.

[105] Keyes to Meigs, August 21, 1862, July 31, 1862, Meigs Papers.

offered and refused command of the army and added immediately: "I learn that Meigs is very anxious for it; much good may it do him!" The next day the quartermaster general wrote to his wife about the commander of the army in harsh terms. Unlike Halleck, whom Meigs admired because "He does not seek publicity" and departed from his army in the west "without a demonstration" from the troops, the commander of the Army of the Potomac was dangerous:

> McClellan is the only one of our generals commanding who seems to have won the fervent affection of the troops-They cling to him with love and confidence even through these fatal delays & these terrible retreating combats. It would perhaps be dangerous to our state to have a great leader with this power of wielding the minds affections & thoughts of men & of directing them to victory. . . . [106]

The difficulty, from the administration's viewpoint, lay in finding someone militarily competent but politically benign. In short, Meigs yearned "for a Napoleon with patriotism enough not to seize on our government & skill & genius to save it."[107]

Meigs concluded that McClellan's popularity with the army posed a greater danger to the administration than was generally allowed and Confederate troops in Richmond a lesser one. This realization represented an important shift in Meigs' evaluation of the circumstances. As late as July 13, the "ascription of overwhelming numbers to the rebels army [sic]" had caused Meigs more distress than he had experienced after the North's loss at Bull Run a year earlier.[108] He reversed that judgment two weeks later when on July 28 he estimated to Halleck that about 105,000 Confederates faced McClellan's force, a figure he reached from culling various Confederate sources.[109] The quartermaster

---

[106] McClellan, *Own Story*, p. 458; Meigs to Louisa Meigs, July 31, 1862, Rodgers Family Papers.

[107] Meigs to Nannie Rodgers, September 5, 1862, Rodgers Family Papers.

[108] Meigs to Nannie Rodgers, July 13, 1862, Rodgers Family Papers.

[109] *OR* 11, pt. 3, pp. 340-341.

general's figures, substantially below McClellan's (and Keyes') estimate, suggested that McClellan did not need the 20,000 to 30,000 reinforcements he sought.

So matters stood when Halleck, the new general-in-chief, arrived in
Washington the night of July 22. Meigs viewed his arrival in cosmic
terms:

> What a position is now his. Except the President no man in the world now
> holds so high & responsible a place. The fate of free government not only
> on this continent-but in the world. Not only this year but for a century
> hangs upon the balance which he is holding.[110]

Halleck wrote to McClellan at once and told him that immediately
upon his arrival in Washington, "high officers, in whose judgment I had
great confidence" advised him to order the army's removal from Harrison's Landing.[111] Certainly Meigs was among those "high officers."
The quartermaster general sailed with Halleck the next day, Thursday,
July 24, to Harrison's Landing. Meigs knew that the new general-in-
chief had Lincoln's confidence: "I think that the Pres'd & Secy will
very much defer to his judgment as to the conduct of the war."[112] He
left with Lincoln's authorization to keep or remove McClellan from
command as he saw fit.[113] They arrived at 1:30 p.m. Friday.

Halleck and Meigs both spoke with Keyes, who described for
Halleck what he believed was the army's extremely dangerous position
and worsening state.[114] At twilight, Meigs gathered more intelligence
indicating "a bad spirit in the Army." Sitting around a campfire near the
tent where Halleck and McClellan were conferring, the quartermaster

[110] Meigs to father, July 26, 1862. Meigs Papers.

[111] George Brinton McClellan, *The Army of the Potomac: Gen. McClellan's Report* (New York, 1864), p. 602.

[112] Meigs to father, July 31, 1862, Meigs Papers.

[113] Pease, *Diary of Orville Hickman Browning*, p. 563.

[114] Keyes to Meigs, August 21, 1862, Meigs Papers.

general heard "officers of rank" speaking of "a march on Washington" to "clear out those fellows." Burnside broke into the circle opposite Meigs and warned the group that they were talking "flat Treason, By God!" Meigs thought the incident important enough to report to Halleck who brushed it off as "Camp-talk."[115]

Having heard alarmist estimates of Confederate strength from Keyes and with talk of "treason" among officers fresh in his mind, Meigs returned with Halleck to Washington.[116] Meigs found waiting for him a letter from Keyes dated July 21 but not posted until July 23, which meant that Meigs had seen Keyes since the letter had been mailed. Keyes must have guessed the letter would be passed on to others, so he uncharacteristically avoided the subject-army politics-that suffused all previous and subsequent correspondence with Meigs. Instead, the corps commander focused on the need to recall the army from outside Richmond. Meigs passed the letter on to Halleck, who discussed its recommendations with Lincoln, Stanton and Burnside at the war department on Monday morning, July 28.[117]

Keyes' letter sounded a steady drumbeat of despair and near-panic about the military situation: the South's forces, far healthier than the Union's, vastly outnumbered the army of the Potomac. The Union faced collapse and would be at the South's mercy unless Lincoln sent 100,000 reinforcements or recalled the army from Harrison's Landing.[118] Two days later, on July 30, Meigs passed on to Halleck a second letter from Keyes, which reiterated in even starker terms the defeat the corps commander foresaw if the administration did not withdraw the army.[119] In the next 48 hours, Meigs assured Keyes that orders had been issued

[115] Meigs, "The Relations of President Lincoln," p. 294.

[116] *OR* 11, pt. 3, pp. 340-341. Meigs apparently came to discount Keyes' estimates of Confederate strength.

[117] Meigs Pocket Diary, July 28, 1862, Meigs Papers; Pease, *Diary of Orville Hickman Browning*, p. 565.

[118] Keyes to Meigs, July 21, 1862, Meigs Papers. See also Keyes to Meigs July 27, July 31, August 14, August 21, and December 17, 1862, Meigs Papers.

[119] Keyes to Meigs, July 27, 1862, Meigs Papers.

which "would probably put [the] Army in motion," and on August 3, Halleck instructed McClellan to move his army to Aquia Creek.[120]

"I must remark," the general-in-chief explained to McClellan, "that a large number of your highest officers, indeed a majority of those whose opinions have been reported to me, are decidedly in favor of movement."[121] In funneling Keyes' opinions to Halleck, the quartermaster general ensured that the corps commander's pessimistic views were among the most thoroughly "reported" to Halleck.

On July 29, Lincoln, Stanton and Halleck were again "working out the problem of McClellan. What to do with whose army is the great question of the war just now."[122] Meigs thought potential disaster lurked in all the alternatives not because the army lacked sufficient numbers, nor even because of conditions at Harrison's Landing. Meigs was "inclined to think" that "hurling [the army] upon Richmond. .would be the true policy," but it could not be carried out because it required "an active enterprising dashing leader who kept heart amid disasters [and] saw hope flashing through the blaze of artillery."[123] McClellan could not carry it off: "He has never attacked. He has never followed up an advantage. He has always believed the enemy stronger than himself. . . .Never to attack always to fight on the defensive & never to follow up the repulsed & defeated enemy. . . ."[124] The army and its leaders would therefore be "expecting defeat & thus ensuring it." In Meigs' mind, McClellan was the problem:

I fear moreover that the young general[,] overwhelmed with the responsibility of knowing that another repulse would almost ruin his army &

[120] Ibid.

[121] McClellan, *Report*, p. 603.

[122] Meigs to father, July 29, 1862, Meigs Papers. Meigs observed that the pressure of wrestling with this issue had taken a toll on Stanton: "Our secretary's explosive energy so conspicuous when he first assumed charge of the war office cannot go on exploding continually & lately we have seen fewer of his fulminations." Ibid.

[123] Ibid.

[124] Ibid.

would greatly injure our cause[,] would hesitate & halt in his ad-
vances & substitute for the rush of victorious assault the slow trench
of the engineer.[125]

Meigs concluded that a "march in retreat to Fort Monroe" seemed
the only alternative and that it did offer the possibility of "victory in the
open fields" and destruction of the Confederate army should it attack
Union forces. But the retreat also risked disaster because the Southerners might then "dash at Pope & at Washington while McClellan is going
around Robin Hood's barn by the path by which he came in."[126]

The diminution of McClellan's power and the removal of the army
from near Richmond pleased Meigs and came exactly 30 days after
Lincoln had rebuffed the quartermaster general for trying to "stampede"
him into that very course of action. In the final analysis, what mattered
to Meigs were not so much the realities in the area of operations (about
which he was unsure) or the condition of the troops, but that a dangerous
McClellan led the army, and his forces should never have been on the
Peninsula in the first place. In late July, Meigs told his father:

One principle much influences me[-]it is that it is always (almost)
best to abandon an error than to endeavor to patch repair conceal it-it
was wrong to go to Yorktown. The effect of this blunder weakens
us[;] our army can be consolidated to strike the enemy only by undo-
ing what has been done wrong.[127]

Meigs' strenuous lobbying to recall the army accompanied similar
intense efforts by Stanton, Chase and the Radical Republicans, but
Meigs' views probably had greater weight. Because the quartermaster
general was a West Point professional who had been intimately involved
with policies since March 1861 and who enjoyed a reputation for competence and loyalty going back to the administration's first weeks, Lin-

---

[125] Ibid.

[126] Ibid. Maj. Gen. John Pope's Federal Army of Virginia was massing in central Virginia.

[127] Ibid.

coln and Stanton placed a high value on his counsel, thus giving him a stature within the high command both unique and extremely influential during the Peninsula Campaign. Although Meigs continued to advise Lincoln, Stanton and even Halleck, he never again participated in strategic and operational decision making as he had during the spring and summer of 1862. With Lt. Gen. U. S. Grant's appointment as general-in-chief in March 1864, operational authority moved away from the capital, and Meigs' influence retracted to the more limited boundaries of the quartermaster general's official responsibilities.

Mac Wyckoff

Mac Wyckoff holds a B.A. degree in history from Lin-
field College in McMinnville, Oregon. He has researched
Kershaw's Brigade for eight years and is the author of *A
History of the 2nd South Carolina Infantry: 1861-1865*
(Fredericksburg, Va., 1994). His next book, *A History of the
3rd South Carolina: 1861-1865* is nearing completion. He is
the editor of a recent edition of *A History of Kershaw's Brigade* and author of "Kershaw's Brigade at Gettysburg" for
Gettysburg Magazine. He lives in Fredericksburg, Virginia,
with his wife, two daughters and a labrador retreiver.

"Our Loss Was Great..."

Joseph B. Kershaw's South Carolina Brigade in the Battle of Savage's Station

On the night of June 29, 1862, in the aftermath of the Battle of Savage's Station, Gen. Robert E. Lee sent an uncharacteristically sharp dispatch to his lieutenant, Maj. Gen. John Bankhead Magruder. "I regret much that you have made so little progress today in the pursuit of the enemy. . . .We must lose no more time or he will escape us entirely."[1] Rarely did Lee resort to rebuke, but his frustration over the Federals' escape from his Confederate pursuers on June 29, 1862, tried his patience severely. Lee saw that his campaign to drive the invaders from Richmond—soon to be known as the Seven Days Battles—was becoming a series of lost opportunities for the Confederates. Time would show that the chance Magruder missed at Savage's Station was among the more costly to the Confederate cause.

Despite the failure of Lee's generals to execute his plan and achieve important results on June 29, the Battle of Savage's Station provided Southern infantrymen with another opportunity to add luster to their growing reputation as fighters. One brigade of South Carolinians, commanded by Brig, Gen. Joseph B. Kershaw, spearheaded the Confederate attack on the 29th and bore the brunt of the casualties. The only Confederate success that day came through the hard fighting of Kershaw's

---

[1] Clifford Dowdey and Louis H. Manarin, eds., *The Wartime Papers of R.E. Lee* (New York, 1961), p. 205.

Brigade. While the success was soon squandered, the example of Carolinian courage remains.

Joseph Brevard Kershaw, a 40-year-old lawyer from Camden, South Carolina, organized the 2nd South Carolina regiment and served as its colonel. He assumed command of the brigade in February of 1862 and was a popular leader. One of his men described him as "a very fine man and a good officer. . . .He is liked by everyone." Another soldier added that "there is not a man in it [the regiment] who would not follow him to death."[2]

Kershaw's four regiments, the 2nd, 3rd, 7th and 8th South Carolina regiments, had varied experience before they came together at Richmond. Colonel John D. Kennedy's 2nd South Carolina, Kershaw's old outfit, had helped bombard Fort Sumter into submission, joined in the rout of the Federals at First Manassas in July 1861, and participated in several skirmishes. Colonel James D. Nance's 3rd South Carolina and Colonel David W. Aiken's 7th South Carolina regiments had yet to "see the elephant" after a year of army life in the Old Dominion. The men of Col. John W. Henagan's 8th South Carolina tasted combat at Manassas, but the experience prepared them only slightly for the hardships and horrors to come. Kershaw's four regiments became part of Maj. Gen. Lafayette McLaws' Division of General Magruder's command.

In June 1862, Southerners dug field fortifications around their capital city while Maj. Gen. George B. McClellan slowly planned his next move. Because "Little Mac" split his force to straddle the swampy Chickahominy River, Lee realized he had an opportunity to strike a telling blow. The Southern commander developed a bold plan to seize the initiative and repulse the larger Union army. Lee decided to leave Magruder's 25,000 men, including Kershaw's Brigade, south of the Chickahominy blocking the eastern approaches to Richmond against about 75,000 Northerners. The rest of the Confederate army would move north of the river and hopefully achieve numerical superiority against McClellan's isolated right wing. With 60,000 men, the Southern

[2] Francis Marion Goodlett to father, May 19, 1861, William H. Goodlett Papers, University of South Carolina, Columbia, South Carolina; *The Sumter Watchman*, June 17, 1861, p. 2.

Brig. Gen. Joseph Brevard Kershaw

commander hoped to crush 30,000 Federals or at least drive them eastward, thereby threatening the Union supply line—the Richmond and York River Railroad—which linked McClellan's army with its depot at White House Landing on the Pamunkey River.

Lee's attacks began on June 26th with a series of uncoordinated Confederate thrusts north of the Chickahominy at Mechanicsville. Though the Federals held off the Southerners, the Army of the Potomac's commander decided to retreat the next morning to a strong position near Gaines' Mill. After a full day of combat on June 27, Lee pried McClellan from his supply line, forcing the Federals to "change base" and head south toward the safety of their gunboats on the James River.

Meanwhile, Magruder postured and bluffed south of the Chickahominy, thereby creating the illusion of strength. On the 27th, while Lee fought nearby at Gaines' Mill, Kershaw sent two companies of the 7th and 8th South Carolina forward to learn if the Federals still held their position at Fair Oaks. The Palmetto soldiers found the enemy in a dense wood, and the Federal pickets unleashed a heavy fire that killed Pvt. Albert Miles, the first combat fatality in the 7th South Carolina. Canister and shell from Federal artillery wounded three other South Carolinians in the foray. Having accomplished their task, the Carolinians withdrew. The virgin 7th had been bloodied, and the regiment was "much complimented" on its comportment in this little fight.[3]

Magruder grew increasingly nervous as McClellan consolidated his army on the south side of the Chickahominy on June 28. If the Federals attacked, the Chickahominy would isolate Magruder's relatively small force from the majority of the Southern army. Magruder could not know, of course, McClellan intended no offensive movements. On the night of the 28th, McClellan ordered his advanced units at Fair Oaks to withdraw. McClellan intended to form a strong rear guard of three corps near army headquarters at Savage's Station, where he hoped to protect the flank of the army as it fled southward to the safety of the

---

[3] John S. Hard letter, July 3, 1862, *The Charleston Mercury*, July 24, 1862. Hereinafter cited as Hard, *Mercury, July 24, 1862.*

gunboats on the James River. After issuing this order, McClellan shifted his command post to the south side of White Oak Swamp, but he left no one in charge of his rear guard. The three corps commanders at Savage's were left to act independently of each other.

Having forced the Federals out of their formidable defenses, Lee wanted to bring McClellan to battle and crush the Army of the Potomac. The road network east of Richmond favored the Confederate pursuit, and Lee made his plans accordingly. Four main roads led east and southeast toward the fleeing Federals. Lee planned a five-pronged assault. Magruder's command would push back the Federals at Fair Oaks along the Williamsburg Road and slam into the flank of the retreating column. Major General Benjamin Huger's Division would advance on the Charles City Road and intercept the head of the column at a crossroads called Glendale. Two other divisions under Maj. Gen. James Longstreet and A. P. Hill would make a long march and approach Glendale from the southwest. Major General Theophilus Holmes' Division would move on the River Road toward the high ground at Malvern Hill, which McClellan hoped would be his safe haven. Major General Thomas J. "Stonewall" Jackson's command—the largest of the Confederate columns—was to cross the Chickahominy and pursue the tail of McClellan's force.

But General Magruder was not well and would soon prove that he was not up to his assignment. Suffering from lack of sleep and acute indigestion, Magruder consumed a mixture of drugs that included morphine. Lee met with his subordinate commander on the night of June 28 to outline his plans, but, perhaps due to Magruder's physical state or possibly because of the extreme aggressiveness of Lee's ideas, "Prince John" failed to grasp Lee's intentions.

* * *

Private William L. Daniel of the 2nd South Carolina remembered that Sunday the 29th, "dawned brightly upon us, and none knew that this beautiful day of rest was to become a day of blood and death." General Kershaw sent four companies of the 2nd South Carolina at an early hour to learn if the Federals remained in position at Fair Oaks. "We moved cautiously through the dense woods to the open space in which their camp was situated," reported Daniel, and finding it abandoned "took possession of it."[4]

Kershaw's men found that the Federals had set much of the matériel in their camps afire before retreating, but the Carolinians still managed to gather food, clothing and other items that the flames had not reached. William Crumley, a 15-year-old courier for Kershaw, chopped down a large U.S. flag left behind in the camp before bluffing three Federal stragglers into surrendering to him. Crumley presented the flag and prisoners to General McLaws with words to shame the three grown-ups for being captured so easily by a mere boy.[5]

About 8:00 a.m., the rest of the brigade joined the reconnaissance party. Major Franklin Gaillard advanced his skirmishers of the 2nd South Carolina, and they soon became engaged with the men of the 71st Pennsylvania. The Southerners lost a few men in this small skirmish before the Pennsylvanians retreated. The Carolinians renewed their pursuit on the Nine Mile Road toward the Richmond & York River Railroad, and about a mile later, they again engaged Federal skirmishers and came under artillery fire from their left.[6] Worried that this artillery fire might be coming from Jackson's force, Kershaw restrained his men and sent forward a detachment to reconnoiter. When the firing grew heavier, Kershaw concluded that the shots came from the Federals.

Although Federal Brig. Gen. Edwin Sumner had withdrawn his advanced units from Fair Oaks, he moved only as far as Allen's Farm along the railroad near Orchard Station, where Col. George Thomas "Tige" Anderson's Georgians encountered two Pennsylvania regiments.

[4] William L. Daniel to Ma, July 13, 1862, from Camp McLaws, Daniel Family Papers, University of South Carolina, Columbia, South Carolina. Hereinafter cited as Daniel Family Papers.

[5] William M. Crumley, Personal Reminiscences of the Civil War From Feb. 1862 to Apr. 1865, Confederate Miscellany Collection, Emory University, Atlanta, Georgia.

[6] One of the projectiles fired at Kershaw's men, a spherical case, burst a few yards from Private Daniel, "the bullets flying in every direction." A piece of metal hit the handle of Daniel's saber-bayonet splitting it in half. Daniel picked up a part of the shrapnel as a souvenir. Daniel to Ma, July 13, 1862, Daniel Family Papers.

About noon, following what one Union soldier considered a two-hour fight, both the Georgians and Pennsylvanians withdrew in opposite directions. The Federals retreated under the mistaken impression that Jackson's forces had arrived on the field.

Unfortunately for the Confederates, "Stonewall's" command remained north of the river throughout the day, leaving Magruder's men unsupported in their attempt to interdict McClellan's retreat. Colonel Anderson's retreat from Allen's Farm, however, convinced the nervous Magruder that the Federals were advancing, not withdrawing. Magruder sent word to Lee asking for help. Lee could not believe that the retreating McClellan would assume the offensive, but, eager for Magruder to attack, he sent two brigades of Huger's command with the stipulation that they must be returned to Huger if not engaged by 2:00 p.m.[7]

By the time Huger's men arrived, Magruder had learned that Jackson had been delayed. "Prince John" decided to await Stonewall's arrival before attacking. With Huger's and Jackson's men, Magruder would have more than 45,000 troops of all arms to pit against about 40,000 in the Federal rear guard. When Magruder did not act promptly, however, Huger's troops rejoined their own command. Most of Huger's column, like Jackson's, remained inactive throughout the day.

Around 3:00 p.m., the rest of Magruder's column came up to join Kershaw's men near Allen's Farm. Skirmishers of the 2nd and 3rd South Carolina resumed the advance eastward toward Savage's Station until they saw strong Union earthworks perpendicular to the Williamsburg Road. Assuming the works to be strongly manned, Sgt. Robert W. Shand of the 2nd South Carolina described the fortifications as being "impregnable from a frontal attack." Shand thought that the works were 15 feet high, 40 feet thick at the base tapering to 20 feet at the top fronted by a moat 15 feet deep and 20 feet wide.[8]

---

[7] U.S. War Department, *The War of the Rebellion: The Official Records of the Union and Confederate Armies*, 128 vols. (Washington, D.C., 1890-1901), series I, vol. 11, pt. 2, pp. 50, 680, 706. Hereinafter cited as *OR*. All references are to series I unless otherwise noted.

[8] *OR* 11, pt. 2, p. 726. Robert Wallace Shand, *Incidents in the Life of a Private Soldier in the War Waged by the United States Against the Confederate States 1861-1865*, p. 70, Robert Shand

Kershaw halted his command about 4:00 p.m. and ordered Capt. Delaware Kemper's Battery to shell the earthworks while the 2nd and 3rd South Carolina regiments moved through a thickly wooded ravine in an attempt to flank the Union position. Luckily for the Southerners, a few shots from Kemper's Battery scattered the small force of defenders before the flanking force could launch an attack on the works. "I don't think we ever could have stormed them successfully," Lt. Thomas H. Pitts of the 3rd South Carolina later wrote with relief. The South Carolinians occupied the abandoned camp, where they discovered more food and letters. While some men ate and rested, others took time to read the Yankee epistles, many of which were written in German, leading Sergeant Shand to conclude, "we realized we were fighting the United States and Europe too."[9]

Kershaw's Brigade continued to lead the advance against the Federal rear guard. His brigade was aligned with the left of the 2nd on the railroad, the 3rd and 7th South Carolina extending the line south to the Williamsburg Road, Kemper's Battery on the road, and the 8th in line to the right of the road. Soon after the advance resumed, the Carolinians entered a dense woods that stretched east for about four hundred yards on slightly undulating ground toward Savage's Station. Lieutenant Pitts described this foilage as "the thickest undergrowth of bushes you ever saw. . .you could not see a man ten paces ahead of you and it was utterly impossible to keep anything like a line of battle."[10] As Kershaw's men slogged through the thicket, units quickly lost lost formation and cohesion. Bullets began zipping through the brush as advance elements of both armies exchanged gunshots. Those in the front of Kershaw's advance ran the risk of being mistaken for the enemy and shot by friends in the back. Sergeant D. Augustus Dickert of the 3rd South Carolina was struck by a Federal bullet in the left lung which sent him reeling to the

---

Papers, University of South Carolina, Columbia, South Carolina. Hereinafter cited as Shand Memoirs.

[9] Thomas Pitts to Lizzie, July 7, 1862, Pitts-Craig Letters, Emory University, Atlanta, Ga. Hereinafter cited as Pitts-Craig Letters; Shand Memoirs, p. 70.

[10] Pitts to Lizzie, July 7, 1862, Pitts-Craig Letters.

ground, where another bullet, which he believed came from one of his own men to his rear, struck him in the thigh.[11] Regaining consciousness, he put his hand to his chest and felt a gaping wound, "the blood gushing and spluttering out at every breath." As he staggered to his feet his brother, Pvt. B. Fletcher Dickert, helped him to the rear. Reaching a fallen tree trunk, they stopped to examine the wounds. Fletcher Dickert, a physician, proclaimed the wound fatal. "A bit of very unpleasant information," recalled the patient. Upon further examination, Dr. Dickert assured his brother that his chances of survival looked good. Sergeant Dickert survived this and three other wounds during the war and later wrote an excellent history of the brigade. Dr. Fletcher was not so lucky. He fell mortally wounded while standing next to his brother at Chickamauga in September 1863.[12]

The Carolinians continued pushing through the woods until they came upon the Federal skirmish line, which they immediately charged. The assault drove the 72nd and 106th Pennsylvania regiments of Brig. Gen. William W. Burns' Philadelphia Brigade from the woods and into a field, in the center of which lay Savage's Station. The attack caught the Federals by surprise, for they believed that Maj. Gen. Samuel P. Heintzelman's Federal III Corps occupied the woods in their front. Unfortunately for the Northerners, Heintzelman had marched his command away from the battlefield, contrary to orders and without telling anyone. The swiftness of Kershaw's attack caused generals John Sedgwick and William Franklin to flee from the pursuing Confederates to avoid capture or worse. One Federal recalled that they had "great difficulty in riding away with the dignity and deliberation due to a Brigadier!" As a result of Heintzelman's unplanned departure, the Battle of Savage's Station began with General Kershaw's four regiments and a battery outnumbering the two Federal units from Pennsylvania.[13]

[11] D. Augustus Dickert, *History of Kershaw's Brigade* (Newberry, 1899), pp. 129, 132.

[12] Ibid.

[13] *OR* 11, pt. 2, p. 727. R.I., Holcomb *History of the First Regiment Minnesota Volunteer Infantry 1861-1864* (Stillwater, 1916), p. 148; George A. Bruce, *The Twentieth Regiment of Massachusetts Volunteer Infantry* (Boston, 1906), pp. 115-116.

Library of Congress

Brig. Gen. Edwin Sumner

The Federals in the field around Savage's Station were in what Brig. Gen. William F. "Baldy" Smith later described a "muddle." Although the Northerners still had three divisions present, no single officer directed the action. While the Carolinians struggled through the dense woods, Burns managed to place his two regiments in the field east of the station and between the railroad and the Williamsburg Road before calling for assistance. General Sumner, the senior officer on the field, hurried forward the 1st Minnesota of Col. Alfred Sully's brigade. Burns placed the newcomers on his left straddling the road and with their left bent back to protect the flank. He then withdrew the 72nd Pennsylvania from the center and placed it on the right, with the extreme right refused, or bent back. While these moves strengthened the flanks of Burns' line, they left the center vulnerable. Burns called for more help.[14]

Kershaw's Carolinians entered the field, flaunting their flags almost in the faces of the Pennsylvanians. When Sgt. Robert Shand emerged from the woods, he saw the Federals less than 150 feet away. "The bullets whistled past my ears without interruption and not singly, but in two's and three's at a time," recalled Shand. "Men were falling all around." Shand considered this the hottest fire he had ever been in, and Private Daniel agreed. "I never saw balls fly thicker," he wrote, claiming that it was a "miracle almost that so few were hurt, but still our loss was great."[15] The 7th South Carolina withstood the fire and charged to within fifteen paces of the 1st Minnesota. "You may be sure that they poured a fire into us," wrote Carolinian Sgt. James B. Suddath, who took a spent ball on the lip. Another shot broke Sgt. W. W. Denny's arm and a Federal cannon shot tore off both of Sgt. Tom Hill's legs.[16] As Pvt. Ben Taylor of the 7th South Carolina turned to the rear rank and said, "give it to them boys," a bullet struck him in the head. Jim, his brother,

[14] William F. Smith, *Autobiography of Major General William F. Smith, 1861-1864* (Dayton, 1990), pp. 42-43; *OR* 11, pt. 2, p. 91.

[15] Charles H. Banes, *History of the Philadelphia Brigade* (Philadelphia, 1876), p. 80; Shand Memoirs, p. 71; Daniel to Ma, July 13, 1862, Daniel Family Papers.

[16] James B. Suddath letter, July 4, 1862, in *South Carolina Historical Magazine*, vol. 63 (1962), p. 93.

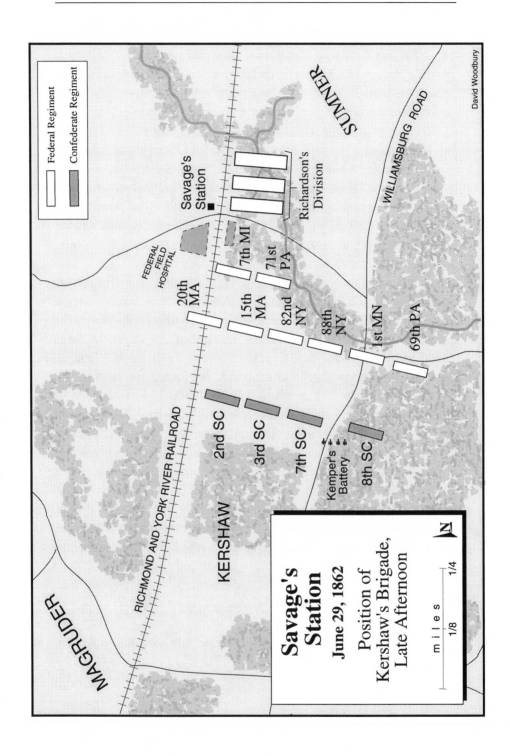

Savage's Station
June 29, 1862

Position of
Kershaw's Brigade,
Late Afternoon

miles
1/8   1/4

N

David Woodbury

turned toward Ben and "gazed upon him in mute sorrow." Captain John Hard put his hand on Jim's shoulder and said, "I have no consolation to offer you, except that Ben has fallen at his post; there he lies, yonder is the enemy, avenge him." The 7th poured a withering fire into the 1st Minnesota from the front and diagonally to the right. The enfilading fire devastated the Minnesotans, who began to fall in greater numbers.[17]

Before Burns could receive reinforcements, the 2nd and 3rd South Carolina broke through the weak Union center wounding Burns and forcing back the Pennsylvanians. With their right flank now exposed, the men of the 1st Minnesota held on briefly before retreating on the double quick. The Northerners withdrew across the field and up the slope of a hill before rallying. One Federal reported that the Carolinians were "coming in swarms." With still no division or corps commander at the front to direct the action, Burns remained on the field despite his wound and placed the newly arrived 82nd and 88th New York regiments in the center. He replaced the two worn out Pennsylvania regiments on the right (the 72nd and 106th) with the 15th and 20th Massachusetts regiments. Finally, he put the 69th Pennsylvania on the left and held the 71st Pennsylvania and 7th Michigan in reserve. North of the road, the Carolinians had lost their numerical advantage and were outnumbered about two to one.[18]

Still the battle raged. Teenaged Capt. Leonard Bartlett of the 2nd South Carolina fought with such gallantry that he became a prominent target. Even after receiving a severe head wound, he continued to lead his company forward, inspiring his men by his actions. He pressed on until faint from blood loss. Unable to continue fighting, he lay down under a tree and remained there all night. By morning, he was dead.[19]

Another member of the 2nd South Carolina, Sgt. Richard Hilton, had told a friend that he "intend[ed] to go through or die in the attempt."

---

[17] Hard, *Mercury*, July 24, 1862; Richard Moe, *The Last Full Measure: The Life and Death of the First Minnesota Volunteers* (New York, 1993), p. 153.

[18] Moe, *The Last Full Measure*, p. 153; Ernest Linden Waitt, *History of the Nineteenth Regiment Mass. Vol. Inf. 1861-1865* (Salem, 1906), p. 87. *OR* 11, pt. 2, p. 91.

[19] *The Charleston Daily Courier*, July 22, 1862, p. 3.

After Hilton received two bullets in the bowels, Capt. Benjamin Clyburn ordered Hilton to the rear. Ignoring the order, Hilton continued forward until struck a third time.   Clyburn again ordered Hilton to the rear. Refusing, the wounded soldier fought on until he received his fourth and mortal wound.   "There was doubtless no man in the Confederate nation," wrote Clyburn, "who deserved more worthy mention, or whose acts had won for him a brighter fame, both as a willing and dutiful soldier and high toned gentleman."[20]

Sergeant Hilton's company lost several other key men at Savage's Station, including the Perry brothers. The luckier of the two, Lt. Andrew M. Perry, received a severe neck wound but survived only to fall mortally wounded at Chickamauga. Andrew's brother, Sgt. J. Franklin Perry, was struck in the groin and died of his wound in a hospital. Another bullet struck Cpl. Irvine Knight in the lung. About the same time, Pvt. Benjamin Leitner, the color bearer for the 2nd, received a mortal wound.   Lieutenant Colonel Artemus Goodwyn was severely wounded in the left ankle. Another bullet struck Cpl. William Truesdel in the head, passing through his nose and neck killing him instantly.[21]

The 7th South Carolina also suffered greatly. A bullet struck Lt. Col. Elbert Bland's forearm. Another round hit Captain Hard while he was loading his gun and took off the top part of the knuckle of his first finger. Moments later, a second bullet struck him in the breast, but a pocket bible he had picked up saved his life. The shot caused extreme pain, however, and his whole side was paralyzed for some time. One of

---

[20] *The Lancaster Ledger*, August 13, 1862, p. 2.

[21] Knight lingered at death's door in a hospital before taking a turn for the better, giving surgeons hope for his recovery. However, on the same day and in the same hospital that Sgt. Perry died, he broke an artery and quickly bled to death. *The Lancaster Ledger*, October 28, 1863, p. 2. Leitner died on July 13th in Richmond. Sergeant Richard Kirkland wrote Truesdel's sister, Rosa, about her brother's death. Rosa wrote back asking why William's friends had not helped him. Kirkland responded that we must remember "It is not our will but His will that must be done." *The Camden Confederate*, December 26, 1862, p. 2. Richard Kirkland to Rosa, July 2, 1862, from Richmond, Va., Richard Kirkland Papers, University of South Carolina, Columbia, South Carolina. Hereinafter cited as Kirkland Papers. Richard Kirkland to Rosa, July 24, 1862, from Camp McLaws, Kirkland Papers.

the Minnesotans thought that the 7th fought with the "utmost obsti-
nacy."[22] South of the road, both sides received reinforcements. The
Vermont Brigade had already begun its retreat from Savage's Station
when ordered to about-face and return to the field. The New England-
ers' arrival extended the left of the Union line where they battled Kemper's Battery, the 8th South Carolina, and the three newly-arrived
regiments of Brig. Gen. Paul Semmes' Brigade. The 17th and 30th
Mississippi regiments of Brig. Gen. Richard Griffith's Brigade stood in
reserve behind Kemper's Battery. The entry of additional units caused
no little confusion.

The 10th Georgia of Semmes' Brigade passed over the 8th South
Carolina into a dense woods. Colonel Henegan obliqued his Carolinians
to the left so that they would not fire into the rear of the Georgians.
Soon thereafter, however, Henegan's regiment came under fire from the
Vermonters to their front and from the rear by the other two regiments of
Semmes' command. Henegan ordered his men to lie down while officers desperately sought to halt the firing in their rear. After the friendly
fire stopped, the men of the 8th South Carolina advanced again, only to
find the 10th Georgia again crossing their front.[23]

While Henegan sorted out this deadly confusion, Captain Kemper's
artillery to his left continued to pour its fire into the Federals. According
to one observer, the "little guns leaped with joy. . .and every discharge
tore great gaps through the blue coated regiment. . . ." Private Wilbur
Fisk of the 2nd Vermont confirmed that the canister tore "through our
ranks like hail stones making huge openings at every discharge." The
Carolinians later counted 75 dead Federals in front of Kemper's Battery.
Still, the Federals mounted a counterattack along the road where they
eventually pushed back the 7th South Carolina, making the advanced
position of the 2nd and 3rd untenable. The presence of the Vermonters
on their flank forced the 2nd and 3rd to fall back.[24] The orders to

---

[22] Hard, *Mercury* July 24, 1862. Holcombe, *History of the First Minnesota*, p. 96.

[23] *OR* 11, pt. 2, pp. 720-721, 744.

[24] *The Charleston Daily Courier* July 22, 1862, p. 3. Wilbur Fisk, *Anti-Rebel: The Civil War*

withdraw his regiment angered Major Gaillard of the 2nd. "At this moment of victory," he bitterly wrote in his report, "an order was given to cease firing and to fall back." Lieutenant Pitts of the 3rd also felt that had it not been for that order, "victory was ours." As the 2nd and 3rd South Carolina struggled to realign with the rest of the brigade, the recently-arrived 88th New York charged into the woods and hastened the Southerners' withdrawal.[25]

Kershaw's Brigade finally reformed, but darkness halted the action. Rain pelted the participants that night as the Federals withdrew from the field. General Burns reported from the Federal perspective that "our men showed their superiority, and the victory can be fairly claimed by us. He [the enemy] was the attacking party, and was not only checked, but repulsed and driven from the ground." More important than the tactical details, from General Lee's point of view, was the fact that the Southerners had not been able to force the Federals to stand and fight a decisive battle, nor had they even slowed McClellan's change of base to the James River. The events of the 29th greatly reduced the chance of Confederate success at Glendale the following day.[26]

While Huger and Jackson had remained inactive, General Magruder had advanced with excessive caution and used only two and a half of his six brigades. On several occasions during the Peninsula Campaign, Magruder showed an ability to handle his troops well on the defensive. At Savage's Station, however, he failed to grasp General Lee's aggressive intent and lacked the vigor of a successful offensive commander. Not only did Kershaw's men largely fight without assistance, but Kershaw received little guidance from his division commander. No evidence exists to show a strong guiding hand of General McLaws in coordinating the efforts of his division. While the performance of Magruder, Jackson and Huger, and to a lesser extent, McLaws, contributed to the failure, the

---

Letters of Wilbur Fisk (New York, 1993), p. 39.

[25] *OR* 11, pt. 2, p. 733. Thomas Pitts to Lizzie, July 7, 1862, Pitts-Craig Letters. Holcombe, *History of the First Minnesota*, p. 151.

[26] *OR* 11, pt. 2, p. 92.

real problem was Lee's plan itself. This ambitious undertaking was too complex to be executed by Lee's still inexperienced army. Lee needed better cooperation and coordination from his immediate subordinates; he might have done better with a more simple, realistic scheme for defeating McClellan.

Thrust into what was essentially a no-win situation, the Carolinians fought bravely and suffered tremendously against some of the best troops in McClellan's army. Of Kershaw's Brigade, correspondent Gregory de Fontaine wrote that "no command in the army has won for itself a more brilliant reputation for valor, or performed a nobler share of service in the late series of battles before Richmond."[27]

Kershaw's Brigade, the most aggressive unit on the field, sustained 81 percent of the Southern casualties at Savage's Station. All but nine of the 290 casualties in the brigade occurred in the 2nd, 3rd and 7th South Carolina. Prior to this campaign, neither the 3rd nor the 7th regiments had lost a single man killed in battle. "No description," wrote Private Daniel, "can give you an idea of the suffering and anxiety and care to which we have been exposed. Nothing but actual experience will suffice. The sight hardens some, but I must say it deeply moves my sympathies." Lieutenant Pitts added, "I do hope never again to be a participant in such a terrible battle."[28] Although Kershaw's Brigade arrived on the field too late the next day to take part in the lost opportunity at Glendale, the Carolinians were in action again in the terrible fighting on July 1st on the slopes of Malvern Hill.

[27] *The Charleston Courier* July 22, 1862, p. 3.

[28] William Daniel to Ma, July 13, 1862, Daniel Family Papers. Thomas Pitts to Lizzie, July 7, 1862, Pitts-Craig Letters.

William J. Miller

The series editor of *The Peninsula Campaign of 1862: Yorktown to the Seven Days* William J. Miller is the author of *Mapping for Stonewall: The Civil War Service of Jed Hotchkiss* (Washington, D.C., 1993) and *The Training of an Army: Camp Curtin and the North's Civil War* (Shippensburg, PA, 1990). He is editorial consultant for *Civil War* Magazine.

Scarcely any Parallel in History

Logistics, Friction and McClellan's Strategy for the Peninsula Campaign

For centuries, military men have argued that logistics determine the outcome of campaigns. "Understand that the foundation of an army is the belly," Frederick the Great told his generals in 1747. "It is necessary to procure nourishment for the soldier wherever you assemble him and wherever you wish to conduct him. *This is the primary duty of a general.*" (emphasis added) The Duke of Wellington declared that victory hinged on attention to logistical detail and that a wise commander traces the path of every biscuit from the stalk into the soldier's mouth. Napoleon, who declared that an army moves on its stomach, and the theorists Karl von Clausewitz and Baron Antoine Henri de Jomini all declared logistics decisive. A modern historian states flatly that "logistics make up as much as nine-tenths of the business of war."[1]

---

[1] Martin Van Creveld, *Supplying War: Logistics from Wallenstein to Patton* (Cambridge, UK, 1977), p. 231.

Yet historians—well fed, well clothed and comfortably housed as they invariably are—exist in a world far removed from the physical hardships of the soldier and rarely delve more than superficially into how armies are provisioned. Most writers of history dwell upon strategy and tactics and, impatient to get to the action, too often begin studies of campaigns at the point of the fixed bayonet and work backward. Students of military history would do better to heed Wellington's advice and follow the cracker boxes forward from the quartermasters to the camp-fires and battlefields. Only thus can they understand campaigns at least as well as did the commanders.

No Civil War general could ignore the basic needs of his men and hope to be successful, nor could he make strategic or tactical decisions independent of logistical realities. While there might have been good logisticians who were bad generals, it is unlikely that there were good generals who were bad logisticians.

Successful strategists in the Civil War—or more precisely, those whose campaigns succeeded—realized that armies on campaign must fight for their survival. What an army requires above all else in this struggle—before weapons, ammunition or uniforms—is food. When Maj. Gen. George B. McClellan moved his army to Virginia's Peninsula in March 1862, he, like every army commander in history, had to wage two campaigns: one to defeat the opposing army and another to keep his own army healthy, contented and in combat trim. Clearly, McClellan failed to defeat the Confederates before him, but how did he succeed on his "second front"—that is, his rear? How were his battles with Joseph E. Johnston and Robert E. Lee affected by his struggles with logistical problems?

The enormous size of McClellan's army and the complexity of the operation needed to sustain it made severe demands upon the army's logisticians: the officers of the commissary of subsistence and ordnance departments and especially the men of the quartermaster department. George McClellan asked these supply officers to do what had never been done—what might not have been possible—yet, despite wet weather and bad roads that multiplied the difficulties of their already unprecedented task many times over, the army's quartermasters accomplished their assignment. Unfortunately for the Union, their struggle to surmount these difficulties consumed precious days and weeks that McClellan's strategy had not allowed for and, in the end, could not compensate for. The Federal operations against Richmond might have ended sooner and far more disastrously had not the army's logisticians performed so well. For these Federals, the Peninsula Campaign was an unqualified victory.

Yet McClellan never gave his supply officers their due. He complimented them in his report of the campaign in a way that made it seem they performed rather routine duties creditably, but he never acknowledged their remarkable achievement in overcoming what at the time many thought were insurmountable difficulties. By the time he came to write his memoirs some 20 years after the war, of course, McClellan was more concerned with his own place in history that those of his logisticians, and the general worked solely to vindicate himself and his strategy. He attributed the failure of his campaign to interference from Washington. The general's arguments hinged on two premises: The Lincoln administration did not give him enough men to execute the campaign he hoped to carry out, and the war department forced him to adopt the White House line of operations, which in the 1880s McClellan adjudged faulty.[2] Of these two contentions, historians have more rigorously debated the first—the numerical sufficiency of the Army of the Potomac. Critics claim McClellan overestimated the strength of the Confederates opposing him and advanced too timidly. General McClellan argued that the general's strategy would have succeeded if only he had been given enough men to enact it, and his supporters seem to have adopted this same argument. The Lincoln administration did, together

---

[2] George B. McClellan, *McClellan's Own Story* (New York, 1887), pp. 342-345. The order McClellan claimed forced him to use the White House line of operation is the famous May 17, 1862, edict from the war department informing McClellan that Maj. Gen. Irvin McDowell's I Corps would join him from Fredericksburg. The order did not in itself demand that McClellan adopt the White House line. McClellan was already at White House and had begun establishing his base there. In issuing this order, therefore, the war department was building upon the reasonable supposition that McClellan wished to operate from White House. On May 21, McClellan wrote to Lincoln objecting to the order only on the grounds of its ambiguity about whether McDowell would be subject to his orders. Nowhere in this chatty, 900-odd word letter did McClellan raise any objection to having to operate from White House. U.S. War Department, *The War of the Rebellion: The Official Records of the Union and Confederate Armies*, 128 vols. (Washington, D.C., 1890-1901). series I, vol. 11, pt. 1, pp. 28-29. Hereinafter cited at *OR*. All references are to series I unless otherwise noted.

with many other circumstances, alter McClellan's plans to a degree that by late May the general was leading a campaign that little resembled the movement he had designed. But, recognizing that McClellan failed with a plan that was not entirely his is quite different from confirming that he would have certainly succeeded if permitted to follow a program that was his own. The story of the logistical operation on the Peninsula suggests that perhaps the more important question is not whether McClellan had or did not have enough men to take Richmond as he planned but whether he had *too many* men—too many men to be fed easily, too many men to be moved quickly, too many men to be cared for and wielded as a weapon at the same time by a commander unpracticed in doing either. There is ample evidence, in fact, to indict McClellan's plan to take Richmond from the Tidewater as logistically naive and therefore strategically unsound.

Part 1: Preparations

To say that the army George McClellan took to the Peninsula in the spring of 1862 was the largest in American military history to that point does not do it justice. The entire American force in the Mexican War, for example, did not exceed 41,000 men. Moreover, this force was divided into columns that moved independently under different commanders. This arrangement aided the logisticians, for these columns drew supplies from separate depots. On the Peninsula, McClellan never had to feed fewer than 100,000 men, all of whom were supplied from one principal depot and its few nearby satellites all under the control of one quartermaster and his staff. From a strictly logistical standpoint, the only operation in American military history to that time that could compare to the Peninsula Campaign in complexity and difficulty, if not in size, was the 1857 expedition against the Mormons in Utah. Although the operation involved only about 8,000 people, including troops, civilians and miscellaneous government employees, the difficulties in provisioning them in a mountainous region that was all but inaccessible through a long and severe winter were formidable. The Utah operation required almost 4,000 wagons and 47,000 oxen. Quartermasters super-

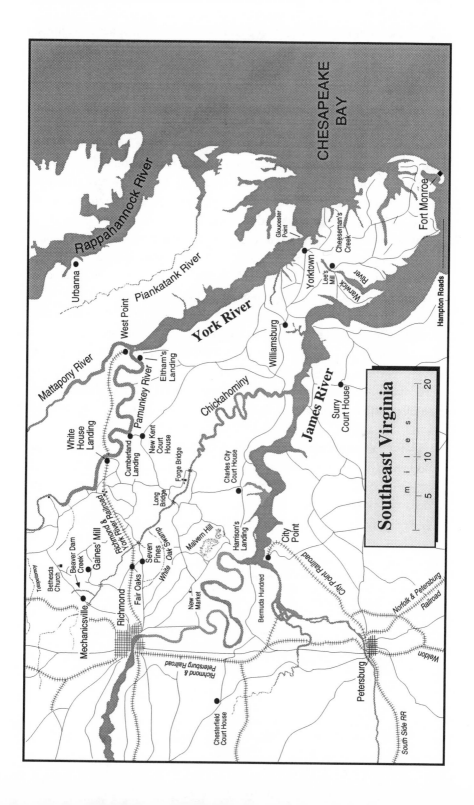

vised the shipment of more than 2.25 million tons of supplies and almost 5 million rations. Many tons of food and supplies had to be conveyed to points in Utah during the fair weather across 800 miles of largely uninhabited prairie from the depot at Fort Leavenworth, Kansas.[3]

McClellan's operation was many times larger. The Army of the Potomac was the first American army to compare in size to some of the powerful European armies of the 18th century. The army's return for April 13 showed an aggregate strength of 105,235 soldiers present, including all those who were sick, on extra duty or under arrest. Each of these men had to eat. McClellan's aggregate present would grow as high as 127,327, where it stood on June 20, just before the Seven Days Battles. Between April 13 and July 10, by which time McClellan had ceased offensive actions on Richmond, the mean number of troops McClellan had present was 115,355. Each of these men needed food each day. In addition to rations, many of the men would need new tents and blankets, shoes and clothing in the course of the five-month campaign. Most would require a substantial amount of ammunition.

An army of 115,355 needed approximately 25,000 horses and mules for everything from cavalry and artillery service to hauling wagons. These animals ate prodigious quantities of fodder. Each of them needed saddles or other harness. All, or almost all, would need to be shod at least once and probably several times between April and July.

If the encampment of the Army of the Potomac on the Peninsula had been a city, which in effect it was, it would have been the ninth largest city in the United States.[4] But McClellan's aggregate present figure does not begin to describe the size of the army's logistical operation. Every army the size of the Army of the Potomac, especially those of the

---

[3] Erna Risch, *Quartermaster Support of the Army: A History of the Corps 1775-1939* (Washington, D.C., 1962, rpt. 1989), pp. 322-327. As will be discussed, McClellan's operation on the Peninsula employed some 3,000 wagons and 19,000 horses and mules exclusive of cavalry and artillery.

[4] New York (813,669), Philadelphia (565,529), Brooklyn (266,661), Baltimore (212,418), Boston (177,840), New Orleans (168,675), Cincinnati (161,044), St. Louis 160,773, Chicago (109,260), Buffalo (81,129). *Statistics of the United States (Including Mortality, Property, &c. in 1860 Compiled from the original Returns and Being the Final Exhibit of the Eighth Census* (Washington, D.C., 1866).

18th and 19th centuries, contended with large numbers of civilian hangers on, collectively known as camp followers. Some of these people were civilian employees, and many performed important services for the army. Many others were simply a nuisance. An army, or a city, the size of McClellan's in the spring of 1862 would have been a congregating point for thousands of such civilians: wagon drivers, river pilots, stevedores, prostitutes, wives, fathers, uncles, politicians, volunteer doctors and nurses, sutlers, laundresses, body servants, speculators, newspaper correspondents, undertakers, mechanics, carpenters. All of these people needed food and shelter. While the army was not responsible for the care of them all, the necessities of their lives were imported to the Peninsula from the North along the Federal supply line, thereby adding to the army's burden. It is impossible to determine how many thousands of such people accompanied the army on the Peninsula, but it is perhaps sufficient in a consideration of the army's logistical difficulties to realize that the official figures regarding the amount of subsistence needed by McClellan's soldiers do not completely represent the strain on the army's supply line.

The men responsible for creating and maintaining the supply line belonged to the quartermaster department. Brigadier General Montgomery C. Meigs, quartermaster general of the U. S. Army with headquarters in Washington, oversaw the supply of all Union armies. One of his subordinates, Brig. Gen. Stewart Van Vliet, was chief quartermaster for the Army of the Potomac and traveled with McClellan's headquarters. Lieutenant Colonel Rufus Ingalls was Van Vliet's chief lieutenant, and Capt. Charles Sawtelle assisted Ingalls. The latter three men planned and directed the movement of the Army of the Potomac's supplies on the Peninsula. All three officers were West Point graduates with years of experience in the quartermaster department.

General Meigs recorded the duties of the department he commanded:

> The object of this Department is to insure an efficient system
> of supply, and to give facility and effect to the movements
> and operations of the army. It is the duty of this department
> to provide quarters, hospitals, and transportation for the
> army, and prisoners of war, and transportation for all military

stores, provisions, camp and garrison equipage, ordnance and ordnance stores; to direct the survey and superintend the opening and repairing of roads, and the construction and repairs of bridges which
may be necessary to the movements of any part of the army. . .to purchase all fuel, forage, straw and stationery required by the army, and
have them transported to the posts where they may be wanted, and issued to those entitled to them; to purchase all horses, oxen, mules, and
harness, and all wagons, carts, boats, and other vessels, with their
equipments, for the transportation of the army and for garrison purposes; to have custody of the same, and be responsible for their proper
use; to purchase all cavalry and artillery horses; to construct, repair,
and maintain all telegraph lines necessary for military purposes.[5]

Officers in four other departments joined the quartermasters in their
labors to provide for the army. The subsistence department procured the
food for the army, the ordnance department provided the arms and ammunition, the paymasters brought the troops their money, and the men of
the medical department obtained and administered the medicines and
treatments needed to maintain the army's health. The officers in these
departments, with the quartermasters, were the businessmen of the
army—the purchasers, negotiators, accountants and distributors—and
their labors touched every aspect of a soldier's life. But while the officers of the other departments labored to perform their specific duties,
their effectiveness depended upon the efficiency of the quartermasters,
who had the crucial job of moving the army. The quartermasters were
responsible for transporting everything—from crackers to bullets to ban-
dages—so if they failed, the best labors of everyone in other departments went for naught. Transportation was the most important and most
difficult part of the quartermasters' job, and it was to solving problems
of movement and distribution that quartermasters in the field devoted
most of their time.

[5] *Annual Report of the Quartermaster General for the Year 1863* (Washington, D.C., 1864), pp.
5-6.

The business of supplying an army is largely a matter of cold numbers. U. S. Army regulations in 1862 decreed that every day every soldier was to be given various foods in varying amounts totaling three pounds.[6] The rules stated each horse was due 26 pounds of fodder daily and each mule 23 pounds. Whatever else changed, the amount of food each man and animal in the army was to be issued each day remained constant in all but the most dire of emergencies.

And, of course, much else did change. Quartermasters had to balance variables, such as the condition of wagons and teams, the size and capabilities of the human labor force, the character of available roads and, most important, the weather with constants like the capacity of wagons, railroad cars and bridges, to find a formula that would allow the fixed amount of food and matériel to be delivered when and where it was needed. Van Vliet's task on the Peninsula was to feed and supply the Army of the Potomac. If, for example, McClellan planned to take 140,000 men and 40,000 animals to the Peninsula, Van Vliet would need to move about 700 tons of food and forage daily just to provide for the army's minimum wants. This tonnage does not include camp equipage, blankets, uniforms, tents, ammunition, horse shoes, nails, axes, shovels, hospital supplies and any of the other thousands of things an army requires in the field. If Van Vliet or his officers failed, some men would go hungry or get wet or not have enough ammunition. If the animals went without food for a day, they would be weaker for work the next day, thus exacerbating transportation problems. The fitness, morale and combat readiness of the army depended to a great degree upon the quartermasters fulfilling their mission day in and day out, regardless of weather or other obstacles.[7]

---

[6] For the composition of the ration, see *OR* III, 1, p. 399, and Patricia L. Faust, ed., *Historical Times Illustrated Encyclopedia of the Civil War* (New York, 1986), pp. 615-616.

[7] Van Vliet estimated in August 1862 that the army required more than 500 tons of food and forage daily and about another 100 tons of matériel each day. *OR* 11, pt. 1, p. 159. By the calculations of a commissary officer not on the Peninsula, an army of 100,000 men and its attendant animals, perhaps 45,000 horses and mules, would require 650 tons of supplies each day. McClellan had more men with him on the Peninsula but fewer animals because his cavalry force was small. See Henry G. Sharpe, "The Art of Supplying Armies in the Field as Exemplified During the Civil War," *Journal of Military Service Institution of the U. S.*, January 1896, p. 63.

*   *   *

Commissary and quartermaster officers attempting to provide for an army on campaign have two options. They can procure forage and subsistence locally in the army's area of operations or they can import it along the army's supply line from the home country. Often throughout history, supply officers have sought to combine the two options to create a third—bringing some supplies from home and gathering others on the march. Napoleon's logisticians were especially adept at this latter alternative, which, perhaps, partially accounts for the Corsican's success.

McClellan envisioned a strategy of overwhelming the enemy with enormous armies like those fielded in the age of Napoleon, but the circumstances that permitted the huge European armies of 100,000 men or more to roam across the Continent in the 18th and early 19th centuries did not exist in America in early 1862.[8] Virginia was not as thickly settled or extensively farmed as were most countries in Europe. Many Old Dominion planters could afford to grow inedible cash crops like tobacco and cotton. While some portions of Virginia were rich in corn, wheat and livestock, other sections of the state were barren of crops. It is doubtful that the state could long subsist two armies of more than 100,000 men each, as parts of Europe did in the age of Napoleon.[9]

Nevertheless, McClellan apparently did hope to subsist Northern armies in the South as part of his grand strategy. He suggested that Federal armies invading the South should gather what they needed from the countryside and pay for it or issue receipts, ". . .giving the obliga-

---

also *Annual Report of the Quartermaster General of the U. S. Army, 1862* (Washington, D.C., 1863), p. 12, printed in *OR* III, 2, pp. 786ff.

[8] For a discussion of McClellan's strategic aims, see Joseph L. Harsh, "Lincoln's Tarnished Brass: Conservative Strategies and the Attempt to Fight the Early Civil War as a Limited War," in *The Confederate High Command & Related Topics,* Roman J. Heleniak and Lawrence L. Hewitt, eds. (Shippensburg, 1991), pp. 124-141.

[9] For a discussion of why Napoleon's principles and practices were not strictly applicable to warfare in America in the 1860s, see John G. Moore, "Mobility and Strategy in the Civil War," *Military Affairs,* vol. 24 (1960), no. 2, pp. 68-77. This article is required reading for anyone wishing to better understand the relationship between strategy and logistics in the Civil War.

tions of the United States for such supplies as may there be obtainable."[10] McClellan believed this respectful, even benevolent, policy toward Southern civilians and their property would shorten the war and aid the post-war reconciliation process. Lincoln apparently agreed, at least at first, and he permitted the general to make his plans for a limited war.

McClellan's conservative requisition policy, of course, would put a tremendous burden on the Federal treasury. Since the quartermasters could take nothing from the populace of the invaded territory without compensating the owner, the U. S. government had committed itself to bearing the enormous expense of paying for everything its soldiers and army animals ate. If the region happened to be barren, the cost and labor involved in feeding the army would be even greater, for the quartermasters would have to import all the army's needs from the North. So it was for McClellan's army on the Peninsula. The campaign began in early spring, even before the seasonal rains, so McClellan could not have hoped to gather much forage at that time of year.[11] He found, in fact, that his army was actually better off than the residents of the Peninsula. The region was, in his words, "very destitute of all the necessaries of life and many of its families are suffering for food."[12] His conservative requisition policy, at least so far as it concerned the Virginians on the Peninsula, was moot.

Van Vliet, therefore, would have to implement a system by which to feed an army of Napoleonic proportions in a predictably rainy season and without the advantage of local requisitions to ease the burden on his supply line. Quartermasters would have to move every morsel that

[10] McClellan to Lincoln, August 2, 1861, in Stephen W. Sears, ed., *The Civil War Papers of George B. McClellan* (New York, 1989), p. 75.

[11] The only crop that Federals on the Peninsula mentioned as being harvestable in that early season was winter wheat, but the army made no attempt to gather it. One Massachusetts soldier mentioned fruit available from abandoned farms north of the Chickahominy River in late June-specifically cherries and strawberries-but in amounts so small as to be negligible. Robert Goldthwaite Carter, *Four Brothers in Blue* (Austin, Tex., 1978), p. 64.

[12] McClellan to S.P. Chase from Cumberland, May 14, 1862. Scrapbook, Army of the Potomac Letters and Telegrams sent, May-June 1862, Record Group 393, National Archives, Washington, D.C. vol. 1, entry 3977. Hereinafter cited as RG 393, NA.

passed into the mouths of McClellan's soldiers and animals on the Peninsula hundreds of miles over a long, expensive supply line from the North.[13]

Obviously, such a difficult logistical operation would require careful planning. McClellan spent the entire fall and winter of 1861-1862 amassing, organizing and training his troops. In December, he began planning a campaign aimed at Richmond, but not until February did he share it with the war department. Van Vliet spent the winter supplying the growing army around Washington. He moved 400 tons of forage alone daily to feed the army's animals in static camps around the capital.[14] In late February, McClellan told his quartermaster to prepare for a waterborne invasion of the Virginia Tidewater. Lincoln, feeling political pressure, demanded McClellan begin his movement by mid-March. Early in that month, the Confederate army in Virginia evacuated its strong position at Manassas, thereby changing the strategic picture upon which McClellan had made his plans. Though much of the advantage of a waterborne movement disappeared when the Confederates left Manassas, McClellan decided to proceed with his amphibious plan and hastily revised the details. He selected a new landing place—the Virginia Peninsula-and the movement began almost immediately. Though he had made general arrangements to supply the army, Van Vliet had had little more than a week to design plans and alternatives specific to the operations on the Peninsula.

---

[13] Officially, McClellan's soldiers were to take nothing from Southern citizens on the Peninsula under penalty of court martial, but the troops did forage illicitly. See Carter, *Four Brothers in Blue*, p. 64. Quartermasters did manage to find some small amounts of edibles. Captain William LeDuc recalled that "Being short of forage, I seized nearly all that a farmer (Charles Baker) had, which was of little value, as it was corn blades, the only kind of coarse fodder the Virginia farmers save for their stock." William G. Le Duc, *Recollections of a Civil War Quartermaster: The Autobiography of William G. Le Duc* (St. Paul, 1963), p. 71. It is unclear what Le Duc means by "seized" but a later revelation in his memoir suggests that he adhered to McClellan's foraging policy. Early in June, he traveled outside the lines to obtain sweet potatoes from a farmer north of the Chickahominy. "The farmer had the potatoes under the cabin floor, and charged three dollars a bushel for them, in gold." Ibid. p. 79.

[14] *OR* 11, pt. 1, p. 157.

Part 2: Operations

The army began to move from Alexandria, Virginia, on March 17
and disembarked at Fort Monroe at the eastern tip of the Peninsula. The
quartermasters established their first depot at the fort and began feeding
the army. As troops continued to arrive, the camps spread westward to
accommodate the enormous city of soldiers until by early April McClellan had created one of the great population centers on the continent. But
what this population lacked was, to use a modern term, an infrastructure
by which to support itself. McClellan's engineers would have to create
the roads, bridges, harbors and warehouses to sustain the city. Quartermasters would have to make the best use of this infrastructure to supply
the needs of the population.[15]

As the troops began probing westward toward the Confederates
known to be at Yorktown, McClellan discovered his maps were wrong
in many particulars. Of greater concern to Van Vliet, however, was that
the small, poorly drained roads were ill suited to a supply operation of
the size he was to direct. The army's engineers also determined that the
region's bridges were inadequate to support the weight of the wagon
trains and would have to be rebuilt. Van Vliet reported that "the nature
of the country and the condition of the roads rendered it impossible to
haul our supplies by wagons" from Fort Monroe.[16]

But the quartermaster had a valuable asset in the York River. The
water permitted him to move supplies quickly and securely, so Van Vliet
sought to float matériel as close to the army as possible before putting it
on wagons. On April 6, Van Vliet established two depots on the York
River-one at Ship Point and a second, larger one at Cheeseman's Creek.

---

[15] At Fort Monroe in these early days of the campaign, the quartermaster department paid 1,153
men, including 1,001 teamsters. The teamsters were employed "driving government mule teams,
hauling fuel, forage, etc." *Report of Persons and Articles Hired, Report of Transfers, Reports of
Persons Leaving Service or Dying with Salary Due, Harrison's Landing, Perryville, Md., "In the
Field," Washington, D.C., White House, Va.* by Capt. C.G. Sawtelle. Asst. QM. U. S. Army, Jan. to
Dec. 1862, Record Group 92, National Archives, Washington, D.C., File 780. Hereinafter cited at
RG 92, NA.

[16] *OR* 11, pt. 1, p. 158.

From these points, the army drew all of its food, forage and supplies for one month, through the entire siege of Yorktown. Three weeks after beginning operations at Cheeseman's Creek, Van Vliet reported to his superior, General Meigs: "We have had great difficulties to encounter, but they have been overcome. . . .there have been no complaints."[17]

But there were complaints and they must have reached Van Vliet. Brigadier General Silas Casey, commander of a division in the IV Corps, badgered headquarters repeatedly for more wagons. He recalled that after going into camp near Newport News, his men suffered severely for want of food. "Not being permitted to take any transportation from Alexandria down the river," he reported later, "I found myself without any means to transport supplies for the men. That duty was for several days performed by the men. After waiting about two weeks, I managed by great effort to obtain an insufficient supply of transportation."[18] A Michigan officer in the III Corps wrote:

> Crackers 3 inches square & of the usual thickness would sell
> readily at 5 cts. apiece but there are none for sale. The man
> who has one looks on it with miserly eagerness & holds it
> tight as it afaid someone would take it away. There is an
> abundance of meat but it does not satisfy the stomach. The
> Capt. got 2 potatoes this m'g & had them cooked but they
> were stolen before he could eat them. [19]

[17] Ibid., p. 161. The Army of the Potomac's chief commissary of subsistence, Col. Henry F. Clarke, noted in his report the great problems experienced by the quartermasters before Yorktown and suggested that they were aided materially in solving them by the men of the commissary department. Ibid., p. 168.

[18] Silas Casey to N. H. Davis, May 28, 1862, RG 393, box 4. "[I]t was ten or twelve days before we could get our division transportation, and for a part of that time my men had to pack their provisions themselves from the depot at that point." Testimony before the Joint Committee on the Conduct of the War, given March 5, 1863. U. S. Congress, Report of the Joint Committee on the Conduct of the War, Part 1: Army of the Potomac (Washington, D.C., 1863: Kraus Reprint Co., 1977), p. 442. Hereinafter cited as Report of the Joint Committee.

[19] Charles B. Haydon, For Country, Cause & Leader: The Civil War Journal of Charles B. Haydon, edited by Stephen W. Sears (New York, 1993), p. 216-217. Haydon retained his perspective by admitting that "our hardships, which indeed are not serious, must be light compared to those of our Revolutionary Fathers at this place. If they could endure so much to found the Govt. Surely we can with light hearts bear the small privations necessary to defend it."

Here, too, the problem was transportation. After noting that the quartermasters were forcing no crackers or bread of any kind forward to the camps and that some of the men were boiling wheat to supplement their diet, the Michigander stated that

> There are plenty of rations at the mouth of the river 10 miles
> off & teams are trying to get through to them. It takes 2 days
> to make the journey & 6 mules cannot draw more than 1200
> lbs. I think they would do better to pack the provision than
> to draw it. A great many mules are killed by the present
> mode.[20]

Many men, like Casey's, realized they would prefer to try to go get the food themselves than to sit hungrily awaiting in camp. In the second week of the siege, an artillery private in the II Corps formed "a committee" with a friend and went with their rations to see division commander Brig. Gen. John Sedgwick. They showed him their food and asked him "if he thought that was enough for men to live on." The general pleasantly replied, "'No! it is almost impossible to get them [rations], but I will see that you get more very soon.'"[21] But the men soon had to act on their own and took eight battery horses to the depot at Ship's Point for rations: "we brought in what could be packed on the horses," the private recalled, "and it was a terribly tough job for the horses to get through." The trip took more than a day, and, after a day of rest, the batterymen set out again to the depot for more.[22]

Overcoming the "difficulties," Van Vliet reported to Meigs, required the investment of tremendous labor. "The whole army set to work," wrote one of McClellan's staff officers, "to cut roads, to con-

---

[20] Ibid., p. 216.

[21] Thomas M. Aldrich, *The History of Battery A First Regiment Rhode Island Light Artillery* (Providence, 1904), p. 71.

[22] "Enroute, they met General Sedgwick who asked if they were getting more to eat. Private Thomas Aldrich shouted back that they were but that they were working hard for it, which brought a laugh from the general and his staff. Sedgwick shouted, 'That's right; bring up all you can, it is the only way we can get anything up here.'" Ibid., p. 71.

struct bridges, to prepare *Places d' armes*, to establish wharves, to dig trenches, and to erect batteries."[23] Worst of all the problems confronting Van Vliet was the character of the roads. They were too narrow—14 feet wide or less in most places rather that the desired minimum of 16 feet, which would permit two wagons to pass one another.[24] The sandy soil did not drain well nor did it bear up well under heavy traffic. Private Thomas Aldrich of Battery A, 1st Rhode Island Light Artillery, described the roads as being something like gelatin. "A man could simply by standing and jumping up and down shake the ground for twenty feet around him."[25] The subsoil seemed to be quicksand. Van Vliet reported every quartermaster's nightmare: "empty wagons even [sink] to their beds."[26] Van Vliet had been led to expect quite different circumstances. In February, McClellan had argued to Stanton that the superior quality of the roads on the Peninsula was one of the great advantages to mounting a campaign there and stated specifically that, "The roads in that region are passable at all seasons of the year."[27]

The engineers and their labor gangs had to widen, artificially surface and maintain the thoroughfares to such an extent that Van Vliet reported that, "Nearly every foot of the roads has been corduroyed." Some of the roads required three or four layers of corduroying before the logs would stay above the surface of the mud.[28] This work consumed valuable time. Near the end of April, after three weeks of siege operations, topographi-

---

[23] Comte de Paris, *History of the Civil War in America*, 4 vols. (Philadelphia, 1876), vol. 2, p. 11. The prince added that, "These immense labors, superintended in detail by the general-in-chief, who gave himself up entirely to his old specialty as engineer officer, were prosecuted with the greatest activity. . . .Nevertheless, in spite of all their diligence, the time was passing away, precious time for military operations, for the winter rains were over, and the great summer heat had not yet set in." pp. 11-12.

[24] W.R. Palmer to A.A. Humphreys, April 30, 1862, A. A. Humphreys Papers, Historical Society of Pennsylvania, Philadelphia, Pennsylvania, letterbook 6, March 1862-May 22, 1862. Hereinafter cited as Humphreys Papers.

[25] Aldrich, *The History of Battery A*, p. 71.

[26] *OR* 11, pt. 1, p. 161.

[27] Sears, *Papers of George B. McClellan*, p. 167.

[28] Haydon, *For Country, Cause & Leader*, p. 221.

cal engineer Maj. William R. Palmer traveled over the roads in the army's rear and made daily reports to his commander, Brig. Gen. A. A. Humphreys, chief topographical engineer for the Army of the Potomac. Palmer recommended which roads needed the repairs and estimated how many days would be needed by a work detail of a given size to restore the road to good condition. So extensive was the damage to the roads by heavy traffic that Palmer recommended immediate reconstruction of approximately 17 miles of roads connecting the army's camps and batteries with the depot. The workforce and the number of days Palmer estimated would be needed to repair the roads amounted to an expenditure of labor equal to 497 man-days per mile.[29] Even corduroying the roads did not solve all of Van Vliet's problems, however. The volunteer troops detailed to surface the roads were inexperienced in the task and the quality of the corduroying suffered. The log surfaces of the roads were, "exceedingly rough, and the consequence is that the wear and tear of our transportation has been very great."[30] The quartermaster's precious wagons were being shaken to pieces.

Still, Van Vliet felt he had circumstances under control. The extreme end of the Union line at Yorktown was only seven miles from the depot at Cheeseman's Creek, and most of the army was camped closer. So negligible is this distance that one could even say that most of the army was camped *at* its depot. This fact began to work in Van Vliet's favor as the labor gang's surfaced the roads and the junior quartermasters made distribution more efficient

On May 4, the Confederates abandoned their positions at Yorktown, and McClellan immediately ordered a pursuit. Portions of the armies clashed the next day at Williamsburg, after which the Southerners continued withdrawing eastward toward Richmond. When the Confederates abandoned their river batteries at Yorktown, they opened the York River to Federal shipping. While most of McClellan's army pursued

---

[29] W. R. Palmer reports to A. A. Humphreys, April 26, 27, 28, 29, 30, 1862, Humphreys Papers, letterbook 6, March 1862-May 22, 1862.

[30] *OR* 11, pt. 1, p. 161.

over the muddy and badly torn up roads in the Confederate wake, one
strong division under Brig. Gen. William B. Franklin steamed up the
York. Franklin was to establish a beachhead near West Point at the
headwaters of the York and attempt to drive inland and interfere with the
Confederate retreat. Though he failed in the latter part of his mission,
Franklin did establish and defend a toehold at Eltham's Landing on the
south bank of the Pamunkey River.

As soon as the Confederates evacuated Yorktown, Van Vliet broke
up his operation at Ship Point and Cheeseman's Creek and ordered all
the hundreds of transports and barges laden with food and supplies to
move to the more extensive wharves of Yorktown.[31] The historic town
would remain a Federal supply and hospital depot for almost two
months. Van Vliet also sent vessels upstream with Franklin's division,
and his quartermasters established a depot at Eltham's.[32] Days later,
another depot sprouted up at Cumberland Landing, just a few miles up
the Pamunkey from Eltham's. For two weeks in mid-May, the Army of
the Potomac drew all of its subsistence from these two bases. Again,
during this period the bulk of the army was only a few miles from
Eltham's or Cumberland, and for several days, much of the army was
camped at Cumberland.

---

[31] The speed with which Van Vliet moved his depots on the York, Pamunkey and eventually
James Rivers reveals another aspect of the complexity of his task. Because the supplies had to be
ready to be moved with the army as it advanced or retreated, the quartermasters could not afford to
lose time in unloading and then reloading (unshipping and shipping) the matériel aboard the ships,
schooners and barges at the depot, so Van Vliet and Ingalls ordered that the supplies be left aboard
the vessels until needed, thus the boats became floating warehouses. Financial considerations
complicated the situation further. Most of the vessels were rented, some at immoderate rates. The
large, ocean-going screw steamers were too expensive and, because of their size and speed, too
valuable to remain idle as warehouses at the depot. In managing the harbor at Cheeseman's Creek
and subsequent depots, Ingalls tried to move the cargoes of the larger, more expensive steamers
and schooners to less expensive crafts so that the big ships could fetch more matériel from depots
in the North. The less expensive barges and canal boats served as the warehouses at the army's
depot, and whatever tugs, steamers or gunboats that happened to be at hand would tow these crafts
to where the army needed the supplies. See *Report of the Quartermaster General for 1862*
(Washington, D.C. 1863), p. 13.

[32] Commissary chief Clarke reported that early in May two officers established subsistence
depots first at Queen's Creek, about 12 miles above Yorktown on the York River, and later at
Bigler's Wharf, five miles farther up river. These depots helped supply that portion of McClellan's
army moving from Williamsburg by land. *OR* 11, pt. 1, p. 168.

Portion of encampment of the Army of the Potomac at Cumberland Landing, May 1862. (Library of Congress)

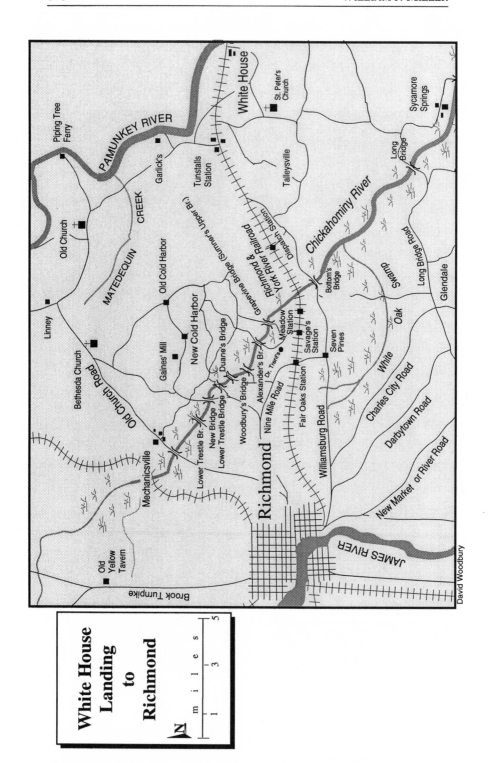

White House Landing to Richmond

On May 16, McClellan moved his headquarters to White House Landing on the Pamunkey. This place, like all of the landings on the river, was important because there the high, steep banks that prevailed along much of the stream's course fell away to permit easy passage between the water and the surrounding farmland. White House Landing was especially important as the place where the Richmond & York River Railroad crossed the Pamunkey. The Confederates had burned the bridge when they left the area, but Federal engineer Lt. Col. B. S. Alexander had visited the site five days before McClellan arrived and reported that the railroad toward Richmond, as far as could be determined, was sound. Alexander liked what he saw of the landing. The broad, flat plains, the deep water, the railroad, a few good roads leading inland, the long sweeping shoreline forming a cove that offered abundant space for moorings convinced the engineer that "this was the proper spot for our final depot of supplies."[33] Both McClellan and Van Vliet concurred, appreciating how valuable the railroad would be in supplying the army as it advanced on Richmond, just 23 miles away.

The quartermasters immediately set to making piers by lashing together barges and canal boats, running them up to the bank at high tide and laying planks across the top. With the main wharf at White House Landing, 10 or 12 such temporary piers would serve the army's immediate needs.[34] Work gangs of soldiers began unloading transports and schooners and packing the wagons that would advance with the army. Engineers and pioneers began felling trees and corduroying roads leading inland. When McClellan ordered his army forward on May 19 after the Confederates, who had by this time withdrawn across the Chickahominy River, Van Vliet's wagons full of crackers, salt beef, beans and other items of the ration trundled along close behind.

---

[33] Ibid., p. 139; The depth of the river and the cove at White House Landing varied with the tide about three and a half feet. Ships at anchor in the vicinity reported depths of up to 30 feet. Log of *U.S.S. Currituck*, May 14, 1862, Record Group 24, National Archives, Washington, D.C. Hereinafter cited as RG 24, NA.

[34] *OR* 11, pt. 1, pp. 159, 165.

The Army of the Potomac's supply line was then longer than it had ever been. The procession of steamers and schooners from New York, Philadelphia, Baltimore, Annapolis and Alexandria snaked up the York to West Point, then about another 45 miles up the tortuous Pamunkey. Once at White House, the supply line stretched inland about 15 miles to the Chickahominy and, eventually, across that stream to within six miles of Richmond. The camps of the army before Richmond in late May represented the farthest distance away from its main depot that the army had ever been. Though this distance was only about 25 miles by winding roads, many of Van Vliet's wagons were now traveling at least twice as far every day as they had from any other base in the campaign. The quartermaster immediately began having problems moving the necessary amounts of supplies forward. As he wrote in retrospect it was with the army's establishment of a base at White House Landing that "the real troubles in supplying the army commenced. . . ."[35]

By the end of May, the Army of the Potomac was spread out along the Chickahominy River 15 to 20 miles from White House. Van Vliet would eventually move most of the necessary supplies over most of that distance by railroad, but at first the railroad required minor repairs, so wagons bore all the army's necessities forward.[36] Because most of the roads on the Peninsula side of Richmond led southeastward from the city rather than eastward or slightly to the north of eastward toward White House, the directors of McClellan's wagon trains had to use a variety of byways and long, indirect circuits to the camps of the army.[37]

---

[35] Ibid., p. 159.

[36] On May 23, Van Vliet optimistically wrote to Meigs "I trust that in two days I shall have the railroad in running order. . . ." Ibid., p. 162. The Confederates had destroyed two small bridges where the railroad crossed over creeks a few miles inland from White House. Engineers and work parties began rebuilding them immediately and, as Van Vliet predicted, opened the railroad from the Pamunkey to the Chickahominy by the end of May. See also Abner Hard, *History of the Eighth Cavalry Regiment Illinois Volunteers* (Aurora, 1868), pp. 120-121.

[37] Although maps vary, and teamsters could follow many routes from White House to the Federal front, only seven (7) routes suggest themselves as practical because of their directness. 1. White House to Mechanicsville via Johnston's Store, Old Church, Linney's and Bethesda Church. 2. White House to Mechanicsville via Tunstall's Station, Cold Harbor and Gaines' Mill. 3. White

One officer thought that "These forest roads are very numerous, [and] they constitute an inextricable labyrinth for those who are not familiar with the locality in all its details."[38]

An infantryman of the 27th New York described the roads as "only personal affairs, leading from plantation to plantation." These thoroughfares usually accommodated nothing larger than "a one horse cart, . . .a double wagon being rarely seen. The roads are very narrow, and although unfenced, on account of the deep cuts caused by age and the woody nature of the country, one wagon could not pass another only at certain places."[39] Brig. Gen John G. Barnard, the army's chief engineer, was shocked by the roads in the region because before the campaign had begun he, like Van Vliet, had been led to believe they would be quite different. "It had been stated so often that I felt it was an assured fact that the roads were hard and sandy; whereas they were everywhere of the most terrible character . . ."[40]

Not surprisingly, Van Vliet struggled to squeeze huge amounts of necessities through these mushy capillaries. On May 23, he told Meigs

---

House to Mechanicsville via Tunstall's, Baltimore Cross Roads, past Sumner's Upper Bridge and through New Cold Harbor. 4. White House to Seven Pines via Tunstall's, Baltimore Cross Roads and Sumner's Upper Bridge. 5. White House to Seven Pines via Tunstall's, Baltimore Cross Roads and Bottom's Bridge. 6. White House to Seven Pines via Talleysville, Baltimore Cross Roads and Bottom's Bridge. 7. White House to Seven Pines via Talleysville, Long Bridge and Glendale. The distinction between roads and routes in this case is important. Some of the routes overlapped in that they shared common roads.

[38] Paris, *Civil War in America*, 2, p.58.

[39] Letter from member of the 27th New York in *Rochester Daily Union and Advertiser* May 28, 1862. Even in their usual condition the roads in this part of the Peninsula were inadequate for the army's requirements. Scouting ahead of the army on May 13, topographer Major Palmer examined the road between Cumberland Landing and White House Landing. The road was not damaged, having borne only light cavalry traffic in recent days, but even in its normal state, Palmer thought it would not support the army. He recommended that a work party of 300 pioneers would have to prepare the road before the army could use it. W. R. Palmer to A. A. Humphreys, May 13, 1862, Humphreys Papers, letterbook 6, March 1862-May 22, 1862. McClellan reported to the secretary of war on May 14 from Cumberland: "Am detained by the necessity of making new roads and repairing old ones." *OR* 11, pt. 3, p. 170.

[40] Barnard made this statement in response to a question about delays before Yorktown, but his phrasing and subsequent testimony implies that he considered the roads everywhere on the Peninsula very bad, which opinion is supported by the statements of other officers, including Van Vliet. Testimony before the Joint Committee on the Conduct of the War, given February 25, 1863. JCC, p. 393.

Quartermaster transports at White House Landing. (National Archives)

that he was experiencing serious problems. "Supplies are now hauled by land from the depot, and owing to the nature of the roads it is about the utmost limit at which an army of this size can be supplied by wagon transportation."[41] The problems in moving rations even dictated to a degree the army's deployment. A member of McClellan's staff reported that the troops north of the Chickahominy in late May helped simplify distribution by camping in clearings right along the main wagon road by which their food was brought to them.[42] The repair of the railroad now became crucially important, and Van Vliet prodded the engineers and laborers to finish their work.

But even after the railroad was repaired, Van Vliet would need all of the more than 3,000 wagons with the army. To ease congestion at White House, quartermasters had established a forage depot a few miles upstream at Garlick's Landing, also known as Putney's Mill. Teamsters hauled forage from this point forward to the army or at least to Tunstall's Station, the nearest station on the railroad. Furthermore, the railroad could only transport matériel close to the army, not right into its camps. The quartermasters would always need wagons to haul food, forage and equipment from the railroad depots to the camps of the various divisions and brigades.[43] This road network in the army's rear required immense labor to build and maintain. The Comte de Paris, a French prince serving on McClellan's staff, wrote that:

> to be able to move and victual the troops with ease; it was
> necessary before joining battle to conquer the treacherous wa-
> ters of the Chickahominy, and to connect both banks by
> bridges numerous and always passable. . . .the Federals
> [spent the first half of June] in repairing the roads which con-
> nected their several camps, in constructing new ones, in extri-

---

[41] *OR* 11, pt. 1, p. 162.

[42] Paris, *Civil War in America,* 2, p. 57.

[43] General Humphreys concluded that "The Army of the Potomac cannot be supplied at a greater distance than 10 miles from a railroad or a river in a country furnishing so little as this does." A. A. Humphreys to Archibald Campbell, July 28, 1862, Humphreys Papers, letterbook 7.

cating from the mud the large supply trains, which scarcely
sufficed for the distribution of daily rations, in strengthening
the bridges and increasing their number. . . .[44]

The spring rains made Van Vliet's work immeasurably more difficult. Rain fell on at least 19 of the 44 days between May 15 and June
28.[45] Tremendous thunderstorms dumped tons of water on the region,
especially in what was by many accounts a storm of biblical proportions
on May 30. April and early May had been wet as well. Van Vliet wrote
to Meigs that "we have had one continued series of storms ever since we
landed on the Peninsula."[46] Because the region was low and wooded,
the sun could do little to evaporate the rain water, so the ground remained wet and swampy.[47]

Van Vliet, who had campaigned in Florida, Mexico, Utah and the
Plains, told Meigs in early June that "I have never seen worse roads in
any part of the country." Dr. Charles S. Tripler, the army's medical
director, thought that the rains "keep the roads in shocking condition."[48]
Brigade quartermaster William LeDuc recalled that the trains moved at a
snail's pace. On May 30, he sent teams to Dispatch Station on the
railroad for supplies. Though the station was only four miles from the
brigade's camp, the wagons "were the entire day going and returning,
nearly all the time being expended in returning, loaded. The ground was
so soft that loaded wagons would cut through the top soil, and have to be
unloaded and dug or pried out."[49] LeDuc remembered coming upon

[44] Paris, *Civil War in America*, 2, p. 75. The prince added that during this time troops worked
on "covering the whole battle-field of [Seven Pines] with vast works." On June 6, Gen. Robert E.
Lee wrote, ". . .the enemy [are] working like beavers, making bridges and causeways." *OR* 11, pt.
3, p. 577.

[45] Brig. Gen. Samuel P. Heintzelman's journal, Samuel P. Heintzelman Papers, Library of
Congress Manuscript Division, Washington, D.C., microfilm reel 7. Hereinafter cited as
Heitzelman Papers. See also Log of *U. S.S. Galena*, May 14, 1862, RG 24, NA.

[46] *OR* 11, pt. 1, p. 164.

[47] See Heintzelman's journal, Heintzelman Papers. See also *OR* 11, pt. 1, p. 159.

[48] Ibid., p. 202.

[49] Le Duc, *Recollections of a Civil War Quartermaster*, p. 71.

another train one night in which, "several of the wagons were hopelessly fast, the teams taken off, and tethered in the woods. I remember one team stuck in mud and water halfway to the horses' bellies, and the driver asleep."[50] The bad weather and the size and weight of the trains passing almost continuously between White House and the Chickahominy severely damaged the corduroyed roads so carefully laid by the engineers and pioneers. Chief topographer Humphreys declared that the destruction was so steady and on such a large scale that "every large train that passes over [a road] should be accompanied by a working party of at least 150 men, having 50 axes and 25 spades, to repair the road and open new track."[51]

Rain and the worsening roads continued to hamper Van Vliet's efforts and soon the quartermasters found themselves locked in a losing numbers game. An army wagon, for example, was an extremely dependable vehicle. Simple and efficient, it had been refined by decades of service until by 1862 it defied improvement. A healthy, well-rested team of six mules on a dry, macadamized road could draw a full wagonload of 4,500 pounds under ideal weather conditions. Rarely, of course, did teams, weather and road surfaces achieve perfection at the same time and place. On the soft roads of the Peninsula, a mule team could haul only about 2,500 pounds, often less.[52] An incident with the siege train at Yorktown illustrates the tremendous effect the condition of the road surface had on the transport of supplies. On April 16, over a good, relatively dry road, 62 siege wagons moved 1,882 10-inch mortar shells from the ordnance depot to the batteries, each wagon bearing about 30 of the 90-pound shells (2,700 pounds) per trip. Nine days later, however,

---

[50] Ibid., p. 70.

[51] A. A. Humphreys, "Instructions for Opening and Repairing Roads," RG 393, U. S. Army Continental Commands 1821-1920, Army of the Potomac, 1861-1865, Letters received, 1862, NA, Box E-L. Humphreys apparently prepared these instructions as a circular for distribution to concerned officers with the army on the Peninsula. In his report of his mid-June ride around the Army of the Potomac, Brig. Gen. Jeb Stuart specifically mentioned the bad condition of the roads around Tunstall's Station, less than five miles from White House Landing. OR 11, pt. 1, p. 1039.

[52] Nathaniel S. Dodge, *Hints on Army Transportation*, (Albany, 1863), p. 7; Risch, Quartermaster Support of the Army, pp. 420, note 88.

after rains and heavy traffic had badly damaged the roads, the wagons could bear only 600 or 700 pounds of black powder—the equivalent of just five passengers.[53]

The animals, too, suffered from the rain. The extra strain of fighting through mud and over rough roads took its toll on the horses and mules hauling the wagons. The horses proved less durable than the mules and broke down so frequently that the quartermasters could no longer depend on them.[54] The experience of one division quartermaster suggests that some of the horses with the army were in bad condition even before they began to work. He considered the horses he drew at Fort Monroe for his teams "poor and almost unfit for work, and ever since I have been in possession of them I have been unable to make them perform more than one half the work required of a good strong team."[55] Even empty wagons often bogged down and blocked traffic when team horses and mules proved too weak to pull them free. The quartermasters did what they could to lighten the load of each wagon leaving the depots, and eventually decided they could not burden the tired teams with any more than 1,000 pounds of cargo.[56]

But the requirements of the army did not lessen with the bad weather. Each man still required the three pounds of daily ration allotted to him by army regulations, each horse was to get his 26 pounds of forage and every mule its prescribed 23 pounds. As Van Vliet stated, these rations had to go forward "rain or shine" every day.[57] The reduced load in each wagon meant the animals would not have to work as hard,

---

[53] *OR* 11, pt. 1, p. 357.

[54] Ibid., p. 161. Van Vliet recommended to Meigs that the quartermaster department do away with horse teams altogether, as the rough service broke them down much faster that it did the mules, which were "far more serviceable and economical. Meigs accepted this recommendation and included it in his annual report to the secretary of war ("Mules bear the exposure and hardships of the campaign much better than horses. . . .") Annual Report of the Quartermaster General of the U.S. Army, 1862 (Washington, D.C., 1863), p. 13, printed in *OR* III, 2, pp. 786ff.

[55] Scrapbook, Army of the Potomac Letters and Telegrams sent, May-June 1862, RG 393, NA, pt. 1, entry 3966, book 531.

[56] *OR* 11, pt. 1, p. 164.

[57] Ibid., p. 159.

but with wagons hauling only a quarter of their capacity, the quartermasters, to move the necessary amount of supplies forward, had to add more wagons to the trains leaving White House and Garlick's for the Chickahominy or keep smaller trains constantly in motion, sending them on multiple trips to and from the front. Either solution increased traffic, making the roads even worse and adding to the fatigue of the animals.

Figures filed at army headquarters by two quartermasters reveal something of the size of the operation on the roads and in the camps each day. On May 28, Quartermaster Capt. M. P. Engle of Brig. Gen. Silas Casey's division of the IV corps reported 194 wagons in use by the division, distributed as follows:

3 wagons for the baggage of division staff
9 for the baggage of three brigade staffs
1 for the baggage of the division artillery staff
84 for use by the 14 regiments of the division
30 for infantry ammunition for the division
13 for forage for artillery animals
10 for artillery ammunition for the division
1 for hospital stores for the division
6 for butcher's tools, scales, store tents, & for brigade commissaries
4 to transport intrenching tools
25 as general forage train
1 to transport Quartermaster's store
2 to transport Rations, cooking utensils &c. for teamsters
2 for the use of the Provost Marshal of the Division
1 to transport Blacksmith's tools, Forge & Coal
1 to transport Mail of Division
1 for Commissary of the *Corps*
194 total[58]

---

[58] Scrapbook, Army of the Potomac Letters and Telegrams sent, May-June 1862, RG 393, NA, pt. 1, entry 3966, book 531.

One of Engle's subordinates, Fred A. Nims, brigade quartermaster and commissary for Brig. Gen. Innis N. Palmer's brigade of Casey's division, reported on May 28 that his brigade retained the following transportation:

2   wagons for brigade headquarters
10 for ammunition
10 for subsistence
3   for forage
5   for use of 81st NY, including 1 wagon for hospital supplies
5   for use of 85th NY, including 1 wagon for hospital supplies
5   for use of 92nd NY, including 1 wagon for hospital supplies
5   for use of 98th NY, including 1 wagon for hospital supplies
45 total[59]

Lacking transportation information about the other brigades in Casey's division, we cannot confirm Engle's figures or accurately evaluate those of Nims, but, if we are willing to allow that there will be discrepancies among overlapping reports like these two and that we do not know a great deal about the daily administration of the supply operation—wagon and team assignments, rotation of vehicles and animals, for example—we can sketch a rough picture of the wagon transportation in Van Vliet's operation.

Using Nims' brigade as a model of a typical brigade, and multiplying his transportation requirements (45 wagons) by the number of brigades in the army (56), we see that the army required approximately 2,520 wagons daily for the transportation of food, forage, ammunition, baggage and hospital supplies.[60] Ingalls estimated that in June he had

[59] U.S. Army Continental Commands 1821-1920, Army of the Potomac, 1861-1865, Letters received, 1862, RG 393, NA, box 6. Nims also reported that the brigade retained 11 ambulances.

[60] The admittedly rough figure of 56 brigades is based on the army as it was organized on June 20, 1862, and includes infantry, cavalry, cavalry reserve, artillery, artillery reserve, engineers, the headquarters guard and the detachment at White House Landing. In enumerating brigades, the author attempted to cluster unbrigaded units into brigade-sized groups.

3,000[61] wagons available with the army and 350 ambulances.[62] To haul these vehicles, he had, exclusive of cavalry and artillery animals "5,000 team horses and 8,000 mules." Subtracting a minimum of two horses for duty with each ambulance, Ingalls' available horse pool dropped to 4,300 for service in the wagon trains. Since horses pulled in teams of four and mules in teams of six, Ingalls had teams enough in late June to move 2,408 wagons (4,300 horses divided by 4 = 1,075 horse teams, 8,000 mules divided by 6 = 1,333 mule teams. 1,075 + 1,333 = 2,408 teams).[63] These rough calculations seem to indicate that in June 1862 the quartermasters on the Peninsula had available to them more wagons than teams to pull them, illustrating, perhaps, Van Vliet's statement to Meigs on June 5, that "Our loss of animals is very great."[64]

Faced with all the problems of wagon transport, Van Vliet came to view the Richmond & York River Railroad as his deliverance.[65] Late in

---

[61] On October 9, 1862, Quartermaster General Meigs advised Secretary of War Stanton that, "The troops generally carry too much useless baggage." Meigs noted that Napoleon believed "500 wagons were enough for an army of 40,000, and that while it would be impossible to fix by any general regulation the number of wagons in the general supply trains" (because such trains would increase with the size of the army and the distance from base), Meigs did feel the war department could regulate the size of headquarters and regimental baggage trains. "These trains have generally in our army been larger than necessary, and, by their magnitude, have offered temptations to officers and men to carry with them useless baggage. The armies have thus been encumbered in their movements, and military operations have been less successful than if our armies had been less profusely equipped." *OR* III, 2, pp. 654-655.

[62] Ibid., I, 11, pt. 1, p. 165. These two figures offer a good example of the difficulty of obtaining accurate figures on the campaign. Ingalls' figures conflict with Van Vliet's, who reported that his department retained 3,600 wagons and 700 ambulances throughout the campaign "with the exception of ordinary losses. . . ." Would the loss of 600 wagons and 350 ambulances be considered "ordinary"? The discrepancy is all the more troubling because both officers are undeniably reliable sources for matters in their department. See Ibid., p. 158. Nims' figure of 11 ambulances with his brigade suggests that the army would have needed 330 ambulances to equip the 30 infantry brigades in the army in late May.

[63] Ibid., p. 165.

[64] Ibid., p. 163. Even allowing for an error of 10 percent in the number of wagons required by the brigades (2,520 - 10 percent = 2,268), the number of teams available would not much exceed the number of wagons to be moved (2,408 teams - 2,268 wagons = 156 extra teams). This small surplus would seem just adequate, considering animals would need days of rest and that some would be injured or fall ill.

[65] McClellan apparently shared Van Vliet's high hopes for the railroad, for late in May the quartermaster informed Ingalls that "The General is most anxious to have the rail road put in running order with the least possible delay. . . ." Van Vliet to Ingalls, May 20, 1862, Scrapbook,

May, he wrote to Meigs that he hoped to soon have the railroad repaired, "when all anxiety with regard to supplies may be dismissed."[66] Construction crews finished their work on the railroad that same week, and the locomotives and cars McClellan had had shipped from the North began running between White House and the army's camps across the Chickahominy.[67]

Van Vliet made forward depots of the small, rural stations on the railroad at which his quartermasters cached rations and supplies. At Tunstall's Station, closest to White House, Van Vliet's lieutenants stored only a small amount, as they did at Dispatch Station and Meadow Station, the next two stops on the road to Richmond. But at four stations south of the Chickahominy, Fair Oaks Station, directly in the army's rear, Orchard Station, Forage Station and especially at Savage's Station, the Federals stockpiled huge amounts of matériel. Divisional, brigade and regimental staff officers of the various departments (quartermaster, subsistence and ordnance) had their requisitions filled at these forward depots, whence wagon trains would move the supplies to the troops.[68] But the whole distribution plan from the forward depots depended on the railroad's ability to move the required matériel forward each day. The railroad proved very quickly that it was barely up to the task, and far from solving Van Vliet's problems, the railroad contributed to them.

The Richmond & York River Railroad was just one of five rail lines serving Virginia's capital, and it was the only one not tied into a large network of rails. The principals of the Richmond & York River Railroad Company had wished to link Richmond with the wharves of West

---

Army of the Potomac Letters and Telegrams sent, May-June 1862, RG 393, NA, vol. 1, entry 3977.

[66] *OR* 11, pt. 1, p. 162.

[67] Colonel D. C. McCallum, director of the U. S. Military Railroads, reported: "March 14, 1862, General McClellan instructed me to have five locomotives and eighty cars loaded upon vessels in the harbor of Baltimore and held subject to his orders with a view to using them in his contemplated Peninsular campaign. They were purchased from Northern railroad companies, loaded as directed, and remained on the vessels until early May, when they were sent to White House, Va., and placed upon the Richmond & York River Railroad." Ibid., III, pt. 5, pp. 974-975.

[68] Risch, *Quartermaster Support of the Army*, p. 421.

Point at the head of the York River. They designed a single 4' 8"-gauge-track road through the swamps to handle light traffic in passengers and freight. It can be assumed that no one involved with the construction of the road between 1853-1856 expected the line ever to support the more than 37,000 residents of Richmond, let alone the 115,335 denizens of the Army of the Potomac. McClellan and Van Vliet were fervently and unreasonably hoping that the single-track, country railroad could perform far beyond its designed capacity and do what it was never intended to.[69]

The weight of the railroad's shortcomings pressed most heavily upon Capt. Charles G. Sawtelle. Of all the junior officers on duty with the quartermaster department in 1862, Sawtelle was selected to fill a crucial role in the war's most important campaign to date. He served as Rufus Ingalls' second in command at White House, where he managed logistics at the depot and oversaw the daily functioning of the supply operation. While Van Vliet directed the operation, dealing with headquarters and Washington, and Ingalls took care of administration, Sawtelle wrestled with the daily operational realities of feeding the huge army.

On June 4, Sawtelle wrote to Meigs and laid bare the harsh truth that the logistical operation on the Peninsula was not working well and might soon stop working at all. He explained that because "frequent and heavy rains" had made the roads impassable for every vehicle except light wagons, "the Army is almost entirely dependent upon the Rail-road." This dependency was, in Sawtelle's opinion, dangerous, for even in good weather with an adequate labor force to accompany it "the road would be barely able to transport all the supplies requisite for an army of this magnitude whilst daily engaging the enemy."[70] And, of course, the

---

[69] *Report of the President of the Richmond and York River Railroad Co. to Stockholders Together With the Report of the Chief Engineer to the Board of Directors, August 9, 1854* (Richmond, 1854), p. 20; Elizabeth C. Johnson, "Alexander Dudley: Entrepreneur," *The Bulletin of the King & Queen County Historical Society of Virginia*, vol. 49, p. 1.

[70] Sawtelle to Meigs, June 4, 1862, from White House Landing, Va., Office of the Quartermaster General, Consolidated Correspondence File. RG 92, NA, Box 1236, entry 225, "White House, Va." Skirmishers, scouts and emplaced batteries were in regular contact throughout

same weather that made the roads quagmires affected the railroad. Storms on May 30 and June 4 damaged bridges, and the rains on the latter day even washed away sections of the railroad, closing it completely until work parties repaired it.[71]

The quartermasters at White House ran the cars forward as soon as they were loaded, so the trains were passing almost continuously over the tracks, which were not holding up under the tremendous strain of well over 600 tons per day. The appointed civilian superintendent of the railroad, C. S. McAlpine, could not find enough laborers and supervisors to maintain and repair the tracks, which, in the continued wet weather and under the strain of heavy traffic, deteriorated dangerously.[72] McAlpine repeatedly asked Col. D. C. McCallum, director of the U. S. Military Railroads with offices in Baltimore, for more men—both trainmen and laborers—to keep the track in trim. McAlpine could not maintain the army's lifeline without laborers and experienced men to run the trains, and he had not enough of either. Sawtelle told Meigs that every day, more employees fell ill and that many of them had to be sent home. "It is impossible to get for them medical attendance here," he wrote, "as there are not half surgeons enough here to attend the wounded."[73] McAlpine feared "a general stampede" of his workers if the war department did not take steps to assist him in his troubles. "Our railroad has become inefficient for want of men," he wrote, "I have sent home 15 to 20 sick. I have as many here off duty from sickness-my well men are

---

this phase of the campaign, and the two armies had fought the Battle of Seven Pines just a few days earlier.

[71] *OR* 11, pt. 1, p. 163.

[72] C. S. McAlpine to D. C. McCallum, June 4, 1862, from White House Landing, Va., Office of the Quartermaster General, Consolidated Correspondence File. RG 92, NA, Box 1236, entry 225, "White House, Va." See also Van Vliet's remarks on the condition of the railroad *OR* 11, pt. 1, p. 159.

[73] Sawtelle to Meigs, June 4, 1862, from White House Landing, Va., Office of the Quartermaster General, Consolidated Correspondence File. RG 92, NA, Box 1236, entry 225, "White House, Va." C.S. McAlpine echoed this request to McCallum, stating that his railroad men "get no attendance whatever from the Army Surgeons, who have their hands full with the unusual numbers of sick + wounded." C. S. McAlpine to D. C. McCallum, June 4, 1862, from White House Landing, Va., Ibid.

becoming frightened and leaving me. . . ."[74] Sawtelle asked Meigs to send 400 laborers from Philadelphia "so that we shall soon be able to fulfill the requirements of the Dept., not only here [White House Landing], but at the several Stations on the Rail-road to Richmond, where it is now necessary to use details of soldiers for unloading cars +c."[75] Sawtelle summed up by flatly declaring that the road was "entirely inadequate for properly supplying the Army of the Potomac now before Richmond, for the want of a sufficient number of experienced Rail-road men."[76]

So as the railroad at first seemed the solution to McClellan's supply problems, its use brought the commander additional problems. On June 9, three weeks after opening the White House line, Van Vliet reported that most of the army's supplies were still transported by wagon.[77] "It now requires every means of transportation we possess," he told Meigs, "both rail and wagon, to keep the army supplied with forage and subsistence."[78]

The quartermasters found it especially difficult to move the required amounts of forage each day. The army's 17,000 horses and 8,000 mules consumed 313 tons of fodder each day, more than half of the army's daily supply intake, and Ingalls could not always get the forage to where it was needed. Early in June, a forage shortage seems to have threatened operations. Captain George Dandy of the quartermaster department served as a distribution officer at the forward depots on the railroad. On June 8, he reported that he did not have enough forage for the troops in his vicinity and could find none nearby. Two days later, the shortage

---

[74] Ibid.

[75] Sawtelle to Meigs, June 4, 1862, from White House Landing, Va., Office of the Quartermaster General, Consolidated Correspondence File. RG 92, NA, Box 1236, entry 225, "White House, Va."

[76] Ibid.

[77] OR 11, pt. 1, p. 164.

[78] Ibid., p. 159. On June 10, Maj. Gen. Ambrose E. Burnside visited McClellan's headquarters and was amazed at the state of the roads. "I was four and a half hours traveling nine miles," he informed the secretary of war. "It is impossible to move artillery whilst they [the roads] are so bad. But for the railroad the army could not be subsisted and foraged." Ibid., pt. 3, p. 224.

seems to have been acute as Van Vliet himself wired Ingalls, "Will there be any forage at Forage Station today—some teams have been there twenty-four hours waiting—the forage is absolutely necessary."[79] Captain J. Howard Kitching of Battery B, 2nd New York Artillery, took matters into his own hands. He borrowed 10 or 12 of the brigade's forage wagons and took them in search of more food for his battery horses. On the banks of the Chickahominy, he found clover "in great abundance" and he set the men of his battery to work. The artillerists mowed and gathered—under intermittent fire from Confederates across the river.[80]

While the animals of the army might have suffered occasional food shortages, they apparently did not complain. The men of the army were not so patient. Throughout history, soldiers have grumbled about their food, and the men of the Army of the Potomac on the Peninsula were no exception. "The soldier lived poorly," recalled one Federal officer after the war, "having no way to add to the insufficient rations, which were furnished quite irregularly."[81] A Pennsylvanian in the V Corps echoed this complaint: "We usually have plenty of coffee and sugar," he wrote home, "when we can get our rations."[82] An artilleryman with the VI Corps thought that the management of the supply operation, "seemed susceptable of a good deal of improvement, both in respect to preserving in good wholesome condition the bread and meat, and in regularly distributing it a necessary intervals." He especially lamented the loss of packages from home containing "preserved fruit, salt fish, cakes, cheese, sometimes tobacco. . .perhaps stockings and underwear," which would arrive with the contents turned rancid during long delays in transport.[83]

[79] Scrapbook, Army of the Potomac Letters and Telegrams sent, May-June 1862, RG 393, NA, pt. 1, entry 3977, book 6 of 7, vol 37/38.

[80] John B. Kitching, *Memorials of Col. J. Howard Kitching* (New York, 1873), p. 69.

[81] Regis De Trobriand, *Four Years in the Army of the Potomac*, translated by George K. Dauchy (Boston, 1889), p. 216.

[82] Oliver W. Norton *Army Letters, 1861-1865* (Chicago, 1903), p. 98.

[83] A.J. Bennet, *The Story of the First Massachusetts Light Battery* (Boston, 1886), p. 41-42.

Officers explained the irregular issue of rations by stating that the transportation operation from the depots was still incomplete, but one New York colonel thought that "the quartermasters are incompetent." A cavalryman thought the quartermasters were guilty of "negligence of duty, incapacity, indulgence [and] actual villainy."[84]

The complaints aside, and despite the transportation problems, the army seems not to have suffered any serious shortage of food. Whatever deficiencies the men of the Army of the Potomac suffered with regard to food seem to have sprung from the composition of the ration rather than the amount.

The greatest and most significant shortage seems to have been in vegetables. At the end of June, one Maine infantryman recalled, he and his comrades were desperate "for something green." Their craving was "fierce," the New Englander explained, "for scarcely any of us had tasted even a potato for weeks."[85] The quartermasters had difficulty enough keeping the army supplied with imperishables without worrying about fresh foods subject to spoilage in the summer heat. Captain George L. Thorndike, commissary of subsistence for Brig. Gen. Winfield S. Hancock's brigade in the VI Corps, reported in mid-June that he could not obtain enough tea, flour, pork or bacon to ration the brigade. Furthermore, when he tried to draw vegetables for the brigade, the commissary officer at the forward depot, Savage's Station, only allowed him five barrels of potatoes, two of which Thorndike refused because they had spoiled.[86]

A predictable result of the poor diet, bad water and disagreeable climate was widespread sickness. A Pennsylvanian wrote in July that "Hundreds of our soldiers have not seen a day in six months when they

---

[84] De Trobriand, *Four Years in the Army of the Potomac,* p. 216; Capt. John Weidman, 4th Pennsylvania Cavalry in *Lebanon Advertiser* August 6, 1862.

[85] Thomas W. Hyde, *Following the Greek Cross* (Boston, 1894), pp. 77, 78.

[86] Thorndike to John Hancock, June 16, 1862, U. S. Army Continental Commands 1821-1920, Army of the Potomac, 1861-1865, Letters received, 1862, RG 393, NA, Box S-Z. John Hancock was assistant adjutant general of the first brigade, commanded by his older brother, Winfield S. Hancock.

were what I should consider well."[87] Brigadier General Daniel E. Sickles reported in mid June that of the 4,280 men in his brigade that landed on the Peninsula less than three months earlier, fewer than 1,800 were fit for duty. Although Sickles' Excelsior Brigade had lost some men to combat, the vast majority of the men out of the ranks were felled by illness. "Daily," he reported to headquarters, "between three and four hundred men are reported by the [regimental] surgeons as incapable of service, while nearly as many more . . .are really unfit for active duty."[88] Of the 29,511 men absent from the ranks according to McClellan's return for June 20, more than 25,000 were on the sick list with their regiments or recuperating in hospitals or at their homes. Dr. Jonathan Letterman, who on July 1 assumed the duties of medical director of the Army of the Potomac, specifically mentioned the deficiency of vegetables in the army's diet as a reason for the great sickness. After examining the sick lists of the army, he estimated that an astounding 20 percent of the army was ill and unfit for duty.[89] As the sick lists lengthened, McClellan not only lost combat power, but Van Vliet felt even greater strain on his transportation. "Each train that takes out stores," reported Sawtelle from White House, "returns loaded to its utmost capacity with sick, wounded, + prisoners. . . ."[90] McAlpine estimated at one point the number of sick and wounded incoming from the front at 300 per train.[91]

[87] Oliver W. Norton *Army Letters, 1861-1865* (Chicago, 1903), p. 97.

[88] Sickles to Chauncy McKeever, June 18, 1862, Army of the Potomac Letters Received, 1862, RG 393, NA, box 7. Dr. J.T. Calhoun of the 74th New York specifically cited the lack of vegetables among the men as one of the factors contributing to illness. See Calhoun's letter dated June 16, 1862, included in Sickles' report.

[89] Paris, *Civil War in America*, 2, p. 76. *OR* 11, pt. 3, p. 238. McClellan reported 115,102 men present for duty on June 20; Jonathan Letterman *Medical Recollections of the Army of the Potomac* (New York, 1866), p. 7-8. McClellan reported on July 14 that 16,619 men were on the sick list. Four days earlier he had reported an aggregate present strength of 117,714. Sears, *Papers of George B. McClellan*, p. 357. *OR* 11, pt. 3, p. 321.

[90] Sawtelle to Meigs, June 4, 1862, dated White House Landing, Office of the Quartermaster General, Consolidated Correspondence File. RG 92, NA, Box 1236, entry 225, "White House, Va."

[91] McAlpine made this estimate immediately after the Battle of Seven Pines, so presumably a higher number of wounded rode the trains to White House at this time than had in May and later in June. McAlpine to McCallum, June 4, 1862, dated White House Landing. Ibid.

The trains running to and from White House were never empty, so wear and tear on the road was unremitting. The constant toil of keeping the trains moving to and from the front was also wearing down the ever-shrinking labor force available to the quartermasters. "All the employees of our department," Sawtelle told the quartermaster general, "are being worked continuously, night and day, not only at the legitimate duties of the Dept., receiving and forwarding supplies, but in assisting in caring for the sick and wounded; as the combined force of the Hospital Department and the Sanitary Commission is not nearly sufficient to properly take care of them."[92]

By mid-June, McClellan's supply operation was groaning under almost unbearable burdens.[93] The quartermasters struggled to move the 600 tons of food and supplies needed each day by the army. The large numbers of sick men placed additional strain on the already overburdened transportation. And, finally, rain turned the already inadequate roads to mud, exacerbating all other transportation problems. Van Vliet and his men would have enjoyed a much greater prospect of success had the army been smaller or more healthy or had the roads been drier and firmer, but with these circumstances conspiring against them rather than for them, the quartermasters were all but overwhelmed.

The story of Federal logistics on the Peninsula offers an excellent illustration of the role of mobility and transportation in protracted campaigns. A logistician's failure to surmount problems of transportation,

---

[92] Sawtelle to Meigs, June 4, 1862, dated White House Landing, Ibid. The U. S. Sanitary Commission was a privately funded and operated organization of volunteer doctors, nurses and hospital attendants who traveled with the armies to assist in caring for the sick and wounded. The Commission's performance on the Peninsula, its first campaign, was excellent. The army's medical department was unprepared for the deluge of sick and wounded soldiers that flooded field hospitals on the Peninsula. Through the Commission's efforts, thousands of soldiers, Federal and Confederate, received medical care the army hospitals were unable to give.

[93] Major Henry G. Sharpe, a commissary officer in the post-war army, suggests an interesting principle of supply with important implications about both the size of the depot at White House and the extent of the strain on the first, or waterborne, leg of McClellan's line of communication. Sharpe quotes German military theorist Field Marshal Count Kolmar von der Goltz (1843-1916), as stating that supply officers must leave much room for error in their calculations. Because of spoilage and the fortunes of war, "Two and three times as much as an army needs must be supplied, if it is to be kept from want; double and treble in respect to the good quality of the provisions, double and treble of the quantity," quoted in "The Art of Supplying Armies," p. 57.

even for a few days, can initiate a downward spiral in which unsolved problems compound upon each other, multiplying the difficulties to be overcome. By the third week in June, when Robert E. Lee launched a preemptive attack, McClellan's quartermasters had made significant progress toward improving the efficiency of their operation, but they had not yet vanquished their mobility troubles. As Van Vliet mused in one report to Meigs, "The difficulties of supplying an army of 100,000 men are not generally comprehended."[94]

Part 3: Evaluations

McClellan's fight to keep his army fed and equipped on the Peninsula had no clear winner. The campaign did not founder because of logistical difficulties, but the strength of McClellan's supply link was tenuous in May and June 1862, and the problems of supplying the army severely taxed the abilities and resources of the quartermasters. Who was to blame for these extraordinary difficulties? Did the army's transportation troubles derive from the unprecedented nature of McClellan's campaign, from sub-par performance in the field, or from circumstances beyond anyone's control?

It is difficult to fault the quartermasters. In his report of the campaign, Rufus Ingalls wrote that the logistical operations on the Peninsula ". . .had scarcely any parallel in history, certainly no precedent in our country."[95] He was probably correct. Larger armies had swept across the world's battlefields, but considering the constraints against which the Federal supply officers struggled, the Peninsula Campaign, from a logistical standpoint, may have been without precedent.

In referring to the vast European armies of the 18th century, Martin van Creveld, author of a landmark study of military logistics, wrote of a hypothetical situation:

---

[94] *OR* 11, pt. 1, p. 159.

[95] Ibid., p. 165.

> Had an army of, say, 100,000 men, wanted to bring up all its
> supplies for the duration of the campaign-usually calculated
> as 180 days-from base, the resulting burden on the transporta-
> tion system would have been so great as to make all warfare
> utterly impossible. . . .To even imagine that the huge quanti-
> ties of fodder that were required by the 60,000 horses which
> accompanied such a force could ever be brought up from
> base borders on the ridiculous.[96]

Yet McClellan did so imagine. Certainly van Crevald's judgment is
not perfectly applicable to McClellan's circumstance on the Peninsula.
McClellan had fewer animals with him, for example, but more men.
The Army of the Potomac also had significant advantages in that it had
an ample number of good wagons, its front lines were only between 20
to 30 miles by road from its base, and it had the services of waterborne
transports and of a railroad.[97] There were, however, more than enough
mitigating factors to counterbalance these advantages. The daily ration
of McClellan's soldiers was larger and therefore heavier than those issued previously to soldiers in Europe.[98] The railroad was a small single-
track rural affair of limited capacity and demanded a large investment in
time, money and manpower to keep in running condition. Rainy
weather hindered all movement. Wounded from battles and large numbers of sick became an unexpectedly heavy burden that further hindered
the subsistence transportation. All things considered, McClellan's ad-

---

[96] van Creveld, *Supplying War*, p. 38.

[97] The advent of railroads in the 19th century revolutionized strategy and logistics, but perhaps
not to the degree one might think. No general could ever be *completely* dependent on a railroad for
his supplies, no matter how good the road. Quartermasters would still need wagons to move
matériel from forward depots on the railroad to the army's camps, so all the factors that restrict
wagon transportation would still inhibit a general's strategic and logistical freedom, except,
possibly, the distance the wagons had to move and the amount of time they would require to do it.
See Moore, "Mobility and Strategy in the Civil War," pp. 75-76.

[98] "By the recent increase of the army ration, which was previously larger than in any other
country, a considerable amount of transportation is employed in moving provisions and supplies
which are not necessary for the subsistence of the soldiers." General-in-Chief Henry W. Halleck,
November 1862. *OR* III, 2, p. 878.

vantages did not put him significantly ahead of van Creveld's hypothetical general.

Long before van Crevald declared against the wisdom of foraging an army from the rear, Gen. William T. Sherman affirmed that a general could not entirely supply his army from the rear. A seasoned campaigner noted for his attention to logistical detail, Sherman paused outside Savannah, Georgia, on Christmas Day 1864 to tell Quartermaster General Meigs that it was "a physical impossibility to supply an army with forage" and that "each army should provide itself with forage and a large portion of its grain."[99]

McClellan's quartermasters therefore had a tall task before them even before they encountered the serious problems unique to the Peninsula. Despite years of service in their department, nothing in their experience could have adequately prepared Van Vliet, Ingalls or Sawtelle for the difficulties of providing for a mobile city the size of the Army of the Potomac. McClellan's plan of campaign demanded of his quartermasters not only what probably had never been done, but what perhaps could not be done, yet the army before Richmond seems not to have suffered significant shortages of food or matériel. By these facts alone, the Federal logistical operation on the Peninsula must be declared a remarkable success. But the campaign failed, and the debate over the reasons for that failure still rages. McClellan cannot be faulted merely for asking his quartermasters to join him in attempting what had never been done. Officers in the Civil War learned their trade on the job and often those who dared great things achieved great successes. "It was," in the words of one staff officer at McClellan's headquarters on the Peninsula, "a war in which he who pushed and found out for himself, was the most likely to achieve results."[100] Still, a general can push the limits of

[99] W.T. Sherman to Meigs, December 25, 1864, Montgomery Cunningham Meigs Papers, Library of Congress Manuscript Division, Washington, D.C. My thanks to Prof. Carmen Grayson for sharing this letter with me. For insight on Sherman's attention to logistics, see James J. Cooke, "Feeding Sherman's Army: Union Logistics in the Campaign for Atlanta," in Theodore P. Savas and David A. Woodbury, eds., *The Campaign for Atlanta & Sherman's March to the Sea,* 2 vols. (Campbell, CA, 1992), vol. 1, pp. 83-98.

[100] Alexander S. Webb, *The Peninsula: McClellan's Campaign of 1862,* (NY, 1881), p. 52.

the possible only so far before he begins asking too much of his troops. Fairly determining what is "too much" is difficult for a general and even more difficult for an historian whose judgments are sometimes guided by hindsight. But with respect to McClellan's demands upon his quartermasters, the premises of his strategy speak as loudly as do the results of the campaign in suggesting that he asked too much.

McClellan and his contemporaries had developed their strategic ideas under the influence of the Swiss military theorist Baron Antoine de Henri Jomini. Jomini's strategic precepts advocated very large armies and "rapid and continuous marches" in enemy country. "A general who moves his masses rapidly and continually," Jomini wrote, "and gives them proper directions, may be confident of both gaining victories and of securing great results therefrom."[101] McClellan's plan of campaign as presented to Lincoln in February 1862 called for "A rapid movement" by his army of 140,000 men from Urbanna, Virginia, on the Rapahannock River to Richmond, which the general hoped to occupy before the Confederate army in central Virginia could offer opposition. McClellan was careful to point out that the plan was flexible—that if the army could not disembark at Urbanna, the movement would still succeed from Fort Monroe on the Peninsula, "altho' with less celerity & brilliancy of results. . . ." In this plan time was a crucial element in what amounted to a race for Richmond. McClellan explained to the president the importance of surprising the enemy and gaining an advantage by rapid maneuvers—". . .slow progress," he wrote, "will enable him to devine our purpose & take his measures accordingly."

In his letter to the president, McClellan did not reveal his plans for subsisting his army. In principle, McClellan's grand strategy provided for buying "supplies" from the Southern citizens, but in fact, he could not have hoped to gather any significant amount of forage in the early

---

[101] Antoine Henri de Jomini, *The Art of War* (London and Novato, CA, 1992), p. 176.

spring on the Peninsula.[102] McClellan intended to carry his subsistance with him, a plan Jomini would likely have viewed with apprehension. The Baron wrote only briefly of the relationship between commissariat transportation and strategy for an invading army, declaring that "the problem of supporting a numerous army in an enemy's country is a very difficult one." He made plain that to move a large army rapidly a general would have to make "all the resources of the invaded country contribute to the success of his enterprises. . . ." but acknowledged that in "thinly-settled and unproductive regions" armies would need to carry their provisions. This caveat rested on the premise that the commanding general would be seeking to make "rapid and continuous" marches and remain ever mindful that idleness and the passage of time (as in siege warfare, for example) increased the difficulty of his supply operation.[103] For McClellan's plan to succeed, therefore, his army would have to keep moving to conclude the campaign quickly and the army's supply operation would have to function smoothly so as not to hinder the army's progress. If McClellan recognized this, he should have been especially reluctant to settle down for a protracted stay, yet he lay siege to Yorktown, consumed 20 days to march his army 65 miles, then settled down once again to a "siege" in which his front lines would scarcely move for more than a month.

McClellan's original plan was a logistical nightmare. It called for an enormous army—an army three-and-a-half times larger than the entire American invasion force in Mexico, three-and-a-half times larger than the force Irvin McDowell had led the previous summer at First Manassas and seven to eight times larger than any McClellan had ever led in the field. The men that composed this army were not veterans but volunteers inexperienced in campaigning, most of whom had spent a

---

[102] McClellan to Lincoln, August 2, 1861, in Stephen W. Sears, ed., *The Civil War Papers of George B. McClellan* (New York, 1989), p. 75. McClellan's ultra-conservative requisition ideology ran counter at least in spirit to Jomini's ideas of practially subsisting an army in the field. The Baron did not advocate plunder, but cited Napoleon and Caesar as having lived at the expense of the countries they invaded. Jomini suggested that generals charge local citizens with gathering and transporting subsistance to the army's camps. Jomini, *The Art of War*, p. 141, 142-143.

[103] Jomini, *The Art of War, pp. 141-146.*

quiet winter in camps around Washington. McClellan's plan called for them to make rapid marches through enemy country, about which he knew little. He further intended to supply his army during this difficult movement by bringing all rations and forage from the rear over one supply route. The components of McClellan's strategy therefore had great potential for working against each other rather than in concert. As Jomini pointed out, it was difficult enough to move a large army rapidly without encumbering it with large trains that would both slow the army's advance and become a liability—a tactical Achilles heel that would cost time and labor to maintain and require that troops be dispatched to protect it.

The greatest weakness in McClellan's strategy to take Richmond from the Tidewater lay in its disregard of time. Geographically, the large, sweeping movement around the enemy's strategic front to his flank and rear was a well conceived alternative to a frontal assault at Manassas, but that fact alone does not make the plan good strategy. Strategy in the military sense is a plan by which to move troops in time and space, and a sound strategy successfully balances these two dimensions. Neither dimension has any significance independent of the other. A commander cannot chart his army's movements as on a chessboard with disregard for the time needed to make such movements or in ignorance of the truth that the enemy is moving against him at the same time. McClellan recognized this in theory and intended for his troops to move rapidly. He thought about how he could make time work in his favor and devised a strategy in which he expected time to be his ally. He does not seem to have carefully considered the myriad ways that time might work against him, however, and one must wonder how far his appreciation of the element of time in strategy extended beyond the theoretical into the practical. Was he sincere, for example, when he estimated for Lincoln that his enormous army of 140,000 inexperienced soldiers and their attendant animals and equipment would cover the nearly 60 miles from Urbanna to Richmond in three marches, crossing three large rivers en route while establishing a supply depot and a line of communications? Time was of the essence, but McClellan seems to have been unconcerned about or unaware of the time-devouring logistical complexities that could hinder his movements.

Karl von Clausewitz, the Prussian military theorist who has influenced generations of strategists, suggested that to be successful, a general must be experienced. "The good general," he wrote, "must know friction in order to overcome it whenever possible, and in order not to expect a standard of achievement in his operations which this very friction makes impossible."[104] In stating this principle, Clausewitz is offering a military corollary of "Murphy's Law"—what can go wrong, will go wrong. A general must first understand that his army will encounter obstacles and that his plans will not unfold smoothly. The larger the operation and the more complex the plans, the more opportunity and therefore the greater likelihood that things will not go as hoped. This "friction" is capable of slowing progress or even stopping an army altogether. Though the commander or his lieutenants may resolve the problems and overcome the friction, such efforts demand much labor and time, the loss of which affects the commander's strategy.

George McClellan was 35 years old when he took his army to the Peninsula. He was widely respected in the army for his intelligence, but he had very little experience in commanding field armies. In western Virginia in the summer of 1861, he led about 20,000 men. This constitutes the sum total of his experience in leading armies in the field. The officers with which "Little Mac" surrounded himself at headquarters were generally excellent at what they did, but none of them had ever belonged to, let alone provided for the functioning of, an army of 115,000 men. Nothing in McClellan's personal military experience could have informed him of the succession of problems inherent in sustaining a huge army and trying to wield it as a weapon at the same time. Because of his inexperience in conducting field operations—especially involving an army of 115,000—McClellan could not "know friction." He could not envision what could go wrong and keep him from his objective. His inexperience may have manifested itself most notably in just the way Clausewitz warned against: The general simply did not

---

[104] Karl von Clausewitz, *On War*, edited and translated by Michael Howard and Peter Paret (Princeton, NJ, 1976), p. 120.

know enough to not expect a standard of achievement from his quarter-masters that might have been impossible to attain due to "friction."

It is little wonder that the Army of the Potomac's supply operation staggered under McClellan's demands. Yet the force was *smaller* than he desired. The war department had withheld more than 50,000 of the troops he had expected to take with him, and only reinforced the Army of the Potomac piecemeal. Throughout the campaign, McClellan repeatedly asked for more troops. His army grew, but slowly. Defenders of McClellan's strategy argue that the reductions and the slow reinforcement prevented the general from implementing his strategy.

In light of the logistical realities of the campaign, there is little logic in these arguments. The roads could only bear so much traffic, and the quartermasters struggled to feed and supply even the men McClellan had with him. It would seem more logical to suggest that McClellan could not carry through with his plan of rapid movements not because he had too few men with him but because he had too many. McClellan, therefore, might have been *fortunate* that the war department denied him all the troops he wished for at the outset of the campaign and only sent them to him at intervals. Far from defeating him on the Peninsula as McClellan claimed, the Lincoln administration might have unwittingly assisted the general in a way neither understood. And the apparently extraordinary amount of rain that fell on the Peninsula that spring is likewise unsatisfactory in explaining away McClellan's failure. The precipitation certainly exacerbated the transportation problem, but did not by itself create that problem. The Peninsula's byways deteriorated into impassiblility not solely because of the rain but because of the combination of rain and heavy traffic. Regardless of the rain the Army of the Potomac would still have had to contend with narrow, unsurfaced thoroughfares, and it is unlikely that increasing the traffic, as McClellan wished Washington would via reinforcement, would have resulted in any significant improvement in the state of the roads.[105]

[105] Van Vliet, in fact, blamed his transportation problems on rainwater. To do otherwise would be to make himself appear incapable or inefficient. *OR* 11, pt. 1, pp. 159, 164.

After the war, McClellan succeded in changing the focus of the debate over his army's defeat on the Peninsula. He deflected criticism from his strategy and conduct of the campaign by concentrating public scrutiny on the actions of the Lincoln administration. Historians have since shifted the public's gaze back to the general, but have considered the failure of the campaign mainly as a function of what many of them perceive to be McClellan's flawed personality. Washington certainly altered McClellan's plans, and the Army of the Potomac did suffer from physical realities beyond anyone's control, but the greater problem for McClellan was probably not that he had too few men to take Richmond but that he had too many men than could be fed, supplied and given medical care on the Virginia Peninsula in the wet spring of 1862. Even with exceptional efforts by his quartermasters, the long line of steamers, railroad cars and wagons was barely sufficient to feed and supply his army. Though his supply officers acquired the necessary food and equipment and the quartermasters kept the matériel moving forward to the army and the engineers and pioneers built and maintained the infrastructure needed to sustain the army, the whole process took longer than McClellan could have dreamed and far longer than he had allowed for in his plan of campaign. The time McClellan lost in fighting the battle in his rear might have been just the time the Confederates needed to save their capital.

Could McClellan's plan of leading a huge army to outmaneuver and overwhelm the Confederates have worked in another time and place? Someplace with broader, better-drained roads? Someplace with fewer malarial mosquitoes? Someplace with less rain? Some time when requisition policies were more liberal, as they were later in the war? Someplace where a less aggressive enemy would have allowed him more time? We cannot know. All we can know for sure is that McClellan was not defeated solely by the machinations of the Lincoln administration or by the audacity of Robert E. Lee. McClellan devised a strategy for an operation unprecedented in size and complexity, yet, because of his inexperience, he could not begin to understand the operational difficulties such a movement would entail. How much McClellan's failure to know friction contributed to the failure of the campaign is difficult to determine but his struggle to keep his army fed and supplied in no way helped him. Had McClellan's logisticians performed less exceptionally, or had the Lincoln administration left McClellan alone to carry out the program he designed, the general's strategy might have sooner died the early and disastrous death it probably deserved.

* * *

Portraits of McClellan's
Chief Supply Officers on the Peninsula

Born July 21, 1815 at Ferrisburg, Vermont, blue-eyed **Stewart Van Vliet** (pronounced Van Vleet) was graduated from the U. S. Military Academy in 1840 with a remarkable record of deportment. By accumulating just 10 demerits in four years, all of them as a plebe, he rose to stand ninth in his class, above his friend and roommate George H. Thomas and Virginian Richard Ewell. Of "Van's" circle of cronies at the academy, only his closest friend bested him in class rank: William Tecumseh Sherman.[106]

After a semester at West Point as professor of mathematics, Van Vliet served in the Seminole War in Florida. He commanded a company of the 3rd Artillery in Mexico, then was appointed regimental quartermaster. He never left the quartermaster corps and served all across the plains, in the Mormon Expedition, and from Oregon to Texas to New York before being appointed the chief quartermaster for the Army of the Potomac in August 1861.[107] In September 1861, the war de-

---

[106] Sherman, Thomas and Van Vliet roomed together as plebes. *Thirty-second Annual Reunion of the Association of the Graduates of the United States Military Academy at West Point, New York* (West Point, 1901), p. 189.

[107] George W. Cullum, *Biographical Register of the Officers and Graduates of the U. S. Military Academy*, 2 vols. (New York, 1868), vol. 1, pp. 30-31.

partment appointed Van Vliet brigadier general of volunteers, but the Senate never confirmed the appointment.

The white-haired Van Vliet arrived on the Peninsula with as strong a resumé as any man in the quartermaster department.[108] He managed the logistics of the campaign well, but was apparently unhappy in his work. On July 10, McClellan relieved the quartermaster at his own request, and Van Vliet reverted to his regular rank of major.[109] The commanding general "cheerfully" acknowledged "the valuable services rendered by General Van Vliet in the organization and administration of his department,"[110] but there was no love lost between the two men. The quartermaster would later openly support Lincoln in the election of 1864, earning the displeasure of "Little Mac" and his camp. In March 1865, Van Vliet attended a St. Patrick's Day dinner in New York, and a newspaper later reported that he had publicly praised his former commander. Van Vliet quickly wrote to General Meigs in Washington to deny he had done so: "The fact is that McClellanites + myself are not on the best of terms, owing to the course I pursued at the Presidential election."[111]

Van Vliet and his old classmate Sherman remained close throughout their lives, and in their old age lived near one another in New York City, where they regularly accompanied each other to society dinners. Van Vliet's affable nature made him a favorite of the social set. One columnist in Washington wrote: "As he passes down the avenue on his daily stroll, more hats are lifted and more ladies smile in recognition to him than

---

[108] George Alfred Townsend, *Campaigns of a Non-combatant* (New York, 1866), p. 97.

[109] Cullum, *Biographical Register*, 1, pp. 30-31.

[110] *OR* 11, pt. 3, pp. 312-313.

[111] Van Vliet to Meigs, March 20, 1865, from New York, Office of the Quartermaster General Consolidated Correspondence, 1794-1915, Record Group 92, NA.

any other man in this Capital. If there is a grand dinner given, official or private, Gen. Van Vliet's name is sure to be reported among the guests, and as for a stag dinner at Chamberlin's or Welker's, it would simply be incomplete without his participation."[112] Van Vliet died in Washington March 28, 1901.

Stewart Van Vliet

[112] *National Tribune*, April 18, 1889. See also *National Tribune*, February 2, 1893.

Born August 23, 1819 at Denmark, Maine, **Rufus Ingalls** was an 1843 graduate of the U. S. Military Academy, standing 11 places below classmate and one-time roommate Ulysses S. Grant. The two men later served together in Oregon, sharing a rented house, and they remained close friends.[113] Ingalls served in the cavalry in Mexico, after which he entered the quartermaster department, where he displayed rare talent. McClellan appointed him chief quartermaster of the Army of the Potomac on July 10, 1862, by the same order that relieved Van Vliet of that post.[114] Ingalls served with the eastern army throughout most of the war, assuming more responsibility and displaying greater capacity with each passing campaign. One colleague wrote: "He loved the Army of the Potomac; he knew its strength and its weakness; its great possibilities and the tremendous difficulties under which it labored."[115] He became quartermaster general of the U. S. Army in 1882, but retired the following year. He died in New York January 15, 1893.

[113] *Twenty-fourth Annual Reunion of the Association of the Graduates of the United States Military Academy at West Point, New York* (West Point, 1893), p. 82.

[114] *OR* 11, pt. 3, p. 313.

[115] *Twenty-fourth Annual Reunion of the Association of the Graduates of the United States Military Academy at West Point, New York* (West Point 1893), p. 85.

Rufus Ingalls

Library of Congress

Charles Greene Sawtelle, born May 10, 1834 in Norridge-wock, Maine, attended prestigious Phillips Academy near Boston before entering the U. S. Military Academy. Four years later, just past his 20th birthday, he was graduated with the class of 1854, standing 38th of 46.[116] After service on the plains and in California, he began the war as a first lieutenant and regimental quartermaster for the 6th U. S. Infantry, but was promoted to captain and moved to the quartermaster general's office with responsibility for administering the important depot at Perryville, Maryland.

For Captain Sawtelle, the abandonment of White House Landing on June 28, 1862, ended a period marked by great labor and responsibility, during which he had performed extremely well. On July 9 from Harrison's Landing, Ingalls sent a telegram to Quartermaster General Meigs specifically to commend Sawtelle. He wrote that during the evacuation of White House, "as well as on all occasions I have received very efficient aid from Capt. C. G. Sawtelle. . . .I know of no officer here who has more zeal energy and sound judgment in business affairs."[117]

Sawtelle performed distinguished service during the war. He rose to lieutenant colonel and served successively as chief quartermaster for the II Corps, for the Cavalry Corps of the

---

[116] Sawtelle excelled in drawing, ranking third in his class in that discipline and forming a strong friendship with another cadet who would become one of America's great artists, James Whistler. Sawtelle's classmates included B. F. "Grimes" Davis, Stephen Weed, W. D. Pender, S. D. Lee, Jeb Stuart, John Pegram, O. O. Howard, Henry L. Abbott, and G. W. Custis Lee, all of whom stood ahead of him at graduation. Cullum, *Biographical Register*, 2, pp. 387-88; *Forty-fourth Annual Reunion of the Association of the Graduates of the United States Military Academy at West Point, New York* (West Point, 1913, p. 76-77.

[117] Ingalls to Meigs, July 9, 1862, Office of the Quartermaster General, Letters Received, 1862, RG 92, NA, book 49, G-M. Meigs' endorsement on the reverse of this telegram, like most writing from that estimable officer's hand, is virtually illegible. What fragments can be deciphered, however, indicate that Meigs had a copy of Ingalls' telegram sent to Sawtelle with a cover note thanking him "in the name of the department for efficient & valuable services. . . ."

Army of the Potomac, for the Cavalry Bureau in Washington, and the Department of the Gulf. In March 1865, he was breveted brigadier general.[118] In 1896 he reached the pinnacle of the department to which he had devoted his life's work when he was appointed quartermaster general of the U. S.

National Archives

Charles Greene Sawtelle

---

[118] Roger D. Hunt and Jack R. Brown, *Brevet Brigadier Generals in Blue* (Gaithersburg, MD, 1990) p. 535.

Army. He would fill the post for less than a year, however, retiring as a brigadier general at his own request and ending more than 40 years of superior service. He died January 4, 1913.

Pennsylvanian **Henry Francis Clarke** was born November 9, 1820, and entered the U. S. Military Academy in 1839. According to one contemporary familiar with the academy and Clarke, the class of 1843 was among the less distinguished to pass through the hallowed halls on the Hudson. "The class. . .embraced, as all classes do, both clever men and studious men, but as a general thing its cleverest men were not studious, and many of the studious were not the cleverest." The class as a whole scored low in scholarship and even lower in conduct; less than half of those who began in 1839 lasted to graduation in 1843. The class had a reputation at the Point of being especially fond of the legendary off-campus saloon of Mr. Benny Haven.[119] "Ruddy" Clarke finished 12th in his class of 39, ahead of U. S. Grant and Rufus Ingalls. "He was a universal favorite," wrote a colleague, "not only with his class but with the whole corps of cadets and with officers and professors. . . .It is not believed he ever had an enemy."[120]

Clarke served in the 2nd U. S. Artillery in Mexico, where he was wounded and breveted. After teaching artillery and mathematics at West Point, he participated in the campaign against the Seminoles in 1851-1852. Clarke entered the subsistence department in 1857 and was chief commissary in the

---

[119] *Eighteenth Annual Reunion of the Association of the Graduates of the United States Military Academy at West Point, New York* (West Point, 1887), p. 71.

[120] Ibid., p. 72.

Mormon Expedition that year, cooperating with quartermaster Stewart Van Vliet. He was 41 when McClellan took him to the Peninsula as the Army of the Potomac's chief commissary of subsistence.[121] Clarke was also a newly married man, having married Belle Taylor just a year before, daughter of his boss, Commissary General Joseph P. Taylor. Clarke remained as chief commissary for the Potomac army until the spring of 1864, outlasting three commanding officers. He moved to the commissary post in New York at his own request just before Grant began his Overland Campaign. After the war he served in the commissary department in a number of cities, was Lt. Gen. Philip Sheridan's chief commissary in the Division of the Missouri and filled the same post for Maj. Gen. Winfield S. Hancock at Governor's Island, New York.

Clarke was highly regarded in the army both personally and professionally. Of his work on the Peninsula, McClellan wrote, "I am quite within bounds when I say that no one could have performed his vitally important duties more satisfactorily than did General Clarke. He never caused me the slightest anxiety. . .he would always carry out my wishes were it in the power of a man to do so. A stranger to all petty intrigue, a brave and able officer, a modest man, intent only upon the proper performance of his duty, he has never received the reward and appreciation his valuable services merit."[122]

---

[121] Cullum, *Biographical Register*, 1, 165-166; Roger D. Hunt and Jack R. Brown, *Brevet Brigadier Generals in Blue* (Gaithersburg, MD, 1990) p. 114.

[122] *Eighteenth Annual Reunion of the Association of the Graduates of the United States Military Academy at West Point, New York* (West Point, 1887), p. 75.

Brevet Brigadier Generals in Blue

Henry Francis Clarke

Charles P. Kingsbury

Charles P. Kingsbury was another of the accomplished men with which McClellan surrounded himself at headquarters. Born near Albany, New York in 1818, Kingsbury was raised by an uncle in North Carolina. He left an outstanding record at West Point, so excelling at French that he served as an assistant professor while still a cadet. Graduated second in his class (ahead of W. T. Sherman and Stewart Van Vliet), Kingsbury spent his entire career in the ordnance department. In the Mexican War, Kingsbury played a major role in organizing ordnance depots and a transportation system to supply the American columns, and served as General John Wool's chief of ordnance. Between the wars, he published *Elementary Treatise on Artillery and Infantry* and was offered a professorship in mathematics at Davidson College, North

Carolina. Remaining in the army, Kingsbury supervised operations at arsenals and foundries across the country, serving in Richmond, Virginia, until the spring of 1861. When Virginia passed its preliminary ordinance of secession, the Federal war department immediately ordered Kingsbury to Harpers Ferry to assume command of the crucial armory there. That General Winfield Scott issued such orders to a North Carolinian says a great deal about Kingsbury and his unquestioned loyalty to the Union. The secessionists moved on Harpers Ferry on the day of Kingsbury's arrival, denying him the opportunity to remove any of the arms and equipment. Captain Kingsbury took it upon himself to order the destruction of the manufactured weapons and the armory when Federal troops evacuated the town.

Kingsbury joined McClellan in the summer of 1861 in the western Virginia operations, and became the Army of the Potomac's first chief of ordnance later that year. Poor health forced him from the field after the Peninsula Campaign, and for the remainder of the war he supervised operations at various arsenals and foundries throughout the North. He was the driving spirit in the construction of the famous Rock Island Arsenal. He retired to Brooklyn, New York, and died there on Christmas Day, 1879.[123]

[123] Cullum, *Biographical Register* , 2, p. 25; *Eleventh Annual Reunion of the Association of the Graduates of the United States Military Academy at West Point, New York* (West Point, 1880), pp. 80-81, 83-88. Kingsbury's West Point obituary was written by his friend and fellow Brooklynite, Maj. Gen. Henry W. Slocum.

Peter S. Carmichael

Peter Carmichael is a Ph.D. candidate at the Pennsylvania State University. He is author of *The Purcell, Crenshaw and Letcher Artillery* (H. E. Howard, 1990), and *Lee's Young Artillerist: William R. J. Pegram* (University of Virginia Press, 1995).

"The Merits of this Officer Will Not Go Unrewarded":

William R. J. Pegram and the Purcell Artillery in the Seven Days Battles

The Seven Days Battles marked an important turning point in the war in Virginia. The armies fought these engagements tenaciously, producing long casualty lists and perhaps setting unnecessarily high standards for acceptable losses in later battles. But the battles also served as an intensive, week-long seminar in tactics.

One of the lessons of the Seven Days was the supremacy of artillery on the tactical defensive. Federal gunners consistently took advantage of the terrain to mass their pieces against poorly coordinated Confederate assaults. Southern artillerist Col. Stephen D. Lee complimented the Federals on their handling of artillery. "Their pieces were in an admirable position," he wrote in his official report of Malvern Hill, "and so arranged that they could concentrate from twenty to thirty guns on any position."[1]

---

[1] U.S. War Department, *The War of the Rebellion: The Official Records of the Union and Confederate Armies*, 128 vols. (Washington, D.C., 1890-1901), series I, vol. 11, pt 2, pp. 747. Hereinafter cited as *OR*. All references are to series I unless otherwise noted.

Conversely, Confederate failure to concentrate artillery undermined their offensive capabilities throughout the Seven Days. A pernicious organization of the army's artillery dispersed firepower by allotting one battery to a brigade, thereby preventing artillery officers from coordinating their efforts. In most cases a brigadier of infantry determined the placement of Confederate batteries, and rarely had these officers any training in the use of the "long arm." Referring to the performance of Southern gunners during the Seven Days, historian Jennings C. Wise concluded in his study of the Army of Northern Virginia's artillery that the "brigade distribution destroyed their power at the outset to cope with [Federal] masses."[2] Without a unified command structure, C.S.A.batteries could not adequately support infantry or provide effective counterbattery fire. The Battle of Malvern Hill epitomized the powerlessness of Confederate artillery in the Seven Days. Thirty-seven Federal cannon crowning a 150-foot hill quickly silenced Lee's scattered batteries, allowing McClellan's gunners to focus upon and destroy Confederate attackers in detail. The outspoken Maj. Gen. Daniel H. Hill considered the efforts of Confederate artillery at Malvern Hill "almost farcical."[3]

But if Gen. Robert E. Lee's artillery suffered from poor administrative doctrine, it didn't lack aggressive leadership.[4] Imbued with romantic notions of courage prevalent during the first two years of war, officers and privates eagerly sought combat as a test of manhood. Long casualty lists confirmed a unit with distinction. As Gerald F. Linderman persuasively argues in *Embattled Courage: The Experience of Combat in The American Civil War,* "courage had for Civil War soldiers a narrow, rigid, and powerful meaning: heroic action undertaken without fear."[5] Officers who disregarded their own safety and relied upon bold

---

[2] Jennings C. Wise, *The Long Arm of Lee, or the History of the Artillery of the Army of Northern Virginia,* 2 vols. (New York, 1959), vol. 1, p. 208.

[3] Wise, *Long Arm of Lee,* p. 231.

[4] Brigadier General William Nelson Pendleton's disappearance with the reserve artillery on the day of Malvern Hill is a notable exception.

[5] Gerald F. Linderman, *Embattled Courage: The Experience of Combat in The American Civil War* (New York, 1987), p. 17. For a further discussion of the concept of courage among Civil War

tactics earned the allegiance of the rank and file and their superiors' approbation.

Twenty-year-old Confederate William R. J. Pegram led his Purcell Battery according to the most extreme definition of courage during the Seven Days. The flawed Confederate artillery organizational system exposed Pegram's aggressive maneuvers to a destructive enemy fire at Mechanicsville, Gaines' Mill, and Malvern Hill. Opening the week with some 80 to 90 men, the Purcell Artillery lost at least 57 killed or wounded in the three engagements. No Confederate artillery company during the Seven Days sustained heavier losses.[6]

When the war began, few could have imagined that the shy, bespectacled young man from Richmond would emerge as one of the finer artillerists in the Virginia theater. Fearless and composed under fire, Pegram displayed the gifts of a natural leader. In four years he rose from sergeant to full colonel of artillery, an impressive achievement earned by sheer hard fighting. Renowned throughout the army for his eagerness to engage the enemy, Pegram sometimes elicited remarks from Lee's infantrymen such as "there's going to be fight, for here comes that damn little man with the 'specs.'"[7] Pegram's Purcell Artillery had been raised in Richmond. The unit saw limited action along the Potomac River and at First Manassas in 1861. The prospect of fighting near home must have pleased Pegram and his cannoneers when they were ordered to the capital of the Confederacy on May 24, 1862.[8]

---

soldiers, see chapter one of Linderman, *Embattled Courage*.

[6] "The Purcell Battery," The *Daily Richmond Examiner*, July 15, 1862, p. 1; *OR*, 11, pt. 2: 983; Peter S. Carmichael, *The Purcell, Crenshaw and Letcher Artillery* (Lynchburg, 1990), p. 41. According to The *Daily Richmond Examiner*, the Purcell lost 65 either killed or wounded. The Official Records show the battery's losses at 60, while the Compiled Service Records of the Purcell Battery at the National Archives place the company's casualties at 57.

[7] Jennings C. Wise, "The Boy Gunners of Lee," *Southern Historical Society Papers*, vol. 42, p. 156.

[8] On William R. J. Pegram, see James I. Robertson, Jr., "The Boy Artillerist," *The Virginia Magazine of History and Biography*, vol. 98, pp. 221-260; Charles L. Dufour, *Nine Men in Gray* (New York, 1963), pp. 160-196.

After a rain-filled march from Guinea Station, Pegram and his be-draggled men reached the northeastern outskirts of Richmond on May 31, in time to hear blasts of musketry resounding from the Seven Pines battlefield. Out of the confusion that enveloped the Southern army after Seven Pines emerged Robert E. Lee, who concentrated his forces around the defenses of the city and ordered the soldiers to strengthen their positions with picks and shovels.

Isolated north of the Chickahominy, the Union V Corps presented Lee with an offensive opportunity. He assembled Maj. Gen. Thomas J. "Stonewall" Jackson's Shenandoah Valley troops and Maj. Gen. A. P. Hill's division for a turning movement on June 26. Hill had orders to hold his Light Division in readiness to advance until Jackson's troops opened the fighting. Unfortunately for Hill, Jackson was unusually slow that day. As the sun drifted to the west, Hill grew anxious and strained his ears to catch the battle cry of the Valley troops.[9] By 3 p.m., Hill relinquished all hope of seeing Jackson's men. He impetuously directed Brig. Gen. Charles W. Field's brigade and the Purcell Artillery to lead the division's movement across the Chickahominy River.

Before the bugle sounded its distinctive call to the front, Pegram rode forward to face his battalion. In a clear voice, he recited the following lines to his cannoneers:

> To every man upon this earth
> Death cometh soon or late;
> And how can man die better
> Than facing fearful odds
> For the ashes of his fathers
> And the temples of his Gods?[10]

---

[9] On the Southern side of the Seven Days Campaign, see Stephen W. Sears, *To the Gates of Richmond: The Peninsula Campaign* (New York, 1992), Clifford Dowdey, *The Seven Days: The Emergence of Robert E. Lee* (New York: Fairfax Press, 1978), and Douglas S. Freeman, *Lee's Lieutenants: A Study in Command*, 3 vols (New York, 1934-1935), vol. 1, pp. 489-669.

[10] Editorial writer in the *Southern Churchman*; "Col. William Johnson Pegram," *Confederate Veteran* vol. 38, p. 113.

Photo courtesy of Mrs. Virginia B. Maloney.

William Ransom Johnson Pegram (1841-1865). A member of the Purcell Battery once wrote of Pegram, "What a man; what a soldier. . . .Amid the roar of his guns on the battle field he became a giant in voice and stature."

The drivers put their whips against the flanks of their horses "with a cheer." As the battery's caissons rumbled behind the Virginia infantrymen and the wheels of Pegram's six guns spun onto the Cold Harbor Road, a number of his artillerists joined in a chorus of "Maryland, My Maryland." After crossing the river and pushing through Mechanicsville, the battery ascended a steep hill that afforded some shelter from incoming Northern shells. Stubborn fighters of Brig. Gen. George A. McCall's Pennsylvania Reserves awaited the Confederates behind breastworks beyond Beaver Dam Creek. Pegram had told his men earlier in the day that there was no better way of dying than in front of "fearful odds," but he scarcely could have imagined the fight his battery prepared to enter.[11]

As the Purcell Artillery rolled forward behind the middle of their advancing brigade, Field's soldiers moved toward the center of the Federal position. Union artillery commanded their mile-long approach, ripping gaps in the advancing Confederate lines. Field thought it was the "most destructive cannonading I have yet known."[12] He knew that he must rush his men across the exposed plain and engage the Union infantry at close quarters; Federal artillerists would then have to focus their sights elsewhere or risk hitting their own troops. Advancing at the double quick, Field's regiments veered to the left, off the Cold Harbor Road, and plunged straight into the bogs around the creek. The musketry intensified to an awful crescendo. As the Virginia infantrymen surged forward, Field directed Pegram to unlimber his pieces and open fire. The artillerists wheeled their guns into position about three-quarters of a mile from the Federal entrenchments. A newspaper reported that "no sooner had they got into position in this field than it was evident the battery had been drawn into an ambuscade." While rifle balls buzzed over their heads like horse flies, the artillerists struggled to get off a few rounds. Aware that his battery could not withstand the weight of Union

---

[11] W. F. Fulton, "Picketing on the Potomac," *Confederate Veteran* vol. 32, p.428.

[12] *OR* 11, pt. 2, pp. 841.

ordnance, Pegram ordered his guns to the protection of a woodlot behind Field's brigade.[13]

For 30 minutes, Pegram sheltered his battery in the timber. After Brig. Gen. James J. Archer rushed his troops to the left of Field's brigade, Pegram ran his battery forward just south of the Old Cold Harbor Road. Although the Federal artillery had many targets, it must have seemed to Pegram and his men that every Union cannon across Beaver Dam Creek focused on them. Indeed, 22 Northern field pieces bombarded the Purcell Artillery.[14] As General William Dorsey Pender's Brigade passed to the right of Pegram's battery on its way to the front, the North Carolinian observed that Federal cannon played on the Virginia artillerists "with great effect."[15] Amid the destruction, Pegram sat "motionless in his saddle, no more concerned at the shells which were ploughing up the dust about him than if he had been lounging on the porch in Franklin Street."[16]

Francis W. Dawson, an Englishman who later served on Lt. Gen. James Longstreet's staff, informed his mother after the battle that he acted as a volunteer for "a very dear friend of mine, Capt. Willie Pegram." Early in the fight a shell fragment shredded Dawson's pant leg, "cutting a hole about 4 inches in length by 1 in. deep in the back of my leg." One of his comrades yelled out: "That Britisher has gone up at last." Like a number of injured men in the Purcell Artillery, Dawson refused to leave his post. He recovered his "senses," tied a handkerchief around the bloody wound, and returned to his position to find that "our battery. . .had to bear the weight of the fire from the Yankee guns, which

[13] "The Purcell Battery," The *Daily Richmond Examiner*, July 15, 1862, p. 1.

[14] Ibid. The *Enquirer* reported that 24 Federal guns concentrated their fire on the Purcell Battery, but the Federals had not that many guns available on the portion of their line opposite Pegram's Battery: Edwards' Battery (six guns), Kerns' Battery (one section, two guns), Smead's Battery (one section, two guns), Easton's Battery (four guns), DeHart's Battery (six guns), Cooper's Battery (one section, two guns).

[15] *OR* 11, pt. 2, p. 899.

[16] Francis W. Dawson, *Reminiscences of Confederate Service 1861-1865*, edited by Bell I. Wiley (Baton Rouge, 1980), p. 49. Franklin Street in Richmond begins on capitol hill and was home to many of the city's wealthy and powerful.

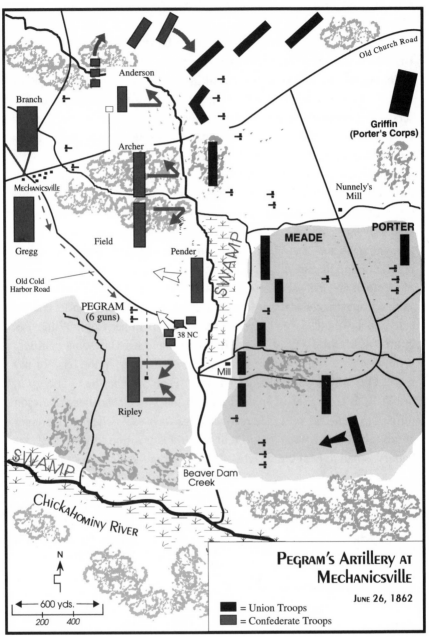

Old Church Road

Griffin
(Porter's Corps)

Branch

Anderson

Archer

Mechanicsville

Nunnely's
Mill

Gregg

Field

PORTER

MEADE

Pender

SWAMP

Old Cold
Harbor Road

PEGRAM
(6 guns)

38 NC

Mill

Ripley

SWAMP

Beaver Dam
Creek

Chickahominy River

N

600 yds.

200   400

**Pegram's Artillery at
Mechanicsville**

June 26, 1862

= Union Troops
= Confederate Troops

Theodore P. Savas

were so placed that they had a cross-fire upon us during the whole of the time."[17]

Enemy shells exacted a heavy toll among Pegram's cannoneers. Dawson recalled that "at each moment some poor fellow would fall, groaning, to the ground, there to lie for hours untended, and uncared for." "The carnage among our men was fearful," the *Daily Richmond Examiner* recorded, "but manfully and coolly they stood to their posts."[18] A single missile killed three horses and one man before tearing the leg and arm off another soldier. Pegram, Dawson, and two other men worked one gun "instead of the complement of ten."[19]

Pegram's stoic behavior undoubtedly steadied the nerves of his men during their first real taste of combat. Seemingly oblivious to the destruction of his command, Pegram refused to retire from the field. Only the benevolence of dusk saved his battery from total annihilation. Out of the 92 men who had galloped into action early in the day, 42 lay wounded, one mortally wounded, and three dead. Four of Pegram's six guns had been disabled during the fight and more than a dozen battery horses killed.[20] Dawson believed these shocking figures spoke an eloquent testament of the battery's courage.[21] An artillerist from another Richmond company scribbled in his diary that evening that the Purcell Battery had "won an enviable fame."[22]

Pegram bore some responsibility for his company's staggering casualties. While inflicting little damage to the enemy, he had needlessly exposed his gunners to the powerful Federal artillery. Most of the responsibility for this disaster, however, rests with the organization of

---

[17] Dawson, *Confederate Service*, pp. 185, 49.

[18] "The Purcell Battery," The *Daily Richmond Examiner*, July 15, 1862, p. 1.

[19] Dawson, *Confederate Service*, p. 185.

[20] Carmichael, *Purcell, Crenshaw and Letcher Artillery*, pp. 15-16; "The Purcell Battery," The *Daily Richmond Examiner*, July 15, 1862, p. 1.

[21] Dawson, *Confederate Service*, p. 185.

[22] William Ellis Jones diary, 26 June 1862, William L. Clements Library, University of Michigan, Ann Arbor.

Lee's artillery. In his later years, Dawson still lamented that the organization of the army enabled the Federals to virtually blast the Purcell Artillery out of existence. "It was one of the greatest errors of the early days of the Confederacy," he wrote, "that batteries were allowed to be knocked to pieces in detail, when, by massing a dozen batteries, the enemy could have been knocked quickly out of time and many lives saved."[23]

In his first battle as commander of the Purcell Battery, Pegram extinguished any doubts about his ability to command men. Facing overwhelming odds, he maintained his composure and led by example when his ranks became thinned. Disregard for his men's safety as well as his own reflected "Willy's" belief that a soldier should willingly resort to any measure to defeat the enemy. That night, while his men slept on the field, Pegram tapped his seemingly endless reservoir of energy and obtained "four splendid Napoleon guns" that had been captured from the Federals. His efforts did not go unnoticed by his superiors. A. P. Hill applauded the efforts of his young artillerist, stating in his official report that "Pegram, with indomitable energy and earnestness of purpose, though having lost 47 men and many horses at Mechanicsville, had put his battery in condition."[24]

The sun rose above a smoldering field on the morning of June 27. As the Confederates peered through the haze across Beaver Dam Creek, they saw abandoned Federal trenches. Brig. Gen. Fitz John Porter had withdrawn his Federals to a defensive line overlooking the lush vegetation of Boatswain Swamp near Gaines' Mill. Undaunted by his costly assaults the previous day, Lee pursued the retreating Federals with the Light Division in the van. Hill's troops collided with the enemy about mid-afternoon. As on the previous day, Hill imprudently flung his units piecemeal against Porter's force.

---

[23] Dawson, *Confederate Service*, p. 48.

[24] "The Purcell Battery," The *Daily Richmond Examiner*, July 15, 1862, p. 1; *OR*, 11, pt. 2: 837. Hill's casualty figure for the Purcell Artillery is slightly off the mark. The company lost 46 men.

While Hill's infantry struggled against a telling fire, Pegram's cannon raced past Gaines' Mill toward the front. About 300 yards east of New Cold Harbor, the Purcell Artillery moved off the dusty road. The battery awaited orders; a few shells exploded harmlessly nearby and stray bullets whined overhead.

Hill's men started to give way about 4 p.m. Stragglers scurried to the rear; other soldiers remained on the field, huddled together in the open but refusing to fire a shot. Hill called for reinforcements, and Pegram rushed his field pieces to the garden of the New Cold Harbor Tavern near the center of the sagging Confederate line. Sighting the muzzles of his guns toward the southeast, he fired on Federal infantry in a patch of timber. As Pegram's guns hurled shells into the marshy ground around Boatswain Swamp, enemy sharpshooters hit a few of the battery's horses but claimed no human victims. Near dusk, a magnificent assault by John Bell Hood's and Evander M. Law's brigades swept across the meadow, scaled the Union works, and drove the enemy back. The Union line finally had been broken, but at a cost of more than 8,500 Confederate casualties. Still, Porter's stand at Gaines' Mill allowed McClellan time to continue his retreat toward the James River. Determined to destroy the Army of the Potomac, Lee stayed on McClellan's trail for the next three days.[25]

Pegram and his men rested under some trees near New Cold Harbor the next day. On 29 June, they crossed the Chickahominy River at New Bridge and encamped at Piney Chapel on the Darbytown Road. Back on the road by 10 a.m. on June 30, the cannoneers marched behind Longstreet's men. The battery moved down the Long Bridge Road while the booming of cannon and the crackle of musketry, drifted from the front. Close to 4 p.m., Longstreet's division attacked Porter's men southwest of the intersection known as Glendale. The Confederate brigades attacked with ferocity, but made little headway against a determined Federal defense. Longstreet called for Hill's division to come forward from its position three-quarters of a mile behind the firing line. Hill's men

---

[25] "The Purcell Battery," the *Daily Richmond Examiner*, July 15, 1862, p. 1.

would learn that fate had brought them another chance at their opponents from four days earlier-the Pennsylvanians of McCall's division, this time supported by Brig. Gen. Phil Kearny's division of the III Corps.

Working his way down the clogged road, Pegram brought his company into position in Nathan Enroughty's pasture, better known as the Darby field. According to the *Daily Richmond Examiner*, Northern projectiles fell around Pegram's men in "a perfect storm." One shell chipped the side of a caisson, sending splinters in every direction. "Had it struck a few inches lower," the *Examiner*'s correspondent observed, the caisson would have exploded with "frightful" results. Woods separated Enroughty's pasture from the ground contested by Hill's infantry, so Pegram had no clear shot at the Federals. His men stood at their posts "without firing a gun, and without the loss of man or horse" until darkness settled over the field.[26]

Despite tactical gains by Longstreet's and Hill's infantry, the engagement on June 30th, referred to by the Confederates as Frayser's Farm, proved indecisive for Lee. The Northerners were able to retire in good order that evening and march southward toward a nearly perfect defensive position at Malvern Hill, a prominent rise above the James River. On July 1, the gray light of morning revealed that the Army of the Potomac held ground to chasten even the most resolute fighter. Rows of Federal cannon crowned the 150-foot-high hill, dominating open fields below. Porter arranged his infantry behind the Union gunners and posted a heavy skirmish line in front. In the words of Jennings C. Wise, "the setting was complete for a tremendous disaster."[27]

Lee felt ill on July 1 and exerted little authority. He left most of the tactical arrangements to subordinates who botched their assignments. Not until midday were the Southern troops in position. Jackson's men occupied the left flank, Daniel Harvey Hill's forces filled the center, and Maj. Gen. John B. Magruder's troops anchored the right. Longstreet believed that Jackson's artillery near the Poindexter farm and Ma-

[26] Ibid.

[27] Wise, *Long Arm of Lee*, pp. 221-224.

gruder's guns on the right would produce a crippling converging fire, but he failed to organize his batteries in such a fashion.[28]

Without adequate artillery support, Brig. Gen. Lewis A. Armistead pushed his Virginia brigade within a few hundred yards of the Union left flank on the Crew farm, followed closely by Brig. Gen. Ambrose R. Wright's Georgia Brigade. Both officers called for support. Two pieces of Capt. Cary F. Grimes's Battery—the Portsmouth Light Artillery—hurried to the scene, only to receive fierce counterbattery fire from over 30 Federal guns. To support this lone company, Capt. Marcellus N. Moorman's Battery rushed forward and found one of Grimes's cannon disabled and the remaining gunners abandoning their posts.[29]

With the loss of Grimes' Battery, Moorman's gun crews became the focal point of the enemy's metal. They could not hold on for long. Close to 3 p.m., Pegram and his Purcell Artillery galloped up Carter's Mill Road to the Confederate right flank. His men unhitched their horses and unlimbered their guns 200 yards to the left of Moorman's company. As Pegram's men loaded their cannon, Moorman's artillerists withdrew from the field.[30] Alone, Pegram's battery became the enemy's prime target in a scene reminiscent of Mechanicsville. Referring specifically to the Purcell Artillery, the *Daily Richmond Examiner* reported: "This proved, by all odds, the fierescest [sic] fight our men had been engaged in."[31] Only half a mile from the Unionists, Pegram could see their gunners loading their pieces. Federal missiles thundered down from the sky, plowing into the earth or spraying jagged metal in the air. Pegram's men began falling. Killed instantly was Charles B. Watkins, a 19-year-old private. His younger brother John, a 16 year old who also served in the company, carried his brother's lifeless body off the field while his comrades continued their deadly work.[32]

---

[28] Dowdey, *The Seven Days*, pp. 320-331.

[29] *OR*, 11, pt. 2, pp. 812-813.

[30] *OR*, 11, pt. 2, p. 813.

[31] "The Purcell Battery," The *Daily Richmond Examiner*, July 15, 1862, p. 1.

[32] Carmichael, *The Purcell, Crenshaw and Letcher Artillery*, p. 18.

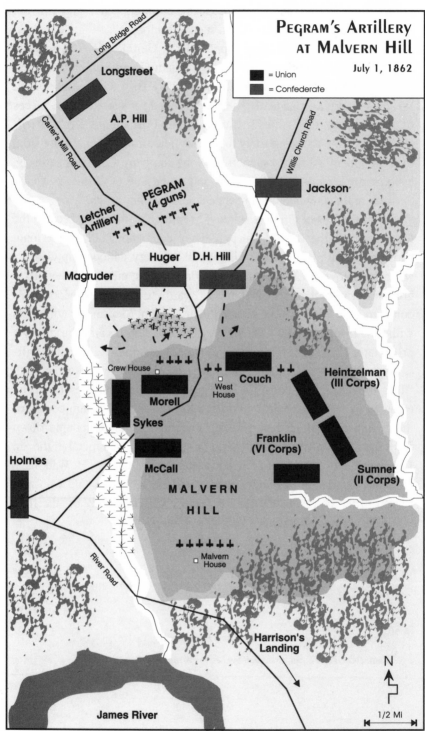

Theodore P. Savas

A. R. Wright observed that the Purcell Artillery had "opened a well-directed fire upon the enemy, which told with fearful effect upon them."[33] Given the overwhelming odds, it is difficult to imagine that Pegram's ordnance had the effect on U.S. guns that Wright suggests. Armistead sought to even the contest, demanding that Magruder and Longstreet forward more batteries, but his requests fell on deaf ears.[34]

In the words of General Wright, Pegram's men "manfully" continued the struggle without additional support. Such were their losses that within an hour there remained only enough men to operate one cannon. With unshaken determination, Pegram's artillerists "firmly held their ground and continued to pour a deadly fire upon the enemy's line." Wright finally saw "the utter hopelessness of the contest," and ordered Pegram to cease firing until more batteries were brought into action. About 4 p.m., the Letcher Artillery went into battery about 300 yards to the right of Pegram's company. "Again the gallant Pegram opened with his single gun," Wright reported, and, with the Letcher Artillery, peppered the Federal line.[35] In the ranks of this Virginia battery was Pegram's friend, Charles Ellis Munford. Engaged to Pegram's sister Jennie, Munford had been Willy's classmate at the University of Virginia. The day after Virginia had seceded, Pegram wrote to Munford and encouraged him to enlist and fight the "black Republicans."[36] Now the two friends stood within sight of each other as they battled the Federals. During the fight, a spherical shell exploded directly over Munford, spraying shrapnel balls, three of which hit Munford. One passed through his eye, another through his head, and the last struck his thigh. He crumpled to the ground dead.[37]

[33] *OR* 11, pt. 2, pp. 813, 819.

[34] Wise, *Long Arm of Lee*, p. 231.

[35] *OR* 11, pt. 2, p. 813.

[36] William Pegram to Charles Ellis Munford, 18 April 1861, Munford-Ellis Papers, (George W. Munford Division), William R. Perkins Library, Duke University, Durham, N.C.

[37] John H. Munford to Sallie Munford, 6 July 1862, Munford-Ellis Papers, (George W. Munford Division), William R. Perkins Library, Duke University, Durham, N.C.

While the air shook with concussions from the enemy's shells, Pegram assisted his men in loading the battery's single gun. When not working the piece, he cheered the remnant of his command. Several of the cannoneers who "stuck to their posts" already had been wounded three times. The *Daily Richmond Examiner* reported that "Pegram's courage and gallantry showed pre-eminent where all were brave."[38] The Purcell Artillery's steadiness under fire also impressed Lewis Armistead, who wrote that "no men could have behaved better than Captain Pegram['s]."[39]

Shortly after 5 p.m., Pegram's single gun and the Letcher Artillery supported the first wave of Confederate infantry assaults. Northern batteries concentrated on the charging infantry, giving the Southern artillerists a needed respite. Within minutes, Confederate attackers stumbled back through the smoky haze that had engulfed the field. The assault had failed utterly.

The day had been a perfect fiasco for Lee. More than 5,000 wounded or dead Confederates littered the field.[40] The Purcell Artillery had lost three of the company's four Napoleons, two men lay dead, another six wounded and 20 horses had been cut down.[41]

Pegram ordered his cannoneers to retire about 6 p.m. Grimy and exhausted, they carried their lone piece into a road jammed with vehicles and headed for the fairgrounds at Richmond to recover from their devastating losses during the Seven Days.

The virtual destruction of Pegram's command might suggest an inauspicious start for his career in the Army of Northern of Virginia. At this early stage of the war, however, officers who exhibited tenacity,

---

[38] "The Purcell Battery," The *Daily Richmond Examiner*, July 15, 1862, p. 1.

[39] *OR* 11, pt. 2, pp. 818-819.

[40] Dowdey, *The Seven Days*, pp. 339-344.

[41] Carmichael, *The Purcell, Crenshaw and Letcher Artillery*, p. 18; The *Daily Richmond Examiner* on July 15, stated that the Purcell Artillery had 20 men "cut down," but the Compiled Service Records and the *OR* do not substantiate this claim.

aggressiveness, and audacity on the battlefield secured the admiration of their men and the confidence of their superiors. Regardless of casualties inflicted or sustained, it was important for Civil War officers (as well as the enlisted men) to behave "manfully" under fire and to encourage others by their calm example. In this, Pegram had succeeded brilliantly.

Pegram's religious convictions inspired him to fight recklessly against a foe whom he considered immoral. Willy saw piety and courage as intimately connected, and hoped he could inspire his men to similar behavior if they realized that heaven awaited those who died in battle.[42] Many Confederate officers typically displayed enthusiasm for battle comparable to Pegram's. William Dorsey Pender, a pious 27-year-old North Carolinian in 1861, informed his wife that "the men seem to think that I am fond of fighting. They say I give them 'hell' out of the fight and the Yankees the same in it."[43] Virginian Greenlee Davidson also thought it desirable to seek battle whenever possible. He welcomed his battery's assignment to a brigade that "is one of the best fighting commands in the army and is always sent in the advance."[44]

Although Willy Pegram led his battery to the edge of extinction during the Seven Days, the army applauded his lust for combat. Superiors pointed to the Purcell Artillery's long casualty list as proof of Pegram's competence and promise. Charles Field wrote glowingly in his official report that "the conduct of Captain Pegram's battery in the engagements excites my admiration. Always eager, always alert, Captain Pegram was in every action where opportunity offered, and always doing his duty, as the loss of every officer killed or wounded and 60 out of about 80 men, sadly attests." Field thought this was the kind of officer

---

[42] There are countless examples of Pegram's zeal in battle and his reasoning for fighting so desperately. For one of the best, see, William Pegram to Virginia Johnson (Pegram) McIntosh, 14 August 1862, Pegram-Johnson-McIntosh Papers, Virginia Historical Society, Richmond; On notions of courage in the Civil War and how they related to religion, see Linderman, *Embattled Courage*, pp. 158-160.

[43] William Dorsey Pender, *The General to His Lady: The Civil War Letters of William Dorsey Pender to Fanny Pender*, edited by William W. Hassler (1962; rpt. Gaithersburg, MD, 1988), p. 191.

[44] Greenlee Davidson, *Captain Greenlee Davidson, C. S. A: Diary and Letters*, edited by Charles W. Turner (Verona, Virginia, 1975), p. 45.

the South needed. "I trust," he concluded, "that the merits of this officer will not go unrewarded by the Department."[45]

Lee must have been impressed by the bravery of Pegram and the countless other officers in his long-arm, but the baneful effects of the artillery's organization turned valor into recklessness. After the Seven Days, Lee, William Nelson Pendleton and Edward Porter Alexander began a long process of arranging batteries into battalions, thereby enabling artillery officers to mass cannon and act independently of the infantry.[46] Lee's gunners reaped the benefits of concentrating their artillery fire at Second Manassas, Antietam and Fredericksburg, redeeming themselves for their lackluster performance during the Seven Days.

---

[45] *OR* 11, pt. 2, p. 843. Field was referring to the Confederate war department, which dispensed promotions.

[46] On the reorganization of Lee's artillery, see, Wise, *Long Arm of Lee*, pp. 412-425; Edward Porter Alexander, *Fighting for the Confederacy*, edited by Gary W. Gallagher (Chapel Hill, 1989), p. 104.

INDEX

Reader's Notes

Reader's Notes

Reader's Notes

Reader's Notes

Reader's Notes